FUGITIVE INDUSTRY

FUGITIVE INDUSTRY
The Economics and Politics of Deindustrialization

By
RICHARD B. McKENZIE

Foreword by
FINIS WELCH

Pacific Studies in Public Policy

PACIFIC INSTITUTE FOR PUBLIC POLICY RESEARCH
San Francisco, California

Ballinger Publishing Company
Cambridge, Massachusetts
A Subsidiary of Harper & Row, Publishers, Inc.

International Standard Book Number: 0-88410-951-8 (CL)
                                    0-88410-952-6 (PB)

Library of Congress Catalog Card Number: 83-22413

Printed in the United States of America

Library of Congress Cataloging in Publication Data

McKenzie, Richard B.

  Fugitive industry.

  (Pacific studies in public policy)
  Bibliography: p.
  Includes index.
  1. Plant shutdowns—United States. 2. Plant shutdowns—Law and legislation—United States. I. Title. II. Series.
  HD5708.55.U6M38   1984   338.6'042   83-22413
  ISBN 0-88410-951-8
  ISBN 0-88410-952-6 (pbk.)

To my son
John Michael McKenzie

PACIFIC INSTITUTE
FOR PUBLIC POLICY RESEARCH

The Pacific Institute for Public Policy Research is an independent, tax-exempt research and educational organization. The Institute's program is designed to broaden public understanding of the nature and effects of market processes and government policy.

With the bureaucratization and politicization of modern society, scholars, business and civic leaders, the media, policymakers, and the general public have too often been isolated from meaningful solutions to critical public issues. To facilitate a more active and enlightened discussion of such issues, the Pacific Institute sponsors in-depth studies into the nature of and possible solutions to major social, economic, and environmental problems. Undertaken regardless of the sanctity of any particular government program, or the customs, prejudices, or temper of the times, the Institute's studies aim to ensure that alternative approaches to currently problematic policy areas are fully evaluated, the best remedies discovered, and these findings made widely available. The results of this work are published as books and monographs, and form the basis for numerous conference and media programs.

Through this program of research and commentary, the Institute seeks to evaluate the premises and consequences of government policy, and provide the foundations necessary for constructive policy reform.

PACIFIC STUDIES IN PUBLIC POLICY

FORTHCOMING

Money in Crisis
The Federal Reserve, Stagflation, and Economic Reform

Forestlands
Public and Private

The American Family and the State

Stagflation and the Political Business Cycle

Urban Transit
Public Failure and Private Renaissance

Rationing Health Care
Medical Licensing in the United States

Oil and Gas Leasing on the Outer Continental Shelf

Taxation and Capital Markets

Impoverishing America
The Political Economy of the Transfer Society

Electric Utility Regulation and the Energy Crisis

Immigration in the United States

Crime, Police, and the Courts

For further information on the Pacific Institute's program and a catalog of publications, please contact:

PACIFIC INSTITUTE
FOR PUBLIC POLICY RESEARCH
177 Post Street
San Francisco, California 94108

CONTENTS

LIST OF FIGURES

LIST OF TABLES

FOREWORD

According to Richard McKenzie, there is an emerging groundswell of support for legislation that would restrict plant closings. Although particulars vary, provisions of proposed legislation encompass requirements for specific periods of notification to employees (up to two years in some cases), severance pay—which would be determined by length of service and past earnings—and continuation of health insurance benefits. Restitution to affected communities has been proposed, as have government subsidies to worker or community groups for purchase of defunct plants or companies. Legislation has been introduced at the federal level and in twenty-four states, although at the time McKenzie compiled his data, only two states and one city had adopted restrictive measures.

The objective of this volume, *Fugitive Industry*, is to present some of the arguments for and the analysis against such restrictions. McKenzie is not neutral: he strongly favors economic efficiency, which is contrary to restrictions on mobility. However, regardless of prejudices, the reader should carefully follow the analysis; it sets the intellectual arena where future battles will or should be fought.

The main economic argument against plant closing restrictions is that if an economy is to realize its full potential, resources must be allocated where they are most productive. Because opportunities arise continuously, a pattern of allocation that is efficient at one time will not necessarily remain so as new options emerge. Resource mobility is a prerequisite for dynamic efficiency.

In this sense, an economy is like a tree or other living organism. The resources are nutrients, and growth and maintenance are simultaneous replacement processes in which nutrients are directed from parts that are less robust to more viable alternatives. As a tree grows, we are little concerned that some leaves die while others develop. Yet we are quite concerned when an industrial plant closes and jobs are lost, even though capital diverted elsewhere results in new plants and new jobs.

There is no question that employees caught in plant closings experience real costs. Not only are they faced with finding new jobs but, to the extent that they have acquired skills that cannot be easily transferred, their future earning abilities are impaired. Yet these costs are the same as those faced by anyone losing a job regardless of whether the loss stems from an ordinary reduction in force of a firm that continues operations or from a plant closing. The only study that I have seen on this subject suggests that displaced workers have more difficulty finding new jobs in areas where unemployment rates are high, but there is little to differentiate workers whose plants had closed from those losing jobs for other reasons. The simple evidence was that those displaced by plant closings remained unemployed about two weeks longer than other displaced workers.

Since the mid-1930s we have had unemployment insurance to compensate workers for job loss. Involuntarily separated workers are eligible irrespective of whether the separation followed a plant closing. Moreover, recent provisions in unemployment compensation trigger extended benefits during periods of relatively high national unemployment and during periods when a states' unemployment is significantly above its longer-run average. The new proposals for plant closing restrictions would provide compensation over-and-above unemployment insurance. The provisions for severance pay in the legislation proposed for plant closings does not depend on lengths of ensuing spells of unemployment, as does ordinary unemployment insurance. Those immediately transiting to alternative employment would receive the same compensation as others who are unable to easily find new positions.

Before such laws are passed, several issues should be considered. First and most important is the question of whether affected workers are differentiated according to job loss through a plant closing or job loss for some other reason. Only if effects are more severe for plant closings is there a case for legislation, which distinguishes them and, as previously noted, the case for differential effect has not been made. Second, even if workers caught in plant closings are more affected, should they receive explicit compensation? Any job carries risks of unemployment and eventual termination. To entice workers to accept riskier jobs, higher wages must be paid. Provisions for explicit compensation reduce worker incentives to self-insure through saving and to protect their own interests by avoiding or by requiring higher compensation for working in jobs with greater risk. Third, if compensation is to be made available, who should pay? The plant closing laws that load costs on affected firms simply increase the latter's costs of production and thereby raise product costs to consumers. As such, plant closing legislation may actually speed the demise of less robust firms.

To the extent that plant closing laws hold jobs in places where they would otherwise be lost, they preclude new job openings elsewhere. I agree with McKenzie's arguments that these laws represent a form of the myopia characterizing much of our regulatory structure. When a plant closes, the losers are easily identified. The gainers are not. In most cases, we cannot predict either the industry or the location of the opportunities that might emerge.

Perhaps I could characterize plant closing laws by raising the issue of what the United States would be like today had we prohibited farm closings for, say, the last one hundred years. Most of us are familiar with the agricultural history of very rapid technological advances that permitted mergers of small farm concerns into increasingly larger producing units. The transition process was not easy for farm labor. Increasing productivity drove farm product prices down and farm workers usually earned only 60 to 75 percent as much as their urban counterparts. The typical intergenerational picture was one where less than one farm boy in ten would remain in agriculture.

There is no doubt that, had we precluded farm closings, both farm labor and the U.S. economy would have been hurt. Most of us would live and work on farms where the technical advantages of economies of scale could not have been realized. Rather than seeing a 25–40 percent urban/farm wage differential, we would find urban workers earning several times as much as farm workers. There is absolutely no question the process that transformed us from a rural to an urban economy imposed high costs on some of the rural people caught in the transition. Yet, if there was a case for government intervention, it would have been to introduce programs to facilitate, rather than to retard, the process. Is the issue of urban employment in transition between plants, whether in the same geographical area, any different? I think not.

Finis Welch
University of California, Los Angeles

PREFACE

Job security is central to the emerging public debate over a national industrial policy. In all probability it will continue to be a dominant industrial relations issue of the late 1980s because the economy will probably continue to follow its unstable and uncertain course, a victim, over the past decade, of the growing instability of government policies. During the 1970s and early 1980s, the search for job security became translated into a drive to restrict plant closings, organized at both the federal and state government levels. The list of restrictions included required severance pay for workers, prenotification to workers of a plant closing, tax penalties, and compensation to communities for lost taxes. The assumption underlying the campaign for closing restrictions is that the source of the nation's unemployment problems is plant closings; and a conclusion all too readily drawn is that jobs can be saved by prohibiting or impeding the ability of plants to close their doors.

The case for restrictions has generally been developed by well-meaning groups who earnestly believe that "social improvement" can be achieved directly and simply through government control of capital flows across regions and states of the country. The purpose of this volume is straightforward: to challenge the assumptions, arguments, and empirical case for plant closing restrictions. The overriding conclusion of the study is that closing restrictions are a bad idea whose time (because of their political appeal) may have come. In the end, restrictions on plant closings are restrictions on plant openings. Contrary to the good intentions of their proponents, restrictions on closures will tend to destroy more jobs than they save and to dampen the country's economic growth. The emotional upheaval surrounding the closing of a major plant in a community is understandable because many people suffer. The often overlooked question this study addresses, however, is whether the proposed remedies will not increase the economic harm to current and future generations of Americans.

This book is the product of several years of work on plant closings and proposed plant closing restrictions. During the several years of work on this subject, I have depended upon many people for help in obtaining information, reviewing manuscripts, and hearing me out on arguments. While I cannot hope to name all of the people who have helped, I must name several people whose criticisms and comments have been particularly helpful: Terry Anderson, Yale Brozen, Rex Cottle, Catherine England, Bernard Frazier, Thomas Haggard, Milton Kafoglis, Dwight Lee, Hugh Macaulay, Delores Martin, Thomas Schaap, Trey Senn, B. R. Skelton, John Warner, Clinton Whitehurst, and Bruce Yandle. Participants at a conference organized around a preliminary draft of the book and sponsored by the Liberty Fund provided important feedback on the arguments contained in the book. I am also especially indebted to Francis O'Connell for his contribution to Chapter 5 of the volume.

I am also deeply indebted to Carole Helsel, Sue Jones, Lisa Kiel, Mary Ann McKenzie, and Jean Savage for editing and/or computerizing the manuscript. James Huffman, Nancy Mathews, Mark Mitchell and David Poor provided invaluable assistance in gathering data and checking calculations in the text. Finally, the manuscript was expanded and finalized while I was on leave from Clemson University to assume a senior fellowship at the Heritage Foundation. The support Heritage provided was invaluable.

My son John is a remarkable teenager. He has contributed indirectly to all that I have written by adding an unimaginable amount of joy to the lives of those around him, especially to mine. For this reason I am very proud to be able to dedicate the book to him.

Richard B. McKenzie

Chapter 1

RESTRICTIONS ON CLOSING
Federal and State Proposals

Youngstown, Detroit, Camden, Cleveland, Pittsburgh, Gary, and Akron: the names of these cities strike a sensitive chord among concerned readers of the daily press. In the minds of many, these cities epitomize urban decay, recession, and despair. All have suffered through the closing of one or more major plants, and much has been written about the resulting "devastating effects":

> Michael R. Kusner suddenly found himself without a job two years ago when AM International, Inc., his employer of 17 years, started thinning out corporate staff to get ready for its move from Cleveland to Los Angeles. During the five months he searched for a new job, Kusner, a 50-year old father of six, lost 15 pounds.
> — *Cleveland Plain Dealer*, 16 September 1979

> Akron was "Tire Capital of the World." . . . All that is history now. Early last year [1978], Goodyear and Firestone, the World's largest tire companies, announced that they were ending production at the last two plants making passenger-car tires in Akron. One month after Goodyear's shutdown in Akron, the company announced that it was investing $34 million in a new tire plant employing 2,000 workers—in Chile.
> — *Washington Post*, 9 February 1979

> Southern Airways, Inc. said it plans to fire 14 percent of its workforce so it can afford $65 million of airplanes. The carrier said it is firing 500 employees over the next two weeks. . . .
> — *Wall Street Journal*, 7 August 1978

Since before this century began, the destiny of millions of men like Jim Woods . . . has lain in mills like Youngstown Sheet and Tube Company's Campbell Works, a mammoth group of grey-rust buildings . . . stretching along the Mahoning River. . . . Today the huge mill was operating much as it has since 1900. . . . But a tornado or flash flood might as well have wiped it all from the face of the earth, for yesterday Youngstown Sheet delivered a blow to this city's solar plexes by announcing that it was shutting down the mill.

—New York Times, 21 September 1981

The following headlines, taken from Ohio's largest newspaper, the *Cleveland Plain Dealer,* over a period of two weeks, vividly express the way many northerners appraise the problem of plant closings: "Southland has northern industries whistling Dixie"; "Workers view sunbelt as land of promise"; "Company's exodus cuts its veteran employees adrift"; "North Carolina sells itself as cheap labor state"; and "North vs. the Sunbelt." Of course, workers in sunbelt states like Alabama and California harbor similar sentiments toward other areas of the country when they see their firms shutting down or moving out.

Barry Bluestone and Bennett Harrison's explanation of the source of the problem of plant closing has attracted national attention. They argue that the source lies in the greed of corporate America and in the inclination of corporate managers to "restore, or preserve, the rates of profits they had become accustomed to in the halycon days of the 1950s and 1960s" by shifting "capital as rapidly as possible, from one activity, one region, and one nation to another. In the process, the industrial base of the American economy began to come apart at the seams."[1] On the other hand, Harvard Professor Robert Reich, in his widely read book *The Next American Frontier,* contends that American managers have become wedded to assembly line production processes of the past and that "social and economic policies were at odds with each other and that America lacked any mechanism to accelerate economic change or to forge a social concensus that would allow adaptation."[2] Obviously, considerable disagreement exists about the presumed decay in our industrial base.

1. Barry Bluestone and Bennett Harrison, *The Deindustrialization of America: Plant Closings, Community Abandonment, and the Dismantling of Basic Industry* (New York: Basic Books, 1982), p. 15.

2. Robert Reich, *The Next American Frontier* (New York: Time/Life Books, 1983), p. 11.

Labor blames management, management blames labor, the people in the North blame the people in the South and West, while the South and West ask the North to look to its own policies as a source of its problems. Perhaps it is only natural for people to want to blame anybody but themselves.

CAUSES AND CONSEQUENCES

Workers and communities across the country, not just in the industrial northeast, who see themselves as victims of the "irresponsible" and "callous" profiteering of free enterprise are ready to do battle, and the fight has been joined in the political arena with legislation designed to restrict plant closings. This legislation, which is a key element in the efforts of many groups to "reindustrialize America" or to institute a new "national industrial policy," effectively attempts to restructure economic power and to revamp, by law, what is perceived as a growing incompatibility between the mobility of "financial and physical capital" and the desire of people with "human capital" to stay put, retain their jobs, and develop their communities — or so the argument goes.

Proponents of this restrictive legislation contend that plant closings not only contribute to greater unemployment, but also

1. To a reduction in national income because many workers remain idle for long periods of time and because firms that move to lower wage areas necessarily lower their total wage bill[3]
2. To an increase in physical and mental illness because researchers have found that a 1 percent increase in the national unemployment rate is associated with

   • 37,000 deaths (including 20,000 heart attacks)

   • 920 suicides

   • 650 homicides

   • 4,000 state mental hospital admissions, and

   • 3,300 state prison admissions[4]

3. John S. Hekman and John S. Strong, "Is There a Case for Plant Closings?" *New England Economic Review* (July/August 1980): 34.
4. From the research of Harvey Brenner, as cited in Barry Bluestone, Bennett Harrison, and Lawrence Baker, *Corporate Flight: The Causes and Consequences of Economic Dislocation* (Washington: The Progressive Alliance, 1981), p. 20.

3. To the "external or social costs" (to use economists' jargon) of reduced tax collections and increased social welfare expenditures (because plant closings mean a reduction in taxable income and property and to more unemployed workers)[5]
4. To a decline in self-esteem and morale: "For twenty-seven years I worked for one employer, and I gave him everything. I was there on time, accepted overtime with a smile, never stole a thing. I put suggestions in the suggestion box. I am not going to do any of that again. . . . They fooled me the last time. They are not going to get anything from me this time but eight hours of regular output, and they damn well better accept that because it's all they've got coming this time around"[6]
5. To a growth in marital and family problems, from divorce to child abuse because any increase in mental and physical problems are felt first and most keenly in the home as mortgage and medical bills mount.[7]

Advocates of restrictions on plant closings see the consequences of plant closings to be pervasive—and destructive. All of these social problems are connected either directly or indirectly, to the free play of market forces; and they undergird the moral fervor of those seeking to restrain what has been called "capital flight" or the "runaway plant phenomenon." The perceived social and economic causes of the growth in "capital flight" are:

1. Low wages in the South, Southwest, and other parts of the world that attract industries, especially heavy manufacturing industries, away from their northern bases
2. Growth in the economies of the South and West that gives those areas a dynamic, self-reinforcing character

5. Ed Kelley, *Industrial Exodus* (Washington: Conference on Alternative State and Local Policies, 1978), pp. 7 and 8. See also Bluestone and Harrison, *Deindustrialization of America*, chapters 3 and 4.

6. Arthur Shostak, "The Human Cost of Plant Closings," *The Federationists* (August 1980): 25.

7. Barry Bluestone and Bennett Harrison, *Capital and Communities: The Causes and Consequences of Private Disinvestment* (Washington: The Progressive Alliance, 1980), chapter 3. For an expanded and updated version of the authors' arguments, see *The Deindustrialization of America*. For a summary of twenty studies on the economic and social consequences of plant closings conducted over the past two decades, see also Jeanne Prial Gordus, Paul Jarley, and Louis A. Ferman, *Plant Closings and Economic Dislocations* (Kalamazoo, Mich.: W.E. Upjohn Institute for Employment Research, 1981).

3. Changes in the relative prices and availability of energy and environmental resources in different regions, which have led to changes in the relative cost of living
4. Changes in the regional population structure, imposing heavier than usual welfare burdens on urban and traditional manufacturing centers
5. Growth in technology of consumer goods and production capability, reducing the period over which firms amortize their plants and equipment and increasing the substitution of capital for labor
6. Growth in conglomerates and multinational business corporations that have lost their social ties to their plants' communities, that have acquired a high degree of control over their product and labor markets, and that can now pit workers and communities across the world against one another in an endless—and destructive—struggle for jobs and incomes
7. A tax code that favors capital at the expense of labor and that encourages businesses to liquidate their plant and equipment and relocate.

The list could be easily lengthened.

PROPOSED REMEDIES

Restricting plant closings emerges as an obvious solution to the problem of capital mobility. Since 1974, the center of the political contest for restrictions on capital mobility has been in Washington. The legislative centerpiece, something called the "National Employment Priorities Act," was first supported in the Senate by then Senator Walter Mondale (D–Minn.) and now by Senator Donald Riegle (D–Mich.); the chief support in the House has always been from Representative William Ford (D–Mich.).[8] Features of the Riegle-Ford bill are also incorporated into the "Employee and Community Stabilization Act of 1979," sponsored by former Senator Harrison Williams (D–N.J.),[9] the "Employment Maintenance Act of 1980," introduced by Sena-

8. U.S. Congress, House, "National Employment Priorities Act of 1979," H.R. 5040 (96th Congress, 1st Session); and U.S. Congress, "National Employment Priorities Act of 1979," S. 1608 (96th Congress, 1st Session).

9. U.S. Congress, Senate, "Employee and Community Stabilization Act of 1979," S. 1609 (96th Congress, 1st Session).

tor Howard Metzenbaum (D–Oh.),[10] and the "Corporate Democracy (or Governance) Act of 1980," sponsored by Representative Benjamin Rosenthal (D–N.Y.) and originated by Ralph Nader's organization, Americans Concerned about Corporate Power.[11]

Stymied by committees that have refused to allow any of these bills to reach the floor of the Senate or House and by a market shift to the right in Congressional social sentiment, proponents of restrictions have moved their political drive to state capitals. And there in recent years a spate of bills, having common objectives and many similar characteristics, has been introduced in at least twenty-four states including: Alabama, California, Connecticut, Hawaii, Iowa, Illinois, Indiana, Kentucky, Maine, Maryland, Massachusetts, Michigan, Minnesota, Missouri, Montana, New Jersey, New York, Ohio, Oregon, Pennsylvania, Rhode Island, Washington, West Virginia, and Wisconsin.[12] The list indicates that a state legislature in every major region of the country has considered at least one bill. However, the list also shows that the stronghold of this new political activism remains concentrated in the northern industrial tier states, where it started.

The movement has had the active and vocal backing of national organizations like Ralph Nader's Public Interest Research groups, the Progressive Alliance (a conglomerate, now defunct, of 130 labor, environmental, civil rights, and feminist organizations), the AFL–CIO, United Auto Workers, United Steelworkers, Amalgamated Clothing and Textile Workers, National Lawyers Guild, and the Conference on Alternative State and Local Policies. In addition, the state bills are supported by groups such as the Ohio Public Interest Campaign, the Ohio State Council of Senior Citizens, the Ohio Council of Churches,

10. U.S. Congress, Senate, "Employment Maintenance Act of 1980," S. 2400 (96th Congress, 2nd Session).

11. U.S. Congress, House, "Corporate Governance Act of 1980," H.R. 7010 (96th Congress, 2nd Session). See also Mark Green, *et al., The Case for the Corporate Democracy Act of 1980* (Washington: Americans Concerned about Corporate Power, 1980), especially chapter 1.

12. This listing of states that considered plant closing legislation between 1979 and 1981 is based partly on a survey I undertook in the spring of 1981 and partly on a survey of state legislative interest in plant closing laws reported by Bernard Frazier. Frazier reports that during the 1981 legislative sessions, ten states, three of which were not included in my survey findings, considered as many as thirty-eight bills that in one way or another affected plant closings (Bernard W. Frazier, presentation at a Liberty Fund symposium on plant closing legislation, Charleston, S.C., May 9–11, 1981). The American Legislative Exchange Council reported in the fall of 1982 that 100 plant closing bills had been introduced in state legislatures [*First Reading,* (September 1982)].

the Ohio Commission on Poverty and Economic Justice, the Massachusetts Coalition to Save Jobs (which includes several unions and citizen organizations), the Illinois Public Action Council, the Philadelphia Unemployment Project, and the Delaware Valley United Labor Committee for Full Employment. In addition, city ordinances proposing to restrict plant closings have been seriously considered in San Francisco, Pittsburgh, and Philadelphia.

Although the supporters' efforts have been, to a large extent, thwarted in most states, two states (Maine and Wisconsin) and one city (Philadelphia) now have restrictive legislation, albeit limited, on their books. Furthermore, the movement's successes are gradually mounting: The number of cosponsors for legislation introduced in successive terms of Congress has increased; sponsors have been found in states where a sponsor previously could not be found; bills have emerged from committees where they were once buried; progressively more restrictive proposals are being seriously considered; and at least one 1984 Democratic candidate, Walter Mondale, has made plant closing restriction an important component of his "industrial policy" and a plank in his presidential platform. These successes, although limited, speak to the staying power of the bills' political supporters, to the almost missionary zeal with which backers approach their campaigns. In its endorsement of the concept of plant closing laws, the AFL–CIO articulated a commonly-held position:

> Sudden plant closings in this country are occurring with alarming frequency. They affect not only large industrial cities but small towns and rural areas and even the South, a region in which many plants relocate. Governmental decisions to close or relocate federal facilities or functions are also occurring at an alarming rate.
>
> The impact on particular communities can be devastating in economic, social and personal terms. . . .
>
> Workers who lose their jobs because there are plant closings may not be able to find new ones or may be forced to work at reduced pay. Family life is often disrupted. The mental and physical health of displaced workers often declines at a rapid rate. Research over a thirteen-year period finds that the suicide rate among workers displaced by plant closings is almost thirty times the national average. . . .[13]

13. Markley Roberts, *Statement on Behalf of the American Federation of Labor and Congress of Industrial Organization to the Senate Committee on Labor and Human Resources on the Economic Dislocation of Plant Closings* (Washington: AFL–CIO, September 17, 1980), p. 1.

This large, politically potent union declared its full support for the enactment of such legislation in Congress and state legislatures because "it is crucially important to require employers to recognize their responsibilities to their employees and their communities before they shut down a plant and to provide economic protections to workers and their families who must suffer the consequences of rash corporate action. . . .[14]

The literature of supporters of plant closing laws reads as though the proponents understand they are engaged in a long-term struggle to change in a fundamental way the economic power in the United States—to democratize, if not humanize, entrepreneurial decisions. Edward Kelly, director of research for the Ohio Public Interest Campaign, echoes the sentiments of the AFL–CIO and many others:

> Employees and communities throughout the United States are facing the growing problem of plant closings and relocations by large corporations. In Ohio alone, closings and relocations have resulted in 13,075 jobs lost during the first three months of 1979. Other states are experiencing similar difficulties. . . .
>
> Together conglomerate growth and small business decline leave Americans increasingly dependent on the large corporations which are moving away. The future promises more plant closings and relocations, and the prospects of renewed recession. Clearly, the need for plant closing legislation is growing.[15]

Bluestone and Harrison introduce the first version of their extensive study of the problem of plant closings with the following assessment:

> You don't have to be an economist or an unemployed worker to be aware of the epidemic of plant closings and other forms of capital flight now sweeping the country. From day to day or week to week, it may be a shirt factory in Connecticut, a steel mill in Ohio or an automobile plant in California which shuts its doors or reduces its work force. But wherever and however this disinvestment takes place, its repercussions on people, communities and even the productivity of the American economy as a whole are often devastating. In fact, the economic and social wreckage left in the wake of capital flight is fast becoming a major American crisis. . . .
>
> In our belief, the operative myths must be stripped away and the disturbing reality concerning capital mobility clearly confronted and coped with.

---

14. Ibid.

15. Edward Kelly, "Foreword," in Ed Kelly and Lee Webb, eds., *Plant Closings: Resources for Public Officials, Trade Unionists and Community Leaders* (Washington: Conference on Alternative State and Local Policies, 1979), p. 1.

Rationally, private profit should not continue to be the *sole* criterion for corporate investment decisions which can have so great a negative impact on workers, communities and the American economy as a whole. A public balance sheet, which weighs the considerable costs to people, towns and public treasuries of decisions made by conglomerates and other corporations in their own interests, should replace the traditional private balance sheet as the standard for decisions concerning capital mobility. We hope this report will contribute to a wider understanding of this pressing problem and documentation of the critical need for legislation to achieve more equitable criteria for decisions regarding investment and disinvestment in the private sector.[16]

PLANT CLOSING REQUIREMENTS

The various state proposals are contrasted with the National Employment Priorities Act of 1979 in Appendix A. (A slightly less demanding 1983 version of the Act was introduced in Congress at the time this book was going to press, too late for full consideration here. Detailed evaluation of the 1979 bill will help us more fully appreciate the intentions of supporters of restrictions.) Although many differences exist, most of the legislative proposals share several key features.

First, they tend to apply to firms with a minimum number of employees, generally 50 or 100, not all of whom need to be unemployed at the closing of a *single* plant (or "establishment" in the legal parlance of the legislation). For example, a company in West Virginia that has a total of 100 employees in several plants is covered under that state's proposed legislation so long as a permanent "relocation" of operations in *one* plant affects as few as 10 percent of the workers in *that* plant, or if a "reduction in operations" affects 50 percent of the workers over any two-year period. The 1979 federal bill is applicable to any firm that has as few as $250,000 in gross annual sales and that intends to close or relocate any single plant employing as few as 50 employees. (It should be noted that the bills sponsored by Congressman Rosenthal and Senator Metzenbaum [H.R. 7010 and S. 2400, respectively] are directed at very large companies. The Metzenbaum bill applies only to firms with more than 500 employees and $100 million in annual sales, the Rosenthal bill only to firms with more than 5,000 workers and at least $250 million in assets or

16. Bluestone and Harrison, *Capital and Communities*, pp. i and ix.

annual sales.) If enacted, such a law could apply to many fast food restaurants in the country.

Second, the proposals have a significant notification requirement. The bills pending at one time or another in Alabama, California, Illinois, Indiana, Massachusetts, Michigan, Missouri, New Jersey, Pennsylvania, Oregon, and Washington have a one-year notification requirement. In Minnesota, Ohio, and West Virginia, the proposed notification requirement is two years. The Montana bill requires a firm to notify its employees of any planned change in operations once the decision has been made by management. The New York bill requires that firms give their employees nine month's notice and the state give a year's notice. Maine and Wisconsin have in effect a notification requirement of 60 days. Representative Ford's 1979 bill has a mandated notice requirement that varies with the size of the company: two years for firms with more than 500 employees, one year for firms with 100 to 499 employees, and six months for firms with fewer than 100 workers. (In the 1983 bill this requirement has been reduced to one year for firms with more than 100 employees and six months for firms with fewer than 100 employees.)

Third, most of the state proposals have some form of severance pay requirement. Maine's severance pay law is typical of proposals in other states; it requires the employer to pay terminated workers a "lump sum" equal to the worker's "average weekly wage" for the previous twelve months times the number of years employed. (Under Maine's severance pay law, "average weekly wage" means 1/52 of the worker's total wages over the previous year.) Thus a worker who has worked for a company for twenty-five years and has earned an "average" of $400 a week during the past year is entitled to severance pay of $10,000, all in one payment.

"Average weekly" (or in the case of Montana, monthly) wage is not calculated the same way in every state. Those concerned with the particulars of the bills need to read them carefully. In some states, average weekly wage is the true average, that is, gross annual wages divided by the weeks worked. In others, average weekly wage is defined as gross compensation, including fringe benefits, divided by the weeks worked. Other definitions are described in the various state bills.

Legislation in other states (like Oregon and Washington) and federal legislation require "income maintenance payments" that are geared to the employee's average pay and tenure of service and paid for up to fifty-two weeks. These maintenance payments, reduced by other forms of compensation, are limited to $30,000 in the Oregon and Washington bills and to $25,000 in the federal bill. A number of state bills also mandate that employers continue health insurance benefits for a period of six months to a year. Again, the Oregon, Washington, and federal bills require that all benefit programs be continued for as long as the income maintenance payments are made.

These various bills usually specify that the proposed laws cannot be used to nullify more generous severance pay and notification provisions in individual worker and union contracts. Furthermore, any required severance pay typically is viewed as a debt obligation, having the same prior legal claim to liquidated assets in bankruptcy proceedings as any other unpaid wages. Under the federal bill, any income maintenance payment not met by the firm and covered by the federal treasury becomes a debt owed to the federal government.

Fourth, several of the state proposals require the departing company to make restitution payments to the affected community. These bills set the payment at 10 percent (Minnesota, Ohio, and West Virginia), 15 percent (Massachusetts, Missouri, and Pennsylvania), or 25 percent (Montana) of the "total wage bill" of the affected workers during the previous twelve months. Under the Oregon and Washington bills, the restitution payment owed by a firm relocating a plant within the state equals 85 percent of one year's lost tax revenue to local governments. If the move is to a location outside the state, the percentage multiplier is considerably higher, 300 percent; and state tax benefits associated with the move are denied. The federal bill imposes similar penalties on firms relocating abroad.

Fifth, several of the bills grant some form of government assistance to covered firms and affected businesses, provided the assistance promotes "the reemployment of affected workers" or "stabilizes employment opportunities." Several state bills (notably the ones introduced in Illinois, Michigan, Montana, Oregon, and Washington) and the federal bill make some provision for government financial and/or technical assistance to worker and community groups interested in buying out the defunct company. However, how much of each government's resources will be devoted to such purposes is left unspecified. Presumably, the redevelopment, company bailout, and worker buyout aid will be restricted by the restitution payments made by the firms to community readjustment funds. Typically, the restitution payments are to be used, in part, by the affected communities to secure state and federal matching redevelopment grants.

Sixth, most of the bills require the company to submit, within sixty or ninety days after notification is given to its employees and public officials, an "economic impact statement" that lists reasons for the closure or change of operations, provides supporting financial data, and gives the company's assessment of the hardship its change of operations will cause the employees and community. A state official or council, like the director of the Department of Commerce in Indiana or of the proposed Bureau of Employee Protection and Community Stabilization in California, is typically given the authority to investigate closings — to call witnesses, subpoena business records, and make recommendations regarding the dispersal of government redevelopment funds.

Seventh, the various state bills contain a number of qualifying provisions that, in effect, narrow considerably the coverage of the restrictions. Most proposed restrictions do not apply to bankrupt firms, to political subdivisions, to public agencies, and to nonprofit organizations. Further, the one- or two-year notification requirement may be waived when and if the company can show to the satisfaction of the investigating authority that the required notification period is impossible or unreasonable to meet or if continued operations would mean "operating losses."

Because of the presence of such qualifiers, Maine's severance pay law has, since its passage in 1975, had limited but growing use. In June 1982 one court case was still pending; and there were two other cases in which, in the opinion of Maine's Bureau of Labor, the companies owed their workers severance pay.[17] In 1981 several other companies voluntarily met the requirements of the severance pay law. In 1979 a firm paid approximately 200 employees severance pay of $287,000 "after the Union representing the employees negotiated for a settlement after consulting with this office [Bureau of Labor]."[18] However, a number of firms have closed and escaped the severance pay requirement because one of the following conditions was present: The firms that changed their operations (1) had been in operation for less than three years, or (2) had fewer than 100 workers in the twelve months prior to closing, or (3) had gone bankrupt, or (4) persuaded their employees to accept employment at other locations within the companies.[19]

17. Letter from Paul K. Lovejoy, deputy director of Maine's Bureau of Labor, 22 June 1981.
18. Ibid.
19. Letter from Seth Thronton, Acting Deputy Director, Bureau of Labor, State of Maine (January 21, 1980).

FUTURE DIRECTION OF THE MOVEMENT

Plant closing legislation at the state and federal levels is, in itself, an important legislative initiative. Such legislation seeks to usurp management's rights to close up shop. However, this legislative drive is probably the first of many forays by the legislation's backers into social control of investment, reinvestment, and disinvestment decisions:

> ... The problem is capital disinvestment: the running-down or liquidation of the net productive capacity of business. ... The basic issue is not how to stop capital mobility—far from it. It is how to assure that the transfer of capital from one use or location to another will not be allowed to disregard the costs of worker and community dislocation.[20]

Proponents of restrictions on capital mobility see plant closing legislation as only one of several alternative policy solutions. A number of other policies have been advocated:

1. Repeal Section 14 (b) of the Taft-Hartley Act, which permits states to have "right-to-work" laws (a change intended to give workers, through unionization, greater bargaining power over plant closures)
2. Require employers to negotiate plant closings with worker and community representatives (a requirement currently in force in West Germany firms, effectively granting workers "rights to their jobs")
3. Selectively nationalize "key industries," bringing the investment decisions of important firms under the direct control of the government
4. Provide federal funds for worker buy outs and company bailouts (proposals submerged in the National Employment Priorities Act of 1979)
5. Require firms to list all vacancies with the government's Job Service
6. Provide federal funds for public enterprises that can replace closed private centers of employment (as is done in Sweden)
7. Insist that firms have their investment and disinvestment plans submitted to some government board for approval (as is done in West Germany and other countries).[21]

20. Bluestone and Harrison, *Capital and Communities*, p. 17.
21. Ibid., chapter 8. See also Reich, *The Next American Frontier*, chapter 11.

THE DIRECTION OF THE STUDY

Subsequent chapters will explore the many economic and social issues surrounding plant closings and the plant closing restrictions proposed at the federal, state, and local government levels. Because the motivation for restrictions was originally, and for many remains, a curtailment of the movement of northern industry to the South, Chapter 2 describes the extent to which the Frostbelt's economic problems are dependent upon the outflow of industry to the Sunbelt. We will see that the Frostbelt/Sunbelt debate is based on a number of economic myths. Chapter 3 makes the case against plant closing restrictions by considering inconsistencies in the proponent's conceptual arguments. A major argument offered in support of plant closing legislation is that firms, especially large conglomerates, are inclined to close "profitable" plants. Chapter 4 explains why such an argument is self-contradictory. By reviewing a series of National Labor Relations Board and court decisions over the past twenty years, Chapter 5 details plant closing restrictions already implicit in labor law and offers explanations for union support of restrictions. Chapter 6 evaluates the causes and consequences of community concessions financed with local and federal taxes and made under the threat of plant closings. The last chapter recapitulates arguments presented throughout the book and focuses attention on viable market alternatives to government-imposed restrictions.

GENERAL CONCLUSIONS OF THE STUDY

One cannot help reading the literature of the advocates of restrictions without coming away with the strong impression that they seek, ultimately, to have government control the inter-, if not intra-, state flow of investment funds. Before such a dramatic shift in government policy is undertaken by way of seemingly innocuous plant closing legislation, arguments underpinning proposed restrictions need to be carefully scrutinized. Legislators would be well advised to look carefully behind the headlines and the emotional trauma that understandably accompanies plant closings. The purpose of this study is to do precisely that.

Bluestone and Harrison recognize that the "Great Reindustrialization Debate" is over several critically important questions, namely, "How do we build a stable, humane, equitable community and still have economic growth? And how can we go about the business of constructing a productive economy which produces livelihoods without destroying lives?"[22] Nothing could stir more agreement. The issue at stake is not whether proponents of restrictions on capital are more concerned with people's welfares than are the opponents. Opponents of restrictions are just as compassionate toward the people's plight as are proponents. Rather, the issue at the heart of the debate is how do we best go about achieving a compassionate, yet tolerably free society, which concerns us all. The argument of this book is not for economic distress or freewheeling economic greed. It is simply that the arguments for restrictions on capital are misguided and will not achieve their own goals.

On the surface, plant closing laws appear to be a relatively simple, straightforward solution to a complex and destructive social problem. However, the findings of this study lead inexorably to the conclusion that this new form of regulation will cut a swath, both broad and deep, across the private economy. It will inextricably entangle the federal and state governments in the affairs of business in a way never before attempted or even imagined. Governments will, very likely, become the arbiters of literally tens of thousands of closings and changes in operations, for we can expect firms to try to escape the economic burden implied in the restrictions through any one of the loopholes that inevitably exist in any sensible piece of legislation.

Establishing the economic justifiability of many closings will not be easy. Some firms will no doubt try to manipulate to their advantage the business assistance and worker buy-out provisions incorporated into several bills. And the closing restrictions are likely to increase—not decrease—the number of business failures. Clearly, plant closing laws increase the cost of doing business—*and of staying in business.* Furthermore, most of the proposed laws offer firms an economic incentive to order their financial affairs so they can declare bankruptcy when they declare their intentions to close. And state officials can anticipate that many firms will adjust their size and restructure their organization so that the closing laws do not apply to them; competitive pressure to minimize costs, including the costs of closing down, will encourage such maneuvering. We can only wonder whether state governments especially, struggling endlessly to keep afloat financially and efficiently produce traditional services like education and highway construction and maintenance, are actually prepared to cope with these circumstances.

22. Bluestone and Harrison, *Deindustrialization of America*, p. 21.

If enacted, where will these laws leave states? State governments will, in many respects, become more than regulators of entrepreneurship, more than just rule setters. They are likely to become entrepreneurs themselves, for their efforts to retard firm closings and relocations will necessarily affect the timing and regional distribution of the states' and nation's physical and human resources. Restrictions on plant closings are not simply restrictions on physical things like buildings and equipment; they are also restrictions on real people whose legitimately acquired rights will be usurped and managed by state government.

Today, whenever a community dams or diverts the flow of a stream, residents downstream can protest and seek legal redress. Similarly, when one state impedes a company from inter- or intra-regionally shifting its operations, other states are bound to protest, to counterattack with suits and legislation of their own in a grand game of "beggar-my-neighbor," hotly played today by sovereign countries in the world of international trade. Plant closing laws are not likely to dampen the growth of regionalism and "sectional economic warfare"; quite the opposite, these laws are likely to intensify regional political competition.

Contrary to arguments often heard, restrictions on investment decisions will not only affect the "greedy capitalist pigs" described by proponents of restrictions; they also will affect workers—some wealthy, some not so wealthy—who save and want to invest in efficiently run companies, who wish to buy goods and services at the lowest prices possible, and who will be less able to find the type of productive jobs they seek. As will be shown in this study, restrictions on capital mobility can be attacked on the grounds that they are inefficient. More importantly, however, they are an affront to the freedoms of individuals. That is why this study is undertaken with a sense of urgency in the belief that more is at stake than the many goods and services that will not be produced because of restrictions. That is the issue that has caused opponents of restrictions in Illinois to introduce a counterproposal to the plant closing bills: require unions to give a one-year notice of their intentions to strike. The logical consistency, but restrictiveness, of such a counterproposal makes clear that plant closing laws are an affront to individual freedom and decisionmaking.

In 1980 *The Wall Street Journal* began a two-part series on plant closings with a heart-rending story of a worker who heard the news of his plant's intended closing over his car radio. At the time, he happened to be on his way home from the bank, having just signed a $50,000.00 mortgage on a new house.[23] Clearly there are many similar stories to be told by workers across the country. *Plants do close down.* Some give their workers several months notice, as did Youngstown's Lykes Steel Company in 1977, but others give little notice. Sometimes firms lead their workers to believe operations will continue indefinitely, only to announce the closing a week or two later. And we have noted some firms — especially those that intend to go out of business altogether — have an economic incentive to hide their intentions to terminate operations because any announcement of such an intention can cripple a firm's ability to keep its employees and continue production and can increase losses (and the erosion of whatever capital is left).

Must we deal with such problems by state government fiat? It would be nice to be able to suggest that the solution to the controversy is simply one of finding a "compromise," a shorter prenotification requirement (somewhere between no requirement and one or two years) and a smaller, mandated severance pay, possibly one or two week's worth. The dilemma is, however, much more complex. There will be a cost attached to any uniform requirement, and those costs will be borne by real people. Workers will probably bear most of the burden, and the difficulty in the state's mandating severance pay lies in the fact that not all workers within a state will want to make the same trade-off between severance pay and wages or other forgone fringe benefits.

Proponents of restrictive legislation should remember that all workers initially have the right to ten or even fifty-two weeks of severance pay: all they have to do is negotiate it, meaning they must be prepared to make the attendant sacrifices. Most are unlikely to choose to make the wage sacrifices necessary in order for them to "buy" fifty-two weeks of severance pay. If they were, we should see many more worker or union contracts with such provisions. Profit-maximizing firms should not be opposed to severance pay and notification provisions in workers' contracts, *provided workers are willing to forgo the necessary wages.* Is there not a form of "revealed preference" evident in the absence of notification and severance pay benefits in worker contracts? Would not *mandatory* severance pay

23. *Wall Street Journal*, September 22 and 23, 1981, p. 1.

(which would give rise to lower wages) be a "bad deal" for workers who would not otherwise choose to negotiate, on a voluntary basis, extended severance and notification provisions in their contracts?

In a free market, contracts can contain virtually any terms, so long as the parties agree and are held responsible. For the market to work sensibly, however, contracts must be enforceable and enforced through the courts. There are good economic arguments in support of laws against fraud, and such laws should be just as applicable to employee–employer relationships as they are to consumer–seller relationships. Employer fraud concerning severance pay or continued operations of a plant can be disruptive and lead to the misallocation of resources. To insure efficiency as well as equity in the private sector, people—employers and employees—must be held accountable for the bargains they strike. If an employee gives up a portion of his or her wages in exchange for a guarantee of severance pay, then in the event the plant closes, his or her rights to severance pay must be upheld. Otherwise, employers are unlikely to have to pay the full costs of production, distorting the allocation of resources. (The word "unlikely" is used advisedly. An employer who continually reneges on his bargains with his workers is likely to find that he will have to pay higher wages to hire the appropriate number and quality of workers. Workers will demand higher wages in order to be compensated for the risks associated with not knowing what bargains, if any, the employer will keep.)

In order for people to retain economic freedom, they must be deemed tolerably responsible for their own actions, for their own implicit or explicit contracts. If people in general are considered too unintelligent or uninformed to negotiate their own contracts, then there is a case for the government's protection of them. However, we must wonder if governments, operating in a world of uninformed people, can by fiat improve social welfare. Governments will also be peopled with the "uninformed," and they will have one additional problem: they will know little of the *individual* circumstances of their *individual* constituents. To that extent, the protection they offer from people's supposed stupidity may be no protection at all. The remedy to the problem of plant closings developed in detail in this volume is this: let people, taking account of their own individual circumstances and preferences, do their own bargaining over their working conditions and benefits. However, hold them responsible for the bargains they strike. Such are the ingredients of a free economy—indeed, a free society.

Chapter 2

PRIVATE DISINVESTMENT AND EMPLOYMENT LOSSES

The phrase "private disinvestment," now unknown to most Americans, is likely to become a media buzzword during the 1980s. The contemporary literature on "capital flight" is replete with it. In simple terms, "disinvestment" means the closing down or wearing out of plants and equipment. Nothing is particularly disturbing about that; plants and equipment are expected to wear out at some point. However, when the phrase is juxtaposed with pictures of idle plants, interviews with displaced workers, and news accounts of how firms have suddenly closed their doors and moved to new facilities in another section of the country or the world, a cloud of evil intent and social disruption is cast over what may most often be perfectly rational, understandable, and socially productive business behavior. The emotional context of the disinvestment debate begs for facts on how serious the problem of plant closings actually is. For that reason, this chapter extends our discussion of plant closings by examining the empirical case for restrictions on disinvestment.

THE ARGUMENTS FOR RESTRICTING DISINVESTMENT

The concerns expressed by those who support restricting business disinvestment are many. On the subject of job losses. Barry Bluestone and Bennett Harrison write in the first version of their major study:

> ... [A]t least 45,000 closings occurred in Massachusetts over the seven-year period (December 31, 1969–December 31, 1976), and 95,000 in New England as a whole. . . . [These] closings in Massachusetts cost the state's workers some 508,000 jobs. For New England as a whole, the 95,000 closings dislocated a bit over a million workers. . . . The 213,000 jobs destroyed in Massachusetts alone by reason of establishment closings between 1969 and 1972 means that *more than one in six (17%) of the jobs reported to D and B [Dun and Bradstreet, Inc.] in 1969 disappeared for this reason in just three years.*[1]
>
> Extrapolating from the 9.3 million jobs eliminated in the states shown, . . . between 1969 and 1976 at least 15 million jobs appear to have been destroyed in the United States as a direct result of shut-downs. *That is an average of 2.5 million jobs each year.*[2]

The Bluestone-Harrison extrapolation of the nation's job losses between 1969 and 1976 is based on the data contained in Table 2–1, which includes the job losses and gains for an incomplete listing of states. The job losses are attributed to one overriding problem, "the accelerating velocity of capital—its increasingly frenetic, unplanned, and abrupt movement—and the fact that the real social and economic consequences of its mobility hardly ever enter into the decisions of corporate managers."[3]

Several reasons are normally given for the "accelerating velocity of capital." Emphasis is put on the role government taxes and expenditures, especially at the federal level, play in providing businesses with incentives for disinvestment and disincentives for the reinvestment of earnings in old, established plants.[4] In addition, much disinvestment supposedly occurs because of the American proclivity to favor new

1. Barry Bluestone and Bennett Harrison, *Capital and Communities: The Causes and Consequences of Private Disinvestment* (Washington: The Progressive Alliance, 1980), pp. 34–37. Bluestone and Harrison have revised and republished their study as *The Deindustrialization of America: Plant Closings, Community Abandonment, and the Dismantling of Basic Industry* (New York: Basic Books, 1982). My analysis, however, concentrates on the first version for two reasons: First, their argument has not fundamentally changed. Second, the purpose of this study is to counter arguments that have been influential in the past.

2. Bluestone and Harrison, *Capital and Communities*, p. 59.

3. Ibid., p. 17.

4. Michael Sullivan, Peter Tropper, and David Puryear, *Tax Incentives and Business Investment Patterns: A Survey of Urban and Regional Implications* (Washington: Northeast-Midwest Institute, June 1981).

Table 2-1. Employment Gained or Lost Through Start-Ups, Closings, and Relocations of Private Business Establishments in Selected States, 1969-76.

State and Region	Jobs Created (000s)	Jobs Destroyed (000s)	Ratio of Jobs Destroyed to Jobs Created	Net Employment Change[a]
		Frostbelt		
New England				
Massachusetts	446	500	1.13	-54
Connecticut	211	238	1.13	-27
Mid-Atlantic				
New York	1,087	1,494	1.37	-407
Pennsylvania	827	865	1.05	-38
East North Central				
Michigan	639	552	0.86	87
Ohio	789	720	0.91	69
West North Central				
Minnesota	249	243	0.98	6
Missouri	321	305	0.95	16
		Sunbelt		
South Atlantic				
Georgia	594	416	0.70	178
North Carolina	372	374	1.01	-2
East South Central				
Alabama	283	252	0.89	31
Tennessee	354	296	0.84	58
West South Central				
Louisiana	300	233	0.76	67
Texas	1,153	830	0.72	323
Mountain				
Arizona	141	125	0.89	16
Colorado	238	174	0.73	64
Pacific				
California	1,820	1,477	0.81	343
Washington	244	180	0.74	64
U.S. Total	16,505[a]	15,121[a]	0.92	1,302

a. Estimates not provided in the source table.

Source: Barry Bluestone and Bennett Harrison, *Capital and Communities: The Causes and Consequences of Private Disinvestment* (Washington, D.C.: The Progressive Alliance, 1980), p. 40 (last two columns of table). The calculations are based on David L. Birch, *The Job Generation Process* (Cambridge, Mass.: M.I.T. Program on Neighborhood and Regional Change, 1979), Appendix A.

locations over old ones: "Next to antiunionism, the strongest motivation for flight from existing industrial cities would appear to be the American penchant to abandon last year's car, last year's spouse, and last year's community." [5]

According to Bluestone and Harrison, the acceleration in the mobility of capital is also caused to a significant extent by growth in the power and influence of dominant domestic and multinational corporations:

> [T]he whole mode of operation of the modern conglomerate is organized around the acquisition of profitable subsidiary business establishments. The implication is that a corporate and especially a conglomerate closing is more likely to be the result of a *planned* strategy to increase profits, while the closing of an independently-owned business is more likely to constitute a truly involuntary "failure." [6]

Of course, as might be expected, special concern is expressed over the shift of capital to foreign countries:

> Foreign investment by American capitalists [which expanded from about $12 to $118 billion between 1950 and 1974] takes many forms. But whether it is going into the construction of overseas branch plants of U.S. firms or to purchase part ownership in businesses established by other countries, *the dollars invested abroad are unavailable for economic development at home* [emphasis added]. [7]

To which is added, "each $1 billion of direct foreign investment by American firms destroys something like 26,500 domestic jobs on balance." [8]

The social damage of "disinvestment" is seen as affecting the personal lives of workers and their families. Representative William Ford, reporting on the research findings of others, has written, "It is well established that the affected workers suffer a far higher incidence of heart disease and hypertension, diabetes, peptic ulcers, gout, and joint swelling than the general population. They also incur

5. Staughton Lynd, "Reindustrialization: Browfield or Greenfield," *Democracy* (July 1981): 27.

6. Bluestone and Harrison, *Capital and Communities*, p. 39.

7. Ibid., p. 23.

8. Ibid., p. 59. Bluestone and Harrison base this estimate on the work of Robert H. Frank and Richard T. Freeman, "The Distributional Consequences of Direct Foreign Investment," in William G. Dewald, ed., *The Impact of International Trade on Employment, A Conference of the U.S. Department of Labor* (Washington: U.S. Government Printing Office, 1978).

serious psychological problems, including extreme depression, insecurity, anxiety, and the loss of self-esteem." [9]

Although actual growth in regional employment opportunities and capital stock is sometimes recognized, proponents of restrictions emphasize the "decline" of the economy and social infrastructure of northern industrial tier states. Writing for the Northeast-Midwest Institute on the economic health of its constituent region, Jacqueline Mazza and Bill Hogan conclude

> The trends highlighted in the preceding chapters [of *The State of the Region, 1981*] constitute a pronounced threat to the physical and economic well-being of the 100-million Americans living in the Northeast-Midwest region, and to the security of the nation as a whole. Unabated, these shifts will erode many of America's productive resources—its industry, its workforce, and its physical infrastructure—at a time when our country can least afford it. Population loss, high living costs, structural unemployment, low growth rates of business investment, and soaring energy prices are but a few of the signposts marking the region's difficult road ahead. [10]

Mazza and Hogan then quote approvingly columnist Neil Pierce, who writes, "The 1980s could be an era of two Americas—one thriving, one hemorrhaging at every pore; one reaching new levels of growth and prosperity, one on a slippery slide of permanent decline." [11] In another column he adds,

> Such trends [in the abandonment of the older industrial areas] are inherently anti-social, because they encourage population outflows and the destruction of established city neighborhoods. They are also diseconomic: first, because national taxpayers eventually have to pay, at least in part, the bill for high levels of urban distress. And second, because they encourage the abandonment or underuse of buildings and public "infrastructures"—public roads, bridges, sewers, transit facilities—long since paid for by the society. [12]

9. William D. Ford, "The National Employment Priorities Act of 1979," *Congressional Record: House* (2 August 1979), p. 7240. See also Jeanne Prial Gordus, Paul Jarley, and Louis A. Freeman, *Plant Closings and Economic Dislocation* (Kalamazoo, Mich.: W.E. Upjohn Institute for Employment Research, 1981), chapters 5 and 6.

10. Jacqueline Mazza and Bill Hogan, *The State of the Region, 1981: Economic Trends in the Northeast-Midwest* (Washington, D.C.: Northeast-Midwest Institute and the Northeast-Midwest Congressional Coalition, 1981), p. 47.

11. Neil R. Pierce, "Offing the Frost Belt: A Stupid Idea Whose Time Has Come," *Washington Post* (18 January 1981), as quoted in Mazza and Hogan, *The State of the Region, 1981*, p. 47.

12. Neil R. Pierce, "An 'Economic Dunkirk'—For Whom?" *Minneapolis Tribune* (4 January 1981), as quoted in Mazza and Hogan, *The State of the Region, 1981*, p. 48.

With such claims continually sounded by capitalism's protectors, as well as its detractors, it is not hard to see how the average person may imagine private entrepreneurs to be unconstrained social terrorists who care little about others and who go around in pinstriped suits, intentionally or unintentionally pushing people off "economic ledges."

The purpose of the remainder of the chapter is straightforward. It is to investigate a number of the empirical and conceptual claims regarding the economic distress caused by plant closings, observed primarily in northern states. More specifically, our focus is on the following:

- To the extent they can be assessed, the actual changes in employment, incomes, capital stock, and tax base experienced by different regions, states, and selected cities, especially in the North;
- The extent to which the employment losses in the North are due to businesses relocating to other parts of the country;
- The degree to which employment gains in the South and West are due to firms moving in.

In short, the purpose of this chapter is to initiate an analysis of regional economic problems, especially in the North, by dispelling media myths regarding regional economic disparities in growth of jobs and income. Later chapters focus on conceptual arguments surrounding proposed plant closing restrictions. Because the arguments for plant closing restrictions arose in the early 1970s, before the recessions of the early 1980s, and because recent recessions may seriously distort long-term trends in employment, attention in the following discussion is focused on the 1965–1980 period. This does not mean that the employment problems encountered in the early 1970s are unimportant. On the contrary, they *are* important. However, the purpose of plant closing restrictions is supposedly to relieve long-run unemployment problems related to structural shifts in the economy, the kind of unemployment observable in trend analysis, not cyclical unemployment problems.

The general conclusion of this chapter is relatively clear from the evidence: Contrary to what might be expected from reports on plant closures, the North's economy is alive (at least, its health is stronger than one-sided reports on plant closings suggest), but sections of the northern economy are faltering *relative* to other areas of the country in the sense that growth is slower. Of course, the North has economic problems—the whole country has experienced many well-documented problems, including high inflation and unemployment rates, low or nonexistent rates of growth in worker productivity, comparatively low rates of growth in real personal income, and absolute decreases in after-tax, spendable income. The point is that these are problems encountered *in all regions of the country*.

Clearly, public policy should be directed toward relieving these national problems, if for no other reason than misguided public policies are at the heart of our inflation, productivity, and unemployment problems. The question is not whether the northern economy is on the decline; the data presented below, on balance, reveal growth, albeit slow, in the northern states. Rather, the question is threefold. First, is the ongoing restructuring of the American economy, which has resulted in plant closings *and* openings nationwide, a significant symptom or cause of the North's relatively slow growth in jobs and income? Second, are government policies, especially at the federal level, contributing to the North's relatively slow growth rate? Third, should the evolutionary, ongoing restructuring of the economy be augmented by purposeful government policy designed to retard or reshape business investment, reinvestment, or disinvestment decisions—that is, can such policies be expected to generally improve people's welfares? This chapter presents an empirical base for examining those questions.

EMPLOYMENT PATTERNS

Concern over the perceived economic decay in the North and Midwest is shared by many who are sympathetic to the capitalistic system. *Business Week*, for example, began a discussion of the regional impact of "America's Restructured Economy" with this assessment:

> The segmenting of the American economy is threatening to create a nation divided into regions of haves and havenots. While production, population and jobs are booming in the South and West, where energy and high-technology industries abound, they are *plummeting* in the old industrial Northeast and Midwest. So *swift* are the dislocations of labor and capital in the Northeast and Midwest that they are intensifying the social and political problems that high unemployment, urban decay, and eroding the political power inevitably cause [emphasis added].[13]

13. "Dislocations that May Deepen: Regional Impact," *Business Week* (1 June 1981), p. 62.

The fact is, however, that northern and midwestern employment patterns do not support the dire economic picture the magazine paints for the 1965–1980 period.

Regions

Consider Table 2–2 and Figures 2–1 through 2–4, which contain data on the four broad regions of the country, Northeast, North Central, West, and South. Because concern is expressed most often about "plummeting" employment in "old-line industries" (which, for the most part, are covered by manufacturing employment), the table and figures are restricted to total employment set in contrast with manufacturing employment in the several regions. In the figures, the employment is scaled along the vertical axis, and years along the horizontal axis, with the slope of the trend lines noted in the interior of the figures, indicating the compound annual rate of growth or decline in employment during the 1965–1980 period. (Because the employment scales on the vertical axes are not uniform across the figures, the reader must compare the graphs carefully and use the recorded growth rates to interpret the meaning of the slopes of the trend lines.)

The single most important observation that can be made pertains to manufacturing employment in the North. Although North Central manufacturing employment has had its ups and downs during the fifteen-year period, the peaks in the manufacturing employment cycles have remained fairly constant, i.e., the trend is rather flat. Representative Ford has noted, as have others, that the northern manufacturing states have lost a million or so manufacturing jobs.[14] That deduction requires careful selection of years used in the comparison, for example, 1969 (a boom year) and 1975 (a recovery year). In that period, the loss in manufacturing employment for the Northeast and North Central regions combined is 1,171,500.

Granted, over the 1965–1980 period manufacturing employment did decline in the Northeast, but by a compound rate of 1.4 percent, and stayed more or less the same in the North Central region. On the other hand, total employment in the two regions grew by 1 and 2 percent, respectively, meaning that the growth in nonmanufacturing jobs more than compensated for the loss in manufacturing jobs. And

14. Ford, *Congressional Record*, p. 7240.

Table 2-2. Total Non-Agricultural Employment and Manufacturing Employment by Census Bureau Regions, 1965-1980 (thousands).

Year	United States Total	Mfg.	Northeast Total	Mfg.	North Central Total	Mfg.	South Total	Mfg.	West Total	Mfg.
1965	60674.0	18280.1	16693.5	5623.0	17493.1	5969.8	16717.9	4340.7	9769.5	2346.6
1966	63881.9	19209.0	17336.4	5878.2	18432.3	6345.6	17749.5	4672.2	10363.7	2313.0
1967	65785.2	19354.2	17730.5	5888.2	18914.7	6345.2	18428.1	4796.1	10711.9	2324.7
1968	68023.2	19776.0	18170.1	5843.0	19460.4	6466.0	19203.1	4999.1	11189.6	2467.9
1969	70359.0	20155.9	18639.4	5879.6	20059.7	6612.5	19969.3	5193.4	11690.6	2470.4
1970	70624.6	19363.4	18653.6	5611.0	19918.2	6264.5	20278.9	5120.7	11773.9	2367.2
1971	70850.4	18541.1	18395.5	5234.5	19834.0	5981.4	20733.0	5065.7	11887.9	2259.5
1972	73113.9	18942.2	18633.3	5208.3	20269.9	6105.5	21746.2	5270.4	12464.5	2358.0
1973	77229.2	20076.3	19142.5	5350.4	21408.6	6542.0	23389.8	5632.1	13288.3	2551.8
1974	78640.7	20044.2	19221.0	5295.1	21746.0	6484.2	23948.3	5646.5	13725.4	2618.4
1975	76848.2	18204.1	18577.1	4791.3	21073.5	5729.4	23449.0	5166.1	13748.6	2517.3
1976	79673.7	18984.4	18807.2	4863.1	21811.1	6037.9	24694.3	5512.9	14361.1	2570.5
1977	82801.1	19104.4	19235.8	4455.7	22539.8	6219.9	25779.3	5723.6	15246.2	2705.2
1978	87263.3	20523.9	19663.5	5114.5	23540.2	6497.2	27350.5	5976.6	16409.1	2935.6
1979	90304.4	21035.5	20406.2	5201.6	24055.3	6586.5	28566.4	6108.8	17276.5	3138.6
1980	90875.4	20353.2	20496.9	5078.8	23655.5	6068.9	29141.7	6073.7	17581.3	3131.8

Source: *Employment and Earnings*, various issues.

Figure 2-1.
NORTHEAST 1965-1980
Total Employment and Manufacturing Employment.

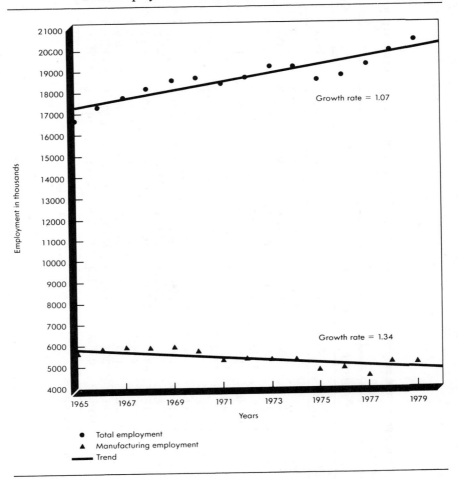

the growth in jobs in the North generally was at a slightly faster rate than the growth in the population, resulting in an increase in the labor force participation rate for northern workers (a change that was more pronounced in other regions).

Although the labor force participation rate did not, generally speaking, expand during the 1970s as rapidly in the North as it did in the South, the participation rate was higher in sections of the North

Figure 2-2.
NORTH CENTRAL 1965-1980
Total Employment and Manufacturing Employment.

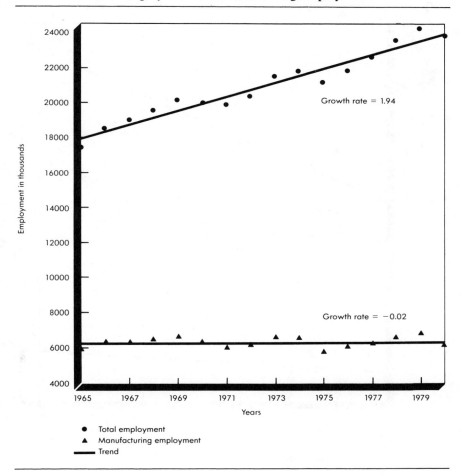

than in sections of the South: New England (65.9); Mid-Atlantic (60.9); East North Central (64.9); West North Central (66.4); South Atlantic (62.8); East South Central (60.4); West South Central (63.4); Mountain (65.4); and Pacific (65.5). The growth in the participation rate in sections of the North can be partially attributed to the lower population growth rate of the North, which, in turn, is due partly to the out-migration from the North during the 1970s.

Figure 2–3.
SOUTH 1965–1980
Total Employment and Manufacturing Employment.

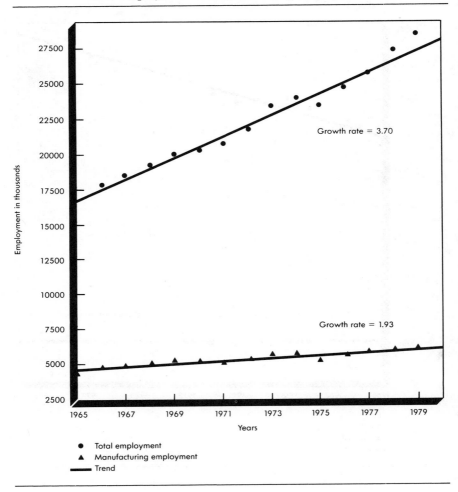

The figures reveal clearly that employment in the South and West grew more rapidly than in the North. What is somewhat startling, given the publicity surrounding the in-migration of Northern manufacturing industries into the South and West, is that the compound growth rate of manufacturing employment for 1965–80 was relatively modest, 1.93 percent for the South and 1.99 percent for the West. Like the North, the southern and western areas of the country

Figure 2–4.
WEST 1965–1980
Total Employment and Manufacturing Employment.

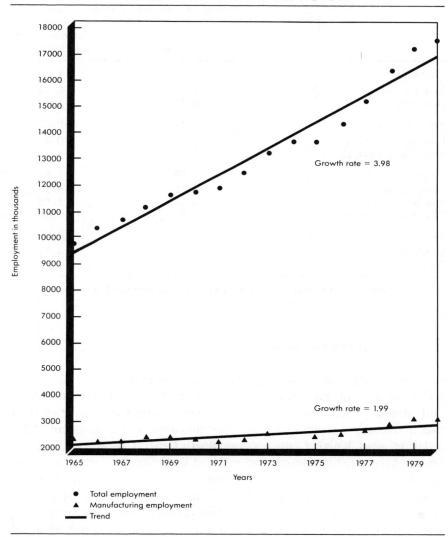

generally found their nonmanufacturing employment in, for example, energy, mining, services, and government growing more rapidly than their manufacturing employment. Table 2–3 gives the details on the specific growth rates for manufacturing employment and total employment.

Table 2-3. Growth Rate in Employment for Census Bureau Regions
and Divisions, 1965-1980.

	Compounded Rate (percent)	
	Total Employment	Manufacturing Employment
Northeast	1.07	−1.34
New England	1.81	−0.34
Mid-Atlantic	0.82	−1.72
North Central	1.94	−0.02
East North Central	1.65	−0.34
West North Central	2.69	1.27
South	3.70	1.93
South Atlantic	3.54	1.36
East South Central	3.24	1.82
West South Central	4.28	3.28
West	3.98	1.99
Mountain	5.41	4.46
Pacific	3.55	1.65

Source: Based on trend values for 1965 and 1980 and computed from data in Table
2-2.

Divisions and States

Of course, the four broad regions considered above may mask sharp
differences in employment gains *and* losses of census bureau divisions
and states. Hence, data on total nonagricultural employment and
manufacturing employment in nine divisions (New England, Mid-
Atlantic, East North Central, West North Central, Mountain, Pacific,
South Atlantic, East South Central, and West South Central) are provided in Table 2-4 and Figures 2-5 through 2-13. Again the employment trends are much the same: manufacturing employment in
the New England and East North Central divisions is relatively flat,
with up and down movements around the more or less horizontal
trend lines. Manufacturing employment in the Mid-Atlantic states,
a division with one of the worst employment records, declined over
the 1965-80 period by 1.72 percent per year compounded, a decline
that was largely but not totally offset by the growth in the West
North Central. Here and elsewhere in this chapter, the compounded

growth rate is based on predicted values for the employment trends analysis for the 1965–80 period.

Total employment in the northern divisions, on the other hand, grew irregularly and less rapidly than total employment in the southern and western divisions. Still, *there was growth in job opportunities.* The growth in employment in the West North Central division, 2.69 percent compounded, is substantially higher than the growth rates of other northern divisions. Even New York and Ohio, two states with relatively poor economic performances for northern industrial tier states, experienced some total employment gains at compound rates of 0.27 and 1.63 percent, respectively (see Figures 2–14 and 2–15). In both states manufacturing employment declined, at compound rates of 2.20 and 0.41 percent, respectively, meaning that jobs in other sectors of their economies were expanding, albeit gradually. (To complete the comparison task, employment data on all other states are contained in the Table B–1 in Appendix B.) Generally speaking, after reviewing the employment records of regions and their states, descriptions of "plummeting" employment conditions in the North over the long-run, like those in the *Business Week* quotation above, are hard to justify.

Cities

True, small geographical areas, like cities, may be hard-hit by employment losses when the economies of their states and regions are expanding. The employment trends of Akron, Cleveland, Detroit, Gary, Newark, Pittsburgh, and Youngstown, cities that are often described as "depressed," follow the employment patterns of their regions in several important respects. First, strong cyclical swings in employment are present (see Figures 2–16 through 2–22). Second, the trend in manufacturing employment is either flat or slightly downward sloping (Table 2–5 gives the details on the compound rates of change in employment). Third, the trend in total employment is upward, albeit slightly, in every one of these cities. Even Youngstown's total employment grew at a compound rate of 1.15 percent over the 1965–1980 period, more than offsetting the 1 percent decline in manufacturing employment, which was accelerating in the 1970s. In spite of these points, it must be reiterated that these cities are not without serious economic problems.

Table 2–4. Total Non-Agricultural Employment and Manufacturing Employment by Census Bureau Divisions, 1965–1980 (thousands).

Year	Mid-Atlantic		New England		East North Central		West North Central	
	Total	Mfg.	Total	Mfg.	Total	Mfg.	Total	Mfg.
1965	12690.6	4163.4	4002.9	1459.6	12864.8	4884.9	4628.3	1084.9
1966	13144.2	4330.6	4192.2	1547.6	13547.6	5163.0	4884.7	1182.6
1967	13439.9	4325.2	4290.6	1563.0	13861.5	5118.4	5053.2	1226.8
1968	13747.9	4290.0	4422.2	1553.0	14285.2	5213.0	5175.2	1253.0
1969	14125.0	4347.8	4514.4	1531.8	14727.6	5334.4	5332.1	1278.1
1970	14129.8	4162.2	4523.8	1448.8	14578.3	5042.2	5339.9	1222.3
1971	13902.5	3888.1	4493.0	1346.4	14463.7	4806.2	5370.3	1175.2
1972	14059.9	3853.3	4573.4	1355.0	14723.6	4882.3	5546.3	1223.2
1973	14374.0	3932.9	4768.5	1417.5	15546.3	5228.8	5862.3	1313.2
1974	14383.5	3859.8	4837.5	1435.3	15722.7	5149.7	6023.3	1334.5
1975	13874.5	3478.8	4702.6	1312.5	15162.0	4506.1	5911.5	1223.3
1976	14034.6	3527.4	4772.6	1335.7	15615.5	4764.6	6195.6	1273.3
1977	14263.4	3048.5	4972.4	1407.2	16088.9	4896.2	6450.9	1323.7
1978	14737.8	3639.6	5225.7	1474.9	16785.7	5106.9	6754.5	1390.3
1979	15012.7	3678.7	5393.5	1522.9	17196.2	5138.6	6859.1	1447.9
1980	15015.8	3554.2	5481.1	1524.6	16752.5	4687.6	6903.0	1381.3

Table 2–4. continued

Year	South Atlantic Total	Mfg.	East South Central Total	Mfg.	West South Central Total	Mfg.	Mountain Total	Mfg.	Pacific Total	Mfg.
1965	8547.0	2348.8	3236.9	1022.7	4934.0	969.2	2175.3	290.9	7594.2	2055.7
1966	9073.1	2507.8	3442.2	1114.0	5234.2	1050.4	2283.7	318.3	8080.0	1994.7
1967	9407.5	2558.4	3531.0	1130.9	5489.6	1106.8	2336.4	320.7	8375.5	2004.0
1968	9846.9	2650.3	3668.7	1178.0	5687.5	1170.8	2434.8	336.9	8754.8	2131.0
1969	10273.9	2736.9	3769.3	1224.6	5926.1	1231.9	2568.0	362.4	9122.6	2108.0
1970	10465.2	2678.4	3825.0	1223.3	5988.7	1219.0	2648.9	363.2	9125.0	2004.0
1971	10746.6	2654.1	3903.9	1220.1	6082.5	1191.5	2778.0	365.2	9109.9	1894.3
1972	11219.3	2740.4	4133.1	1287.2	6393.8	1242.8	2950.0	388.2	9514.5	1969.8
1973	12206.6	2921.8	4391.8	1376.3	6791.4	1334.0	3261.0	433.3	10027.3	2118.5
1974	12382.2	2895.8	4500.7	1376.0	7065.4	1374.7	3393.9	447.4	10331.5	2171.0
1975	11973.0	2632.3	4356.1	1226.1	7119.9	1307.7	3391.6	416.4	10357.0	2100.9
1976	12483.5	2735.5	4621.6	1318.5	7589.2	1408.9	3537.6	444.8	10823.5	2125.7
1977	13009.3	2877.7	4831.5	1376.8	7938.5	1469.1	3822.4	476.7	11423.8	2228.5
1978	13750.1	2991.6	5097.1	1422.4	8503.3	1562.6	4164.5	520.6	12244.6	2415.0
1979	14391.7	3039.4	5218.8	1432.0	8955.9	1637.4	4413.5	561.2	12863.0	2577.4
1980	14694.6	3041.5	5144.8	1362.7	9302.3	1669.5	4501.9	564.1	13079.4	2567.7

Source: Employment and Earnings, various issues.

Figure 2-5.
NEW ENGLAND 1965-1980
Total Employment and Manufacturing Employment.

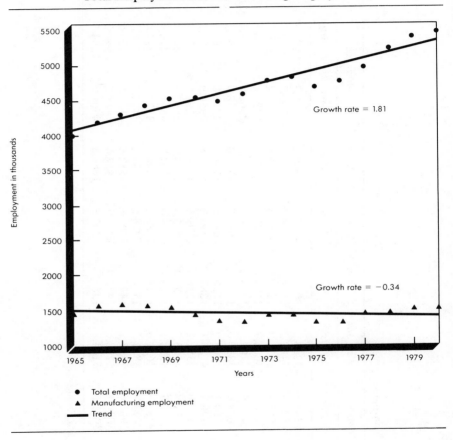

Figure 2-6.
MIDDLE ATLANTIC 1965-1980
Total Employment and Manufacturing Employment.

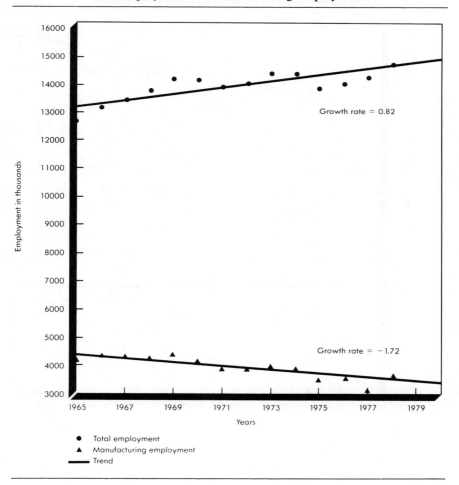

Figure 2-7.
EAST NORTH CENTRAL 1965-1980
Total Employment and Manufacturing Employment.

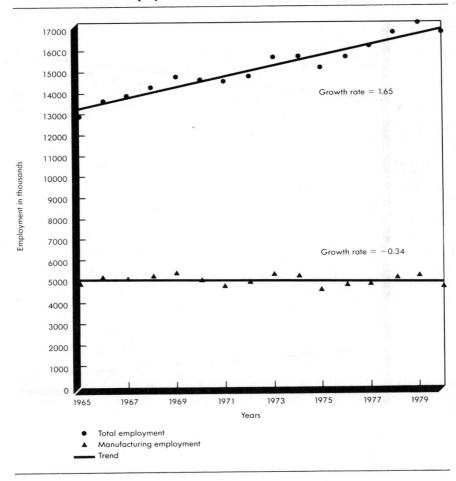

Figure 2–8.
WEST NORTH CENTRAL 1965–1980
Total Employment and Manufacturing Employment.

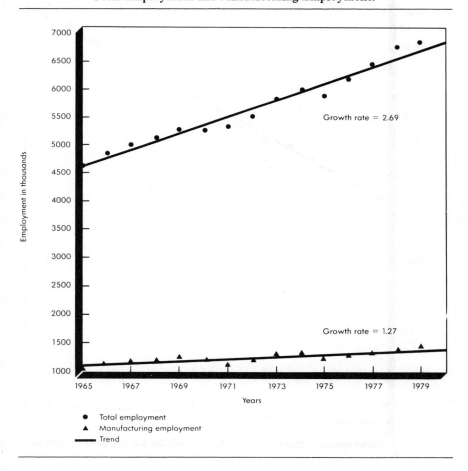

Figure 2–9.
SOUTH ATLANTIC 1965–1980
Total Employment and Manufacturing Employment.

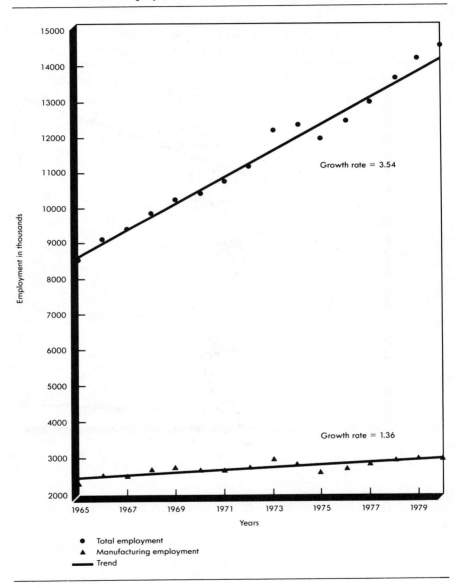

Figure 2-10.
EAST SOUTH CENTRAL 1965-1980
Total Employment and Manufacturing Employment.

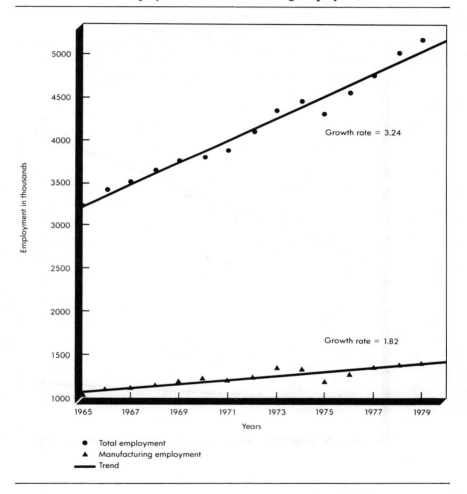

Figure 2-11.
WEST SOUTH CENTRAL 1965-1980
Total Employment and Manufacturing Employment.

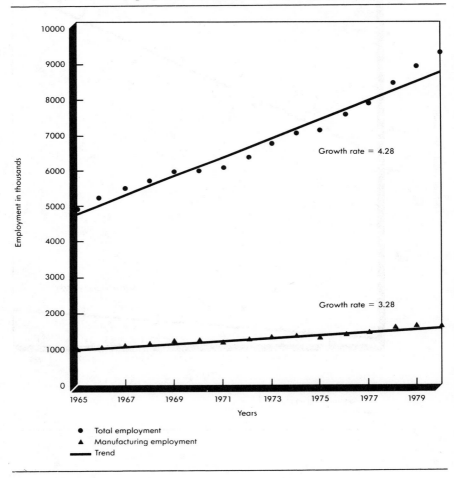

Figure 2-12.
MOUNTAIN 1965-1980
Total Employment and Manufacturing Employment.

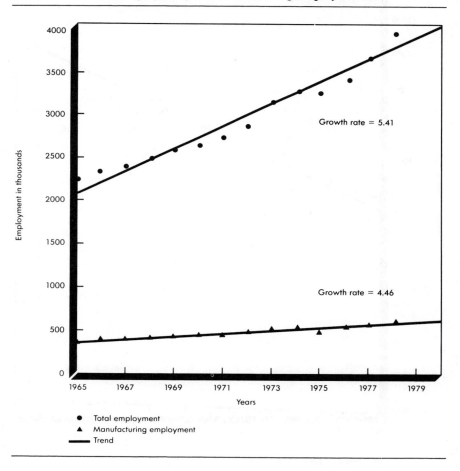

Figure 2-13.
PACIFIC 1965-1980
Total Employment and Manufacturing Employment.

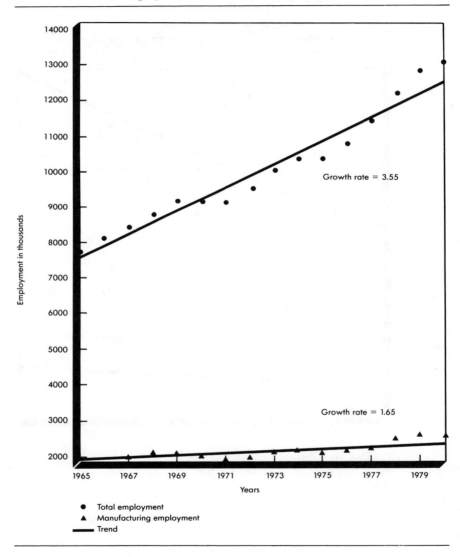

Figure 2–14.
NEW YORK 1965–1980
Total Employment and Manufacturing Employment.

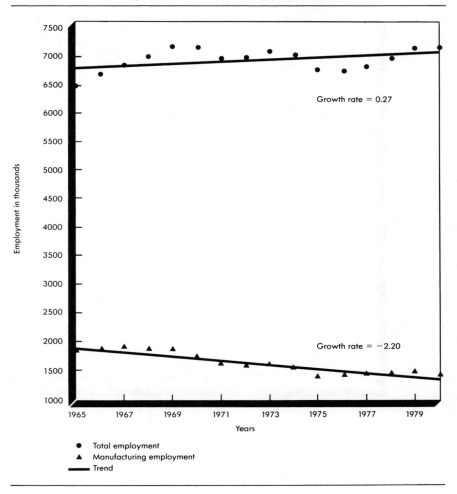

Figure 2-15.
OHIO 1965-1980
Total Employment and Manufacturing Employment.

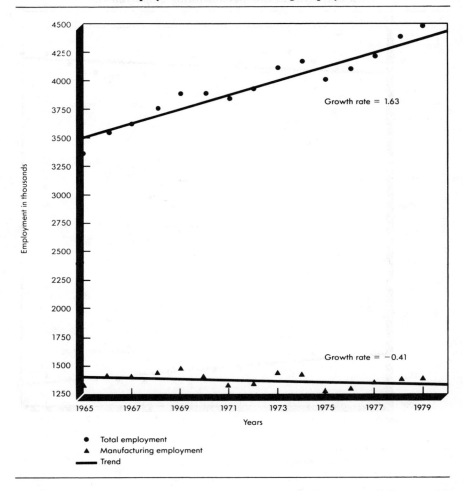

Figure 2–16.
AKRON 1965–1980
Total Employment and Manufacturing Employment.

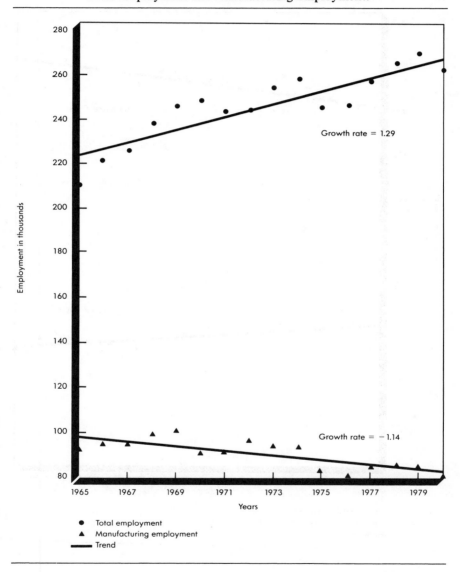

Figure 2-17.
CLEVELAND 1965-1980
Total Employment and Manufacturing Employment.

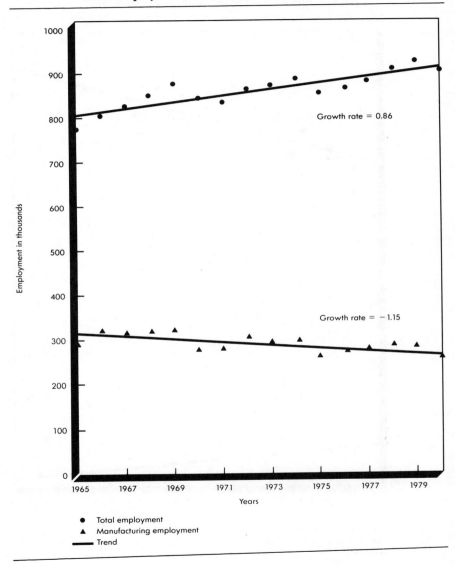

Growth rate = 0.86

Growth rate = −1.15

Employment in thousands

Years

● Total employment
▲ Manufacturing employment
━━ Trend

Figure 2–18.
DETROIT 1965–1980
Total Employment and Manufacturing Employment.

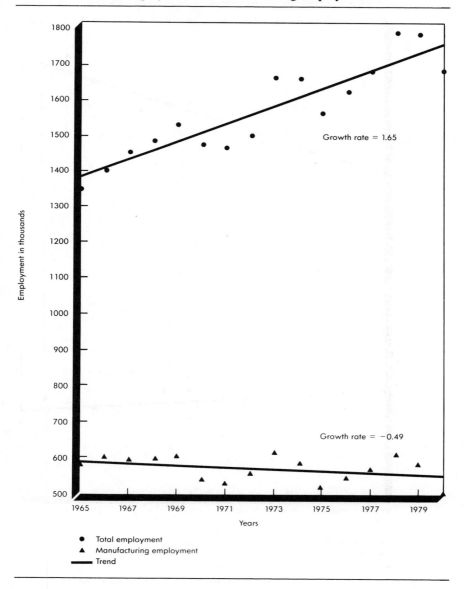

Figure 2-19.
GARY 1965-1980
Total Employment and Manufacturing Employment.

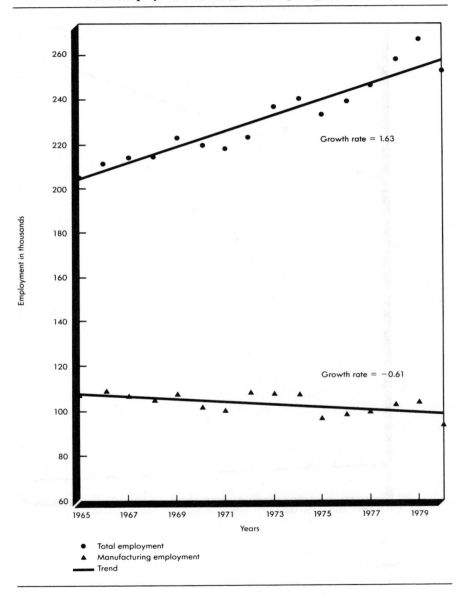

Figure 2-20.
NEWARK 1965-1980
Total Employment and Manufacturing Employment.

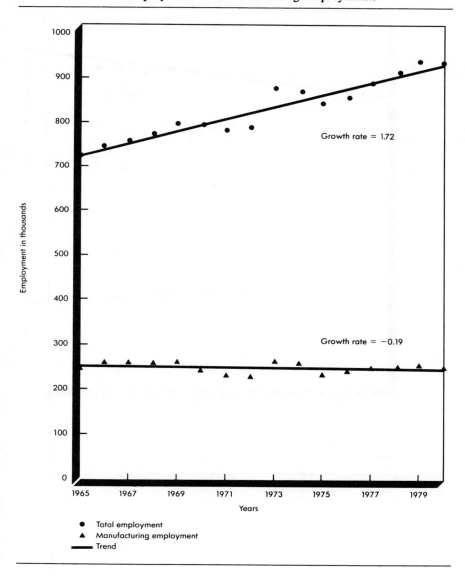

Growth rate = 1.72

Growth rate = −0.19

Employment in thousands

Years

● Total employment
▲ Manufacturing employment
━ Trend

Figure 2–21.
PITTSBURGH 1965–1980
Total Employment and Manufacturing Employment.

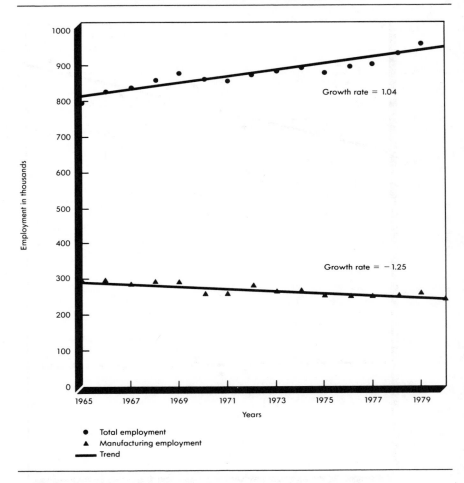

Figure 2-22.
YOUNGSTOWN 1965-1980
Total Employment and Manufacturing Employment.

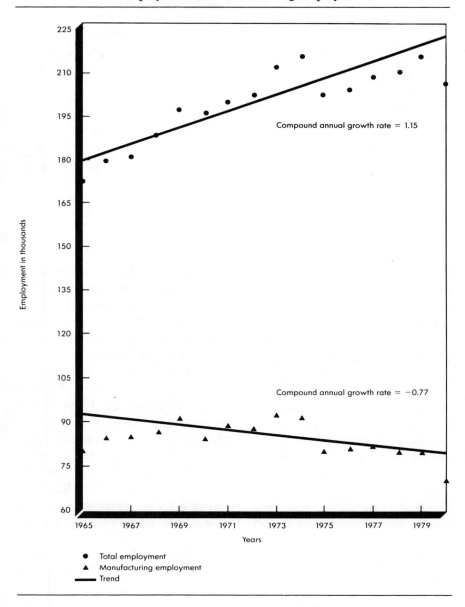

Table 2-5. Growth in Employment for Selected Northern Cities, 1965-1980.

Cities	Compounded Rate (percent)	
	Total Employment	Manufacturing Employment
Akron	1.29	-1.14
Cleveland	0.86	-1.15
Detroit	1.65	-0.49
Gary	1.63	-0.61
Newark	1.72	-0.19
Pittsburgh	1.04	-1.25
Youngstown	1.15	-0.78

Source: Based on trend values for 1965 and 1980 and computed from *Employment and Earnings*, various issues.

Interim Assessment

Is the northern economy being divested of jobs? Is the nation being divided into regions of "haves and have-nots" as far as employment is concerned? The answer, in absolute terms, is clearly no. The northern labor market is still growing *absolutely*, and therefore any case for the economic decline of the North must be made in *relative* terms: The northern economy has not grown as rapidly in employment as the South and West. As manufacturing employment in other regions has grown relatively more rapidly, the North's share of manufactured goods in the nation has shrunk progressively. Its economy has, indeed, been "restructured" *in a relative sense.* However, it should be emphasized that before the 1980-82 recessions, manufacturing employment in the Northeast and North Central combined generally was on the rebound, gaining nearly 900,000 jobs between 1976 and 1979, and that there are Census Bureau divisions, like New England, and states, like New Hampshire, that registered an economic revival equivalent to those registered by certain Census Bureau divisions in the South and West during the late 1970s (see Appendix B, Table B-1). Indeed, some news accounts of regional economic growth have in 1981 begun to refer to New England as the "Sunbelt of the North." As much as economists and public policy officials would like to think they know, they in fact do not know with any reasonable degree of confidence whether the recent upswing in manufacturing employment in the North is temporary or a reversal of long-term employment growth trends. One can only wonder if a policy based on the downward trend in manufacturing employment in the early and mid-1970s would not work to the detriment of the northern economy during the 1980s, once the temporary downturn of the early 1980s passes.

Nothing that has been said here should be seen as an effort to deny that the North has some serious economic problems. On the contrary, the North's economic woes are serious. Relatively high unemployment, cost of living, and taxes; lack of development space and "pollution rights"; and high energy costs and welfare expenditures are several of the more prominent problems. People are moving out of the region *for some reason*, although much of the net out-migration is part of a general population shift away from urban areas (which the northern industrial tier states have plenty of) to rural areas (which the southern and western states have plenty of). The point of this section has been to dispel what can only be described as a myth that the North's economy is "plummeting" into an economic abyss from which it can be saved only by governmental restriction on capital flows.

Does the relatively lower growth in northern employment rates mean that the North is worse off? As will be argued in Chapter 3, in an economy unfettered by government restraints, differential growth patterns across regions is not necessarily a negative or even zero-sum game. The North can be gaining from the relative prosperity of the South. On the other hand, regional growth rates can be distorted by a variety of government policies. If growth rates are distorted, then one has to ask whether the government policies are "desirable." Before we consider that point, other regional economic myths need to be dispelled by the data.

JOB LOSSES AND GAINS

Bluestone and Harrison, as noted earlier, contend that more than 15 million jobs have been lost because of plant closures, contractions, and relocations between 1969 and 1976—a mere seven years. The data on which they base their estimate, covering eighteen states, are contained in Table 2-1. Quite frankly, this extrapolation is a good example of how data can be selectively and creatively manipulated to foster a preconceived and distorted view of the economy. The authors obviously want to give the economy, especially the northern industrial sector, a bad report card in order to reinforce their position that government intervention, in the form of disinvestment restrictions, is needed. To arrive at their estimate of 15 million jobs lost, they use Dun and Bradstreet files of corporate locations to determine the number of jobs "destroyed" in eighteen states (see Table 2-1 for the list of states); they then divide the total jobs destroyed, 9.2 million, by .61, the percentage of the nation's population in the eighteen states listed. The resulting quotient represents the number of jobs that would have been destroyed *if* the employment pattern observed in the eighteen states included in the survey were observed in all states.

A complete analysis of any dynamic economy, however, requires that jobs "destroyed" be set in contrast to jobs "created," a contrast not emphasized by Bluestone and Harrison because many of the jobs "destroyed" can be destroyed by expanding sectors that are creating jobs, driving wages up, and pushing some firms out of business. There were, *on balance*, 788,000 jobs created (jobs destroyed minus jobs created) for the eighteen states surveyed, meaning that there were, on balance, about 1.3 million jobs created for the country as a whole (using Bluestone and Harrison's extrapolation methods) (see Table 2-1). Such a calculation presents a far less pessimistic view of the market economy: Employment opportunities grew.

Even then, the estimated employment growth obviously understates the total number of jobs created on balance in the United States during the seven-year period. Table 2-2 shows the total non-agricultural employment record for the country as a whole. That table reveals that between 1969 and 1976, total employment for the country gew by 9.3 million, or by 13 percent—by over seven times the estimate of net job growth derived by employing the Bluestone-Harrison data base and estimating procedures. Even if 15 million jobs were lost (a figure about which there must now be some question), the net employment gains nevertheless suggest that there were, during the 1969–1976 period, over 24 million jobs created—*more than one job created for approximately every three jobs available in 1969.* And this was accomplished in spite of expanding government regulation and rising tax rates and other problems emphasized by Bluestone and Harrison.

Bluestone and Harrison (and those who have relied on their esti-mates of job losses and gains [15]) pursue their contorted description of the U.S. economy by focusing on the "ratio of jobs destroyed to jobs created." These ratios for the various regions are also reported in Table 2–1. In half the Frostbelt states listed, the ratios are greater than 1.0, meaning more jobs were destroyed than created. In all but one of the Sunbelt states, the ratios are less than 1.0, meaning there were more jobs created than destroyed: "On average, Frostbelt firms destroyed 111 jobs through plant closings for every 100 new jobs they created through openings, while Sunbelt and Far Western com-panies shut down an average of only 80 jobs through business clos-ings for every 100 that they created through openings." [16] Again, we must wonder how this can be if total employment in the North gen-erally rose during the period. Table 2–2 shows that *manufacturing employment* in the Northeast and North Central regions combined was down significantly between 1969 and 1976 (from 12.5 million to 10.9 million); however, *total employment* in the Northeast and North Central regions together expanded by more than 1.9 million (from 38.7 million to 40.6 million).

Perhaps the discrepancy between the Bluestone-Harrison estimates and actual employment can be attributed to sampling error. Perhaps the estimation procedures are too crude for the task at hand; perhaps the data base is faulty. Regardless of the reason, the Bluestone-Harri-son presentation of data leaves the reader with two impressions. The first is that employment opportunities in the North, if not through-out the country, are indeed "plummeting," which they are not. (Again, Table 2–2 makes apparent, between 1976 and 1979 manu-facturing employment has been on the rebound in the North, rising during the four-year period by almost 900,000 in the Northeast and North Central regions combined.)

The second impression is that the North has, on balance, suffered a disproportionate share of job losses due to plant closings and con-tractions, which is also apparently not the case. Table 2–6, which contains data developed by John Hekman and John Strong, based on Bluestone-Harrison employment estimates, reveals that between

---

15. A report distributed by the National Lawyers Guild begins with, "The problem of plant shutdowns has reached crisis proportions. Between 1969 and 1976 fifteen million jobs were lost as a result of plant shutdowns" [*Plant Closings and Runaway Industries: Strate-gies for Labor* (Washington: National Labor Law Center, 1981), p. 1].

16. Bluestone and Harrison, *Capital and Communities*, p. 59.

Table 2-6. Ratio of Jobs Lost 1969-1976 to Total Jobs 1974, Selected States.

Frostbelt States		Sunbelt States	
Massachusetts	.309	Georgia	.311
Connecticut	.287	North Carolina	.287
New York	.334	Alabama	.341
Pennsylvania	.282	Tennessee	.281
Michigan	.265	Louisiana	.343
Ohio	.267	Texas	.212
Minnesota	.305	Arizona	.344
Missouri	.293	Colorado	.341
		California	.355
		Washington	.291
Average Frostbelt	.296	Average Sunbelt	.327

Source: John S. Hekman and John S. Strong, "Is there a Case for Plant Closing Laws?" *New England Economic Review* (July/August 1980): 41, based on calculations from Barry Bluestone and Bennett Harrison, *Capital and Communities: The Causes and Consequences of Private Disinvestment* (Washington: Progressive Alliance, 1980), p. 40.

1969 and 1976 job losses, as a percentage of total employment in 1974, occurred at a slightly greater rate in the Sunbelt states (.327) than in the Frostbelt states (.296) between 1969 and 1976. Of course, as evident in Table 2-6, the job loss rate varied among regions; but the pattern is apparent, as John Hekman and John Strong have recognized: "The Frostbelt states on average and in most individual cases apparently have a lower rate of job loss than the Sunbelt states. The real difference between the two areas is in the rate of job creation. The Sunbelt is expanding faster than the Frostbelt, but not because firms are closing their doors in the Frostbelt at a faster rate."[17]

John Hekman and John Strong corroborate this conclusion by examining the plant closings, contractions, and expansions of selected Fortune 500 transportation equipment companies: "To the authors [Bluestone and Harrison] this [ratio of contractions to expansions] represents a movement of capital out of the North: they note that 'every closing represents a potential capital shift, by freeing up at least some resources whose owners have the option of reinvesting

17. John S. Hekman and John S. Strong, "Is there a Case for Plant Closing Laws?" *New England Economic Review* (July/August 1980): 41 [reprinted in McKenzie, *Plant Closings: Public or Private Choices?* (Washington, D.C.: Cato Institute, 1982), pp. 37-64].

them elsewhere.' However, the data . . . do not show any capital shifting. . . . From this [a rearrangement of data on investment activity] it appears that the proportion of establishments which contracted in the North, 2.1 percent, was virtually the same as that of the South and West, 2.0 percent. Surprisingly, the North had a smaller closing rate, 3.9 percent versus 8.8 percent, and a larger expansion rate, 25.3 percent versus 18.6 percent. The Bluestone-Harrison emphasis seems to be on the absolute number of contractions in the North—five out of the total of seven. In contrast, however, the North has the same number of closings as the South and West, and the North also has three times as many expansions."[18]

It should also be noted that many Sunbelt cities, like Houston, for example, have a higher rate of plant closings and jobs destroyed than Frostbelt cities like Boston.[19] Again, the difference in the relative prosperity of Sunbelt and Frostbelt cities can be pinned partially on the rate of job creation, a fact that must be kept in mind when evaluating claims that northern business closures and relocations to the South and West are an important source of northern economic difficulties, a subject to which we can now turn.

THE OUT-MIGRATION OF NORTHERN INDUSTRIES: MEDIA MYTH OR ECONOMIC REALITY?

Chapter 1 presented news accounts that portrayed the out-migration of northern businesses and their capital as a dramatic, accelerating process that "has burst beyond the bounds that can be accommodated by existing political institutions."[20] A conclusion readily drawn is that the loss of northern jobs and people to the South and West, supposedly because of cheaper labor, cheap energy, antiunionism, and low taxes in those areas, is at the heart of an emerging "second economic war between (or among) the states." Such reporting grossly exaggerates the impact of business relocations on the job losses in the North and the job gains in the South and West.

18. Ibid., p. 39.
19. David M. Smick, "What Reagonomics Is All About," *Wall Street Journal* (8 July 1981), based on calculations developed by David Birch, MIT Program on Neighborhood and Regional Change.
20. "The Second War between the States," *Business Week* (17 May 1976), p. 92.

Building on the work of Peter Allaman and David Birch with Dun and Bradstreet data,[21] James Miller, an economist with the U.S. Department of Agriculture, found that relatively few plant and job losses during the 1969–1975 period were involved in firm relocation decisions.[22] Surveying Table 2–7, we find that as a percentage of the total number of manufacturing businesses in existence in 1969, closures, 38.9 percent, exceeded starts, 33.8 percent, implying that there were fewer businesses at the end of the period than at the beginning. However, what is more interesting for our immediate purposes is that the number of firms migrating to another county (in the same state and region or in another state and region) only once exceeded 3 percent of the total number of firms. (The Mid-Atlantic division lost 3.1 percent of its total number.) Furthermore, national employment losses resulting from relocation were quite modest during the 1969–1975 period, equal to 1.6 percent of total manufacturing employment in 1969. Manufacturing job gains for the country, due to in-migration of business, was equally unspectacular, 2.0 percent of the 1969 manufacturing employment. On balance, however, relocations resulted in slightly more manufacturing jobs being created nationwide than destroyed (for a net gain of 0.4 percent of the 1969 manufacturing employment level).

Of course, job losses and gains resulting from out- and in-migration of businesses varied across regions; however, their impact is not what one would expect from reading news accounts. During the 1969–1975 period, the Mid-Atlantic region, one of the most heavily industrialized regions of the country, had the greatest percentage of job losses caused by relocations, *only 2.8 percent of its 1969 employment level.* Most of the regions show a less than two percentage point change. The Northeast and East North Central regions combined (an area that includes the Mid-Atlantic region) experienced job losses for the six-year period of 1.8 percent of the 1969 employment level for an average annual loss of 33,782 jobs, equaling 0.3 percent of the 1969 employment level.

Allaman and Birch, in one of the first employment studies using Dun and Bradstreet data, have calculated the regional job losses due

21. Peter M. Allaman and David L. Birch, "Components of Employment Change for States by Industry Group, 1970–1972" (Cambridge, Mass.: Joint Center for Urban Studies of MIT and Harvard University, September 1975).

22. James P. Miller, "Manufacturing Relocations in the United States, 1969–1975" (Washington, D.C.: U.S. Department of Agriculture, Economic Development Division, 1980) [reprinted in McKenzie, *Plant Closings*, pp. 19–35].

Table 2-7. Components of Change Due to Stationary Firms, Starts, Closures and Relocations in the Manufacturing Sector, 1969–75.

Item	Total Number 1969	Total Change 1969–75	Net Change Due to Stationary Firms	Natural Change			Relocations		
				Starts[a]	Closures	Net Change	Relocation Gains	Relocation Losses	Net Change
Establishments									
				Percent of Total Number 1969					
United States	326,123[b]	-5.1	0	33.8	38.9	-5.1	2.0	2.0	0
New England	24,894	-5.7	0	29.7	35.8	-6.1	2.5	2.1	0.4
Middle Atlantic	85,014	-16.4	0	22.5	38.6	-16.1	2.8	3.1	-0.3
East North Central	72,500	-7.7	0	27.5	35.1	-7.6	1.7	1.8	-0.1
West North Central	23,900	-8.5	0	29.8	38.2	-8.4	1.4	1.5	-0.1
South Atlantic	36,595	-2.1	0	37.9	40.4	-2.5	2.6	2.2	0.4
East South Central	14,641	-5.9	0	32.1	38.3	-6.2	1.2	0.9	0.3
West South Central	25,519	-0.8	0	41.9	42.8	-0.9	1.2	1.1	0.1
Mountain	9,035	14.7	0	57.3	42.9	14.4	1.5	1.2	0.3
Pacific	34,025	19.5	0	65.2	45.7	19.5	1.4	1.4	0
Employment									
				Percent of Total Number 1969					
United States	19,348,791	-8.0	5.7	8.5	22.6	-14.1	2.0	1.6	0.4
New England	1,566,268	-17.8	-1.3	7.6	26.4	-18.8	3.6	1.3	2.3
Middle Atlantic	4,308,698	-20.3	-1.7	7.1	25.2	-18.1	2.3	2.8	-0.5
East North Central	5,140,825	-2.7	11.3	5.5	19.6	-14.1	1.3	1.2	0.1
West North Central	1,126,675	1.0	14.7	11.4	24.7	-13.3	1.4	1.8	-0.4
South Atlantic	2,458,512	-11.8	2.1	9.3	24.4	-15.1	3.2	2.0	1.2
East South Central	1,051,635	4.3	17.4	8.4	22.0	-13.6	1.1	0.6	0.5
West South Central	1,084,899	1.8	13.4	15.8	27.5	-11.7	2.1	2.0	0.1
Mountain	302,046	0.7	9.9	16.1	28.6	-12.5	4.2	0.9	3.3
Pacific	2,309,233	-3.1	1.5	11.6	16.6	-5.0	0.9	0.5	0.4

a. Because Dun and Bradstreet does not provide the starting dates on branch plants, the percentages are unavoidably biased downwards. The net effect is to bias total percentage change downward by the actual number of new branch starts during the period.

b. This number includes 24,872 firms that did not report employment to Dun and Bradstreet.

Source: James P. Miller, "Manufacturing Relocations in the United States, 1969–1975," Washington, D.C.: U.S. Department of Agriculture, Economic Development Division, 1981); also reprinted in *Plant Closings: Public or Private Choices?*, (Washington, D.C.: Cato Institute, 1982), p. 23. Based on Dun's Market Identifiers, Dun and Bradstreet Corporation, 1969, 1975.

to "deaths," "contractions," and "out-migration" of firms as a percentage of total job losses and regional job gains due to "births," "expansions," and "in-migrations" of firms as a percentage of total gains, all occurring between the end of 1969 and the end of 1972.[23] Although their data, contained in Table 2-8, are now dated, they offer an important insight—one that has not changed significantly with updated revisions of the study: For northern industrial tier states, only 1.5 percent of all employment losses during the two-year period resulted from the out-migration of firms. *This means that for the Northeast and East North Central regions the overwhelming source of job losses—more than 98 percent—was deaths and contractions of firms.*[24]

Was there a distinct southern and western bias in the relocations of northern industries? A tentative answer to this question is provided by economist Miller's work reported in Table 2-9, which reveals that *for the country as a whole about 76 percent of the firms that moved stayed within their own states; another 13 percent stayed within their own region; and only 11 percent moved to another region of the country.* It is interesting to note that the percentage of the firms that moved and remained within their own region was highest in the East North Central region, 87 percent. On the other hand, the percentage of firms that relocated to another region was highest in the East South Central region, 37.9 percent.

Table 2-10 gives estimates of the interregional flow of firms. Of the total number of firms in the country that relocated, 36 percent (2,361 divided by 6,639) were in the Mid-Atlantic region. However,

---

23. Peter Allaman and David Birch found that for the 1969–72 period the employment losses for the Northeast and East North Central regions due to the out-migration of firms equalled 1.5 percent of the 1969 employment base ["Components of Employment Change for States by Industry Groups, 1970–1972" (Cambridge, Mass.: Joint Center for Urban Studies at MIT and Harvard University, September, 1975)].

24. The difference between the Miller and Allaman-Birch percentages for employment losses and gains is worth noting: Miller calculates employment losses and gains as a percent of *total 1969 employment*, whereas Allaman-Birch focus on employment losses and gains (for various reasons, such as deaths, births, and relocations) as a percentage of *total employment losses*. For a similar study of relocation, restricted to New England, see Carol L. Jusenius and Larry C. Ledebur, "Where Have All the Firms Gone? An Analysis of the New England Economy," *Economic Development Research Report* (Washington: U.S. Department of Commerce, September 1977) [reprinted in McKenzie, *Plant Closings*, pp. 65–104]. In his updated study Birch writes, "The most obvious aspect of the [study] is the virtually negligible role played by migration of establishments from one state to another during all time intervals [*The Job Generation Process* (Cambridge, Mass.: M.I.T. Program on Neighborhood and Regional Change, 1979), p. 21].

Table 2–8. Causes of Employment Gains and Losses within Regions, 31 December 1969–31 December 1972.

Region	Total Employment Gains	Causes of Employment Gains (percent)			Total Employment Losses	Causes of Employment Losses (percent)		
		Births of New Firms[a]	Expansion of Firms	In-migration of Firms		Deaths of Firms[b]	Contraction of Firms	Out-migration of Firms
Northern industrial tier	3,516,603	28.6	70.1	1.3	4,672,977	53.8	44.7	1.5
New England	419,614	30.4	68.9	0.7	660,934	53.4	45.8	0.8
East North Central	1,599,179	28.7	70.4	0.9	1,976,375	53.6	45.8	0.7
Middle Atlantic	1,497,810	27.9	70.1	2.0	2,035,668	54.3	43.2	2.6
Sunbelt	2,634,250	34.5	64.3	1.2	2,570,544	57.0	42.5	0.4
South Atlantic	1,206,301	34.5	63.9	1.6	1,172,641	56.5	43.1	0.4
East South Central	543,436	32.5	66.7	0.5	518,122	59.2	40.3	0.5
West South Central	884,513	35.8	63.4	0.8	879,781	56.5	43.1	0.5

a. "The appearance in the 1972 title of a firm with a new DUNS number, for which the year started was 1970–1972" (p. 4 of source).

b. "The disappearance from the title of a firm with a particular DUNS number" (p. 4 of source).

Source: Peter M. Allaman and David L. Birch, "Components of Employment Change for States by Industry Gross, 1970–1972," Joint Center for Urban Studies of M.I.T. and Harvard University, September 1975. The study uses Dun and Bradstreet data, as found in C. L. Jusenius and L. C. Lede-bur, *A Myth in the Making: The Southern Economic Challenge and the Northern Economic Decline* (Washington, D.C.: U.S. Department of Commerce, Economic Development Administration, November 1976), p. 27.

Table 2-9.   The Distribution of Manufacturing Relocations by
Distance Moved—Intrastate, Intraregional (U.S. Census Division),
and Interregional, 1969-75.[a]

Item	Intrastate	Intraregional	Interregional	Total
US				
firms	5,036	852	751	6,639
(percent)	(75.9)	(12.8)	(11.3)	(100.0)
NE				
firms	395	91	139	625
(percent)	(63.2)	(14.6)	(22.2)	(100.0)
MA				
firms	1,804	474	63	2,361
(percent)	(76.4)	(20.1)	(3.5)	(100.0)
ENC				
firms	1,087	86	80	1,253
(percent)	(86.8)	(6.9)	(6.4)	(100.0)
WNC				
firms	241	72	33	346
(percent)	(69.7)	(20.8)	(9.5)	(100.0)
SA				
firms	687	81	187	955
(percent)	(71.9)	(8.5)	(19.6)	(100.0)
ESC				
firms	87	18	64	169
(percent)	(51.5)	(10.7)	(37.9)	(100.0)
WSC				
firms	240	12	56	308
(percent)	(77.9)	(3.9)	(18.2)	(100.0)
MT				
firms	91	0	48	139
(percent)	(65.5)	(0.0)	(34.5)	(100.0)
PAC				
firms	404	18	61	483
(percent)	(83.6)	(3.7)	(12.7)	(100.0)

a. The number of relocations is determined at the destination, e.g., the number of
inmigrants.

Source: Miller, "Manufacturing Relocations in the U.S., 1969-1975," see Table 2-7.

the vast majority of these relocating Mid-Atlantic firms, 96 percent (2,278 divided by 2,361), stayed within the Mid-Atlantic region. Of the remaining eighty-three firms (2361 – 2278) in the Mid-Atlantic region that moved, 60 percent moved to other northern regions, *meaning there were only 33 of the relocating Mid-Atlantic firms in the survey—a little more than 1 percent of the total firms (2,361)— that moved South or West.* These data suggest a point fairly evident throughout the table and confirmed by other studies: No wholesale exodus of businesses from the North to the South or West has taken place. A comparatively large number of relocations emerged from within one region, but most of those relocating firms stayed close to home. The flow of Mid-Atlantic businesses northward to the New England region was greater in absolute and percentage terms than the flow of Mid-Atlantic businesses southward to the South Atlantic region. The observed distribution of moves by distance traveled is not unexpected from an economic perspective: Business movements are costly; the longer the moves, the more costly; the longer the moves, the less frequently they tend to be expected, all other considerations being equal.

Table 2–10 also gives information on the distribution of the employment flows due to business relocations. The Mid-Atlantic division alone experienced 41.4 percent of all job flows. However, most of that division's job flow was either within the Mid-Atlantic division (25.4 percentage points) or to the New England area. Only 0.3 percent of all job flows in the country (309,581) went from the Mid-Atlantic to the South Atlantic. Only one-tenth of 1 percent of the country's job flow went from the Mid-Atlantic to the Pacific.

Dun and Bradstreet data on firms have been seriously criticized for being either inaccurate or not being inclusive and for mislocating firms.[25] For that reason the new firm and employment gains of South Carolina, a relatively high-growth state during the 1970s because of the in-migration of firms, were evaluated from state economic development records.[26] The research generally confirms the

25. David I. Verway, "A Critical Examination of the Dun and Bradstreet Files," paper presented at the Southern Regional Science Association annual meeting, Nashville, Tenn., 6 April 1979. Many of the deficiencies of the Dun and Bradstreet files have been recognized by their users. See David L. Birch, *The Job Generation Process* (Cambridge, Mass.: MIT Program on Neighborhood and Regional Change, 1979), section 2.

26. Nancy T. Mathews and Richard B. McKenzie, "New Plant and Employment Gains in North and South Carolina during the 1970s," *Review of Business and Economics* (October 1982): 31.

Table 2-10. Regional (U.S. Census Division[a]) Flows of Manufacturing Establishments and Jobs Involved in Relocations, 1969-75.

A. Establishment Flows

Region of 1969 Location	Region of 1975 Location									
	NE	MA	ENC	WNC	SA	ESC	WSC	Mt.	Pac.	Total
NE	486	25	6	0	7	4	1	0	3	532
MA	127	2,278	33	3	118	13	14	10	29	2,625
ENC	10	23	1,173	19	39	23	14	11	14	1,326
WNC	1	2	12	313	4	3	9	4	4	352
SA	0	23	11	1	768	10	4	1	5	823
ESC	0	1	9	1	9	105	5	1	1	132
WSC	1	2	3	3	4	6	252	5	2	275
Mt.	1	1	4	3	2	1	3	91	3	109
Pac.	0	6	2	5	4	4	6	16	422	465
Total	625	2,361	1,253	346	955	169	308	139	483	6,639

Table 2-10. continued

B. *Job Flows (Percent)*[b]

Region of 1969 Location	Region of 1975 Location									
	NE	MA	ENC	WNC	SA	ESC	WSC	Mt.	Pac.	Total
NE	5.2	–	.3	–	.2	–	–	–	–	5.9
MA	9.4	25.4	1.7	1	3.1	.5	.5	–	.5	41.4
ENC	.2	.3	14.3	.2	4.6	.8	.3	.4	.6	21.7
WNC	–	–	.5	3.6	–	.1	.2	–	.2	4.6
SA	–	.3	.1	–	12.3	.1	–	–	–	12.9
ESC	–	–	–	–	.1	1.2	.1	–	–	1.6
WSC	–	–	–	–	–	.1	4.6	–	–	4.9
Mt.	–	–	–	–	.1	–	–	2.3	–	2.6
Pac.	–	.1	–	.1	–	–	.1	.3	3.7	4.2
Total	14.8	26.2	17.1	4.1	20.6	3.0	5.9	3.1	5.2	100.0[c]

a. NE = New England   WNC = West North Central   WSC = West South Central
   MA = Middle Atlantic   SA = South Atlantic   Mt. = Mountain
   ENC = East North Central ESC = East South Central   Pac. = Pacific

b. Percent of 1969 employment involved in relocation (309, 581 jobs).

c. Percentages may not add exactly to 100.0 percent due to rounding off.

Note: – indicates values less than .1 percent of all relocation employment in 1969.

Source: Miller, "Manufacturing Relocations in the United States, 1969–1975."

findings of Allaman and Birch and Miller. Nearly 540 new *manufacturing* plants located in South Carolina during the 1970s, of which 338 survived until 1980 and gave rise to 47,308 new jobs by 1980. These new jobs accounted for 13.6 percent of the state's total employment growth during the decade but only 3.9 percent of the state's total employment in 1980. However, nearly 38 percent of the plants had headquarters in the state. While 42 percent of the new plants were from the Frostbelt (i.e., the North Central and Northeast regions), the parent company's headquarters, these Frostbelt plants tended to be larger than average, accounting for 56 percent of employment gains resulting from new manufacturing plants. Still, all frostbelt-based firms accounted for only 7.6 percent of the total employment growth and just over 2 percent of the state's 1980 total employment.

"Large" manufacturing plants, those with 500 or more employees, that were established in the state tend to attract a great deal of media attention. However, such manufacturing plants accounted for only 5.5 percent of the total employment growth in the state during the 1970s and a scant 1.6 percent of South Carolina's 1980 total employment. Large firms from the Frostbelt accounted for 2.7 percent of the state's employment growth during the decade and a scant 0.8 percent of the state's total employment in 1980. Our findings corroborate David Birch's general conclusion: "Whatever they are doing, . . . *large firms are no longer the major providers of new jobs for Americans.*"[27]

By breaking down and rearranging his data further, Miller is able to draw other important conclusions:

- Of the business movement that occurs among counties, the largest percentage, 24.1 percent, is from "core" counties (with at least one million residents, like Cook County, Illinois) to "fringe" counties (ones adjacent to core counties). Somewhat surprisingly, the next largest intercountry flow of firms, 17.4 percent, is from "core" to "core" counties.[28]

- "Relatively new plant operations (under six years old) were proportionately more active in longer distance moves—14.8 percent of the interregional relocations and 11.5 percent of the intra-

27. David L. Birch, "Who Creates Jobs?" *The Public Interest* (Fall 1981): 3.
28. Miller, "Manufacturing Relocations," in *Plant Closings*, Table 3.3, p. 28.

regional relocations compared to only 7.2 percent of the intrastate relocations. Plants over thirty years old, however, also appear to be more active in longer distance moves—19.2 percent of the interregional relocations compared to 13.8 percent of the intraregional relocations and 14.6 percent of the intrastate moves. The evidence is thus not consistent that older plants are more likely to make interregional moves to the most cost-efficient locations in order to overcome low growth and profitability problems."[29] (See Table 2-11).

- Small firms with fifty employees tend to move shorter distances than larger firms with more than fifty employees. Firms with more than fifty employees were relatively more active in interregional moves (see Table 2-11).

- Finally, also apparent in Table 2-11, noncorporate firms were relatively more active in intrastate moves, whereas corporate headquarters and branch plants were relatively more active in interregional moves (which may partially explain the concern over "corporate flight").

All in all, although there is evidence that supports the contention that large corporations are primarily responsible for long-distance moves, the employment impact of the free physical relocations of capital among regions has been relatively meager and cannot explain, in any satisfactory way, the differential employment growth rates among regions. Most firms that pack up shop and move do so within their own regions, and most of these firms stay within their own states. Although such evidence may do little to comfort those who lose their jobs because their plant permanently closes or relocates, the evidence does caution against using federal plant closing laws as a means of improving the relative economic performance of northern industrial tier states. To the extent that plants that move enhance the economic performance of a region, the *intra*regional flows of capital within the North—which would also be impeded by plant closing laws—improve the welfare of people in the North.

Granted that, as critics of corporate flight stress, capital can move in subtle, difficult-to-measure ways, like the gradual shift of the reinvestment of earnings and new investment funds from "old" to "new" locations. If indeed the North were being hit unduly hard by such

29. Ibid., Table 3.6, p. 35.

Table 2–11.   **Age, Size, Ownership and Industry Differences of Intrastate, Interstate, and Interregional Movers.**

Items	Intrastate Movers	Intraregional Movers	Interregional Movers	Total
	Establishments			
	5,036	852	751	6,639
	Percent			
Age:				
under 6 years	7.2	11.5	14.8	8.5
6–10 years	31.5	28.3	24.9	30.4
11–20 years	29.6	29.8	27.0	29.4
21–30 years	17.1	16.5	14.1	16.7
over 30 years	14.6	13.9	19.2	15.0
Total	100.0	100.0	100.0	100.0
Employment:				
Under 20	59.0	54.8	48.3	57.3
20–50	24.1	23.1	21.4	23.7
51–100	8.9	10.7	11.9	9.5
101–500	7.0	10.6	15.6	8.5
over 500	1.0	0.8	2.8	1.0
Total	100.0	100.0	100.0	100.0
Ownership:				
Single operation	74.8	65.5	49.4	70.7
Headquarters	20.5	32.5	47.7	25.1
Branch operation	4.7	2.0	2.9	4.2
Total	100.0	100.0	100.0	100.0
Industry:				
Durables[a]	62.5	48.7	52.7	59.6
Nondurables[b]	37.5	51.3	47.3	40.4
Total	100.0	100.0	100.0	100.0

    a. Lumber and wood products, Furniture, Stone, Clay, Glass products, Primary metals, Machinery, Transportation equipment, Instruments.

    b. Food, Tobacco, Paper products, Chemicals, Petroleum, Leather products, Rubber and plastic products.

    Source: Miller, "Manufacturing Relocations in the United States."

disinvestment-and-shift decisions, one would expect the net disinvestment to show up in an abnormally high closing rate for northern industries (since firms would be closing down plants that have been replaced by plants elsewhere) and an abnormally high layoff rate for workers (since their jobs will be replaced by jobs in plants constructed elsewhere). However, on the basis of data like that contained in Table 2–12 on regional closing rates, Hekman and Strong make this observation:

> It is surprising . . . to see in Table [2–12] that in manufacturing the North Central has the lowest closing rate in the country for every size category. The Northeast has the highest closing rate for smaller establishments, but has a lower rate than the South for plants with over 100 workers. *For the weighted average across size classes, the closing rates of the Northeast and North Central are less than or equal to those for the South and West.* The Northeast ranks better on average than for its individual categories because it has relatively more large plants, where its closing rates are highest (emphasis added).
>
> In trade and services the issue is somewhat different. On the one hand, closing rates should be the same everywhere because trade and services cannot be footloose but are tied to population. On the other hand, closing rates could be lower in the South and West because population is growing more rapidly there and with it the demand for these firms. Table [2–12] indicates that the North Central has the lowest closing rate in most of these categories and the Northeast is again high in many individual rates but ranks well overall. No dramatic Frostbelt-Sunbelt difference is evident here; if anything, the Frostbelt has lower closing rates. *The impression of numerous closings may arise because the Northeast and North Central contain a disproportionate share of the country's manufacturing establishments.* While a number of "mature" industries such as steel and rubber have closed quite a few older plants, either this is not large enough to sway the overall closing rate in the Frostbelt, or else similar closings trends are occurring in the Sunbelt which have not been widely publicized.[30]

Robert Premus and Rudy Fichtenbaum find contrary to expectations, that the layoff rate for the 1960–1980 period was lower in the Frostbelt (1.45 per hundred workers) than in the Sunbelt (1.60 per hundred workers).[31] This regional differential holds up under further study using a regression analysis of cross-sectional industry data:

30. Hekman and Strong, "Is there a Case for Plant Closing Laws?" p. 41.

31. Robert Premus and Rudy Fichtenbaum, "Labor Turnover and the Sunbelt/Frostbelt Confrontation: An Empirical Test," (Washington, D.C.: U.S. Department of Commerce, September 1977) [reprinted in McKenzie, *Plant Closings*, pp. 105–112].

Table 2-12. Proportion of Firms Existing in 1969 That Had Closed by 1976, By Size of Establishment, Region, and Industrial Sector.

Region in 1969 and Industrial Sector	Number of 1969 Establishments in the Sample (000)	Ratio of Firms Closed by 1976 by Number of Employees					Weighted Average of the Size Class
		0-20	21-50	51-100	100-500	501+	
Northeast							
Manufacturing	76	.53	.40	.37	.33	.21	.48
Trade	295	.60	.35	.34	.36	.57	.59
Services	51	.61	.42	.43	.39	.29	.59
Total	514	.59	.37	.36	.33	.26	.57
North Central							
Manufacturing	63	.48	.30	.27	.27	.15	.43
Trade	296	.57	.33	.30	.28	.27	.56
Services	56	.60	.39	.38	.41	.30	.59
Total	519	.56	.32	.28	.27	.17	.54
South							
Manufacturing	49	.53	.36	.36	.34	.28	.48
Trade	335	.59	.33	.30	.23	.23	.58
Services	63	.61	.41	.40	.39	.34	.60
Total	565	.58	.35	.33	.32	.27	.57
West							
Manufacturing	41	.53	.39	.36	.31	.16	.50
Trade	182	.60	.38	.34	.29	.33	.59
Services	35	.62	.41	.40	.42	.36	.60
Total	318	.59	.38	.35	.32	.23	.57

Source: John S. Hekman and S. Strong, "Is there a Case for Plant Closing Laws?" *New England Review* (July/August 1980), Table 5; based on David L. Birch, *The Job Generation Process* (Cambridge, Mass.: M.I.T. Program on Neighborhood and Regional Change, 1979), Appendix D-2: based on Dun and Bradstreet Corporation records.

Table 2–13. Unemployment Rates by Census Bureau Regions, 1970–1980 (percent).

Year	Northeast	North Central	South	West	U.S.
	(Ratio of Region Unemployment Rate to U.S.)				
1970	4.6 (0.94)	4.5 (0.92)	4.6 (0.94)	6.9 (1.40)	4.9
1971	6.2 (1.05)	5.5 (0.93)	4.9 (0.83)	8.1 (1.37)	5.9
1972	6.3 (1.12)	5.0 (0.89)	4.8 (0.85)	9.1 (1.62)	5.6
1973	5.5 (1.12)	4.4 (0.89)	4.2 (0.85)	6.7 (1.37)	4.9
1974	5.3 (0.95)	5.6 (1.00)	5.1 (0.91)	7.1 (1.26)	5.6
1975	9.5 (1.12)	7.9 (0.93)	7.7 (0.91)	9.2 (1.08)	8.5
1976	9.4 (1.22)	6.6 (0.86)	6.7 (0.87)	8.6 (1.12)	7.7
1977	8.4 (1.20)	6.0 (0.86)	6.4 (0.91)	7.8 (1.11)	7.0
1978	6.9 (1.15)	5.3 (0.88)	5.6 (0.93)	6.6 (1.10)	6.0
1979	6.6 (1.14)	5.5 (0.95)	5.4 (0.93)	6.0 (1.03)	5.8
1980	7.1 (1.00)	8.2 (1.15)	6.4 (0.90)	6.8 (0.96)	7.1

Source: Handbook of Labor Statistics and Employment and Earnings, various issues.

The findings are generally consistent with the hypothesis that the "demise of the Frostbelt economy is the result of a low business formation rate and not the relocation of existing businesses to other parts of the country."[32]

Much attention has been given to relatively higher unemployment rates in northern regions. Table 2–13 shows that the unemployment rate has been higher in the Northeast and West than for the nation as a whole and that the unemployment rate in the South and North Central has been lower than for the nation. The higher unemployment rate in the Northeast is often attributed, very simply, to plant

32. Ibid., p. 108.

closings. Given the data reviewed above, however, such an explanation is hard to accept at face value, especially since the unemployment rate of the North Central has generally been below the national average. Also, as noted, employment and the labor force participation rate in the North have generally grown (perhaps not as rapidly as in other parts of the country, but growth has occurred nonetheless); the plant closing rate is lower in the Frostbelt; the layoff rate in the Frostbelt is lower than in the Sunbelt; and the population growth rate in the Frostbelt has generally been lower than in other regions, due in part to the out-migration of people. How can these facts be squared with relatively higher unemployment rates in the North? These are questions that can be only tentatively answered. We stress here that the studies reviewed above provide an important lead: the relatively slow growth in the "births" of new firms and expansions of old firms. However, "plant closings and births" is an inadequate explanation for regional employment problems, requiring us to dig deeper. We must explain *why* plants are, on balance, closing and moving out of the North, even though at a very low rate, and *why* firms are failing to establish more plants in the North. What is the source of the relative attractiveness of the South and West?

REGIONAL INCOME GAINS

At the heart of the controversy over restrictions on disinvestment is the presumption that all of the inter- and intraregional flows of capital are robbing people, especially northerners, of their incomes and tax bases. Again, the facts do not appear to confirm this presumption. Table 2–14 gives per capita personal incomes by regions for selected years, along with the annual compound rates of growth in real per capita income during the 1970s. As revealed in the table, per capita personal income for the nation expanded by more than 54 percent between 1965 and 1979, a disproportionate share of which occurred during the last half of the 1960s.

Also, it needs to be emphasized that *all* regions generally experienced real growth in per capita income during the period, although the growth rates differed significantly across regions and decreased substantially in the late 1960s. Generally speaking, the growth rates during the 1970s were lower in the Northeast than in other areas of the country. The growth rate between 1970 and 1979 for the Mid-

Table 2-14. Personal Income per Capita by Census Bureau Divisions.

Year	United States	New England	Mid Atlantic	East North Central	West North Central	South Atlantic	East South Central	West South Central	Mountain	Pacific
	Real Per Capita Personal Income in 1972 Dollars (Percent of U.S.)									
1965	3459 (100)	3778 (109)	3898 (113)	3772 (109)	3307 (96)	2979 (86)	2426 (70)	2808 (81)	3140 (91)	3966 (115)
1970	4209 (100)	4586 (109)	4746 (113)	4378 (104)	3949 (94)	3850 (91)	3170 (75)	3590 (85)	3845 (91)	4669 (111)
1975	4636 (100)	4781 (103)	5040 (108)	4789 (103)	4515 (97)	4343 (94)	3672 (79)	4164 (90)	4361 (94)	5149 (111)
1980	5331 (100)	5402 (101)	5541 (104)	5583 (105)	5182 (97)	4995 (94)	4303 (81)	5024 (94)	5050 (95)	5977 (112)
	Compound Growth Rate (Percent)									
1965–1970	4.0	4.0	4.0	3.0	3.6	5.2	5.5	5.0	4.1	3.3
1970–1979	2.6	1.8	1.7	2.7	3.0	2.9	3.4	3.8	3.1	2.8

Source: Statistical Abstract of the United States, 1968 and 1980; and calculations by author.

Atlantic region, for example, was only 1.7 percent compounded, *exactly one-half the growth rate for the South Atlantic.* Other southern divisions grew faster than the South Atlantic. Still, there was some growth, albeit slight and much below rates experienced in earlier decades, partly because a greater percentage of the population became employed.

The long-term rate of growth income during the 1970s masks the deterioration in productivity experienced during the late 1970s. During the last three years of the 1970s, productivity either barely changed or went down slightly, by one-half of one percent per year. The negative growth in productivity was offset in part by increases in the labor participation rate. It should also be noted that after-tax income for many families dropped during the 1970s, even though personal income rose generally, because the taxes rose faster than income. Between 1971 and 1981 the after-tax disposable income of the median income family dropped by $467.[33]

While relatively sluggish growth in real income is symptomatic of the Northeast's economic woes, it should lead one to doubt claims that the North's tax base is being depleted by "capital flight." Higher personal income levels spring from a growth in the capital base and become reflected in higher taxable income and a larger property tax base. The data on personal income levels and growth rates, again, raise questions that cannot be fully addressed here: First, why did the growth rates in personal income deteriorate so badly across regions during the 1970s? Second, in what way have government policies contributed to the *relative* reduction of growth in the Northeast and parts of the North Central states?

The relatively slower northern growth rates in personal income do not mean that the North is now necessarily poorer than other regions. What the slower growth rates of northern regions have meant is that regional income levels have tended to converge on the national average: Northern incomes have fallen *relatively* (but have risen absolutely), while southern incomes have risen *relatively* (and absolutely). The convergence of regional income levels, which has been underway for decades, is readily apparent in Figure 2-23. Such a convergence of regional incomes is expected in a market economy as established firms move to low wage areas and new firms spring up in low wage areas. To the extent the flow of capital among regions is dependent on wage and regional income differentials, the ongoing convergence

---

33. Tax Foundation, Inc., *Monthly Tax Features* (July 1981): 1.

Figure 2-23.
Regional Per Capita Income as a Percent of U.S. Average,
Selected Years, 1900-1980.

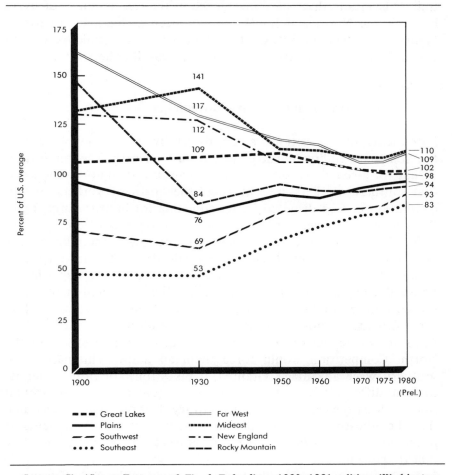

Source: Significant Features of Fiscal Federalism, 1980-1981 edition (Washington, D.C.: Advisory Commission on Intergovernmental Relations, 1981), Table 5, p. 75.

of regional incomes should, in the future, dampen regional capital flows—all very naturally through market forces. The convergence of regional personal income levels does not, to reiterate an important point, explain the falling growth rates across regions.

Some people concerned about the decrease in the North's *relative* income level suggest that northerners are actually much worse off relatively speaking because of the relatively higher costs of living in the North. While the cost of living may be higher, generally, in the North, the rate of inflation between 1969 and 1979 was higher, relatively speaking, in the South than in the Northeast and North Central. This means that the convergence in the *real* standard of living between the North and South has not been as marked as parts of Figure 2-23 may suggest. On the other hand, one would expect the cost of living to rise relatively in growing areas like the South.

Low Wages and Industry Movements

Proponents of restrictions argue forcefully that "low wages" in the South are pulling industry away from the North. The implication is that for given skills southerners are paid less than northerners and that southern workers are "hurting" the northern workers. Such a contention can be disputed. After adjusting for industry mix, Lynn Browne has found very little regional wage differences.[34]

In addition, for the very reason that the low-wage argument has been used for so many decades to explain the southward migration of industry, its validity must be questioned. If lower wages in the South did explain the influx of capital, then it would appear that the advantage would have long ago been completely eliminated. If some firms were moving South, then it doesn't make sense for other firms to locate where labor costs are higher—for example, in the North. Competition would force them all South, eliminating the southern wage advantage. Granted, it takes time for firms to adjust to cost differentials, but the low-wage argument has been around since at least the early part of this century. Is it reasonable to assume that the adjustment would take more than 30 years? Proponents of restrictions seem to maintain that capitalists are too greedy to allow that to happen.

The argument is probably flawed to begin with. Although wages in the South may be lower, they are lower for some reason, such as the lack of worker skills or education. Given the factors that offset lower wages, the firms that are moving South must be doing so for one or both of two reasons: First, technology in production is chang-

34. See Lynn Browne, "How Different are Regional Wages?" *New England Economic Review* (January/February 1978); and Richard B. McKenzie, *Restrictions on Business Mobility: A Study in Political Rhetoric and Economic Reality* (Washington, D.C.: American Enterprise Institute, 1979), chapter 3.

ing in such a way that lower-skilled, lower-wage workers can be combined with more automated, capital-intensive production processes. Second, the industry that is moving South has reached the "mature" stage of the "product-life cycle," meaning the products have been developed to the point that skilled labor is no longer needed in what have become automated production processes. The industry that is moving South is attempting to restructure by combining, again, relatively unskilled southern laborers with a lot of capital, If the low-wage argument did explain industry movements across the Mason Dixon Line, we would expect a high labor-to-capital ratio among incoming industries, whereas the opposite tends to be the case, suggesting that technology and product cycles, and not low wages, go a long way toward explaining industrial shifts.[35] Looked at from the perspective developed here, one must wonder if northerners truly believe that a low-wage, low-skill labor is a southern virtue. One must also wonder if, to the extent northern industry has been lost to the South, southerners have actually acquired the same jobs lost by the North or, if the industries had stayed in the North, northerners would have retained the same combination of jobs. (Of course, industry shifts can also be explained by relative changes in other resources, for example, energy, a subject that cannot be pursued in this volume.)

CONCLUDING COMMENTS

In assessing the economic consequences of capital mobility, investigators have a major problem: Data on business investment and disinvestment decisions are (as they probably should be) largely kept from scholarly scrutiny. From the limited data available, much of which is covered above, only tentative impressions can be offered. First, while the northern economy has grown less rapidly than the economies of other regions, it has, generally speaking, grown slightly, although in an irregular manner.

Second, over the last decade or so, the North does not appear to have been deprived of its capital base. Indeed, its capital base has generally grown, albeit at a comparatively low rate. Its problems

---

35. Caryl Ruppert Ersenkal, *The Product Cycle in Regional Growth: An Application to South Carolina* (Clemson, S.C.: Department of Agricultural Economics, Clemson University, 1981).

appear to stem more from its comparative inability to attract new capital and new business formation rather than from an unusually high rate of plant closings and relocations.

Third, it is hard to agree with those who suggest that the restructuring of the American economy across regions has been, generally speaking, so dramatic that it cannot be accommodated through market mechanisms. Average annual employment losses between 1969 and 1975 due to closings and relocations combine to average no more than about 1 percent of the labor force; and in every region those employment losses were more than offset by employment gains due to births, expansions, or in-migration of firms.

Fourth, growth in personal income has decreased across regions, but especially in the Northeast, implying a convergence of regional incomes.

Finally, a methodological caveat must be added. Studies of regional economies are beset with a particularly pressing problem: the drawing of regional boundaries. Although these boundaries are artificial and more or less arbitrary, the boundaries can, when they are cited repeatedly in statistical commentaries, take on an economic importance they simply do not—and should not—have. Firms and people do not make decisions on the basis of sections of maps. The "South" as a piece of geography has no intrinsic meaning to an entrepreneur interested in making profits—especially to the entrepreneur sitting, for instance, in Harrisonburg, Virginia, contemplating a move to Harrisburg, Pennsylvania. The line that runs on the map between Maryland and Pennsylvania, dividing the Mid-Atlantic from the South Atlantic, probably never crosses his or her mind. Yet regional studies are often written *as if* dividing lines matter in a significant way, as if the entrepreneur is actually interested in being able to say that he is on the "right" side of the line or that his decision is inherently bound to what it means to regional aggregates. Entrepreneurs are concerned, and should be concerned, with the costs of doing and staying in business, not with some sort of territorial imperative carried to the regional level.

This digression brings to light an important point to remember: *Regions do not close or open businesses, contract or grow; people do.* That warning reminds us to look for the true motivations of disinvestment and capital mobility—the economics of remaining open versus closing, of moving versus not moving. All that regional studies can do is to help us group data in a manageable way and to direct our attention to the question of how governmental policies or other economic and political factors may be directing or misdirecting capital traffic in the country—how, for instance, governmental policies may or may not be distorting the free flow of investment funds. Those are topics to which we turn in a future chapter. In the next chapter, we examine the question of how capital mobility among regions can contribute to people's welfares in all regions, the necessary basis on which a critique of proposed government policy must be developed.

Chapter 3

THE CASE FOR PLANT CLOSINGS

Markets enable people to buy and sell what they want at prices they freely choose to accept. They also enable people to adjust to changes in economic and social conditions. Markets are by no means perfect—costs are involved—but markets achieve the degree of efficiency that they do and yield increasing per capita incomes because they give individuals private incentives to adjust to the wants of others and to changes in available capital and technology. As Adam Smith wrote more than two hundred years ago, market participants, by pursuing their own private interests, are led "to promote an end which was no part of this intention."[1] That end is the expansion of the national product and the satisfaction of consumers.

Competition is the benefactor of markets because it forces people to reveal what they are willing to do. At the limit it forces them to reveal both the *minimum* prices they are willing to accept for the products or services being sold and the *maximum* prices they are willing to offer for products or services they want to buy. To the extent that it exists in the marketplace, competition induces people to produce at their limits, given their preferences and cost constraints. It is in this sense that competition maximizes national output and in-

1. Adam Smith, *An Inquiry into the Nature and Causes of the Wealth of Nations*, Modern Library edition, (New York: Random House, 1937), p. 423: "Consumption is the sole end and purpose of all production; and the interest of the producer ought to be attended to, only so far as it may be necessary for promoting that of the consumer."

come. Public or private institutions and policies that restrict trade or the ability of markets to adjust to changes in preferences, prices, and profits, restrict not only individual choices but also national production and income.

This chapter explores on a conceptual level the economic consequences of restrictions on business closings. A general discussion of how markets work illuminates the unsuspected and unintended economic consequences of statutes restricting plant closings and relocations—that is, it says something about what problems will probably arise if restrictions are enacted. Such a discussion will also help us, later, to focus on and understand, albeit partially, the bases for the political support of closing restrictions.

MARKET PROCESSES AS "CREATIVE DESTRUCTION"

No matter how the data on plant closings are arranged, one fact stands out: many businesses fail. In their study of the New England economy, Carol Jusenius and Larry Ledebur found that between 1969 and 1974 nearly 7,000 manufacturing firms died (see Table 3-1). Of the total number of deaths, about 90 percent were relatively small firms employing fewer than a hundred workers, but more than a 100 firms with more than 500 workers also went out of busi-

Table 3-1.   Number of Manufacturing Firms That Died, Were Born, by Employment Size Category, New England, 1969-1974.

Number of Employees	Births		Deaths		Net Change (Births Minus Deaths)
	Number	*Percent*	*Number*	*Percent*	
Total	4,318	100.0	6,706	100.0	−2,388
1–100	4,198	97.2	6,028	89.9	−1,830
101–200	69	1.6	322	4.8	−253
201–300	20	0.5	129	1.9	−109
301–400	16	0.4	67	1.0	−51
401–500	1	0.02	54	0.8	−53
501 or more	14	0.3	106	1.6	−92

Source: Carol L. Jusenius and Larry C. Ledebur, "Where Have All the Firms Gone? An Analysis of the New England Economy," *Economic Development Research Report* (Washington, D.C.: Department of Commerce, September 1977). Reprinted in Richard B. McKenzie, ed., *Plant Closings: Public or Private Choices?* (Washington, D.C.: Cato Institute, 1982), p. 85.

ness during the five-year period. The "death rate" (measured as a percent of firms in existence in 1969) was 31 percent.[2] As Table 3-1 reveals, the deaths exceeded the births of firms by a substantial margin, and 97 percent of the new firms hired fewer than 100 employees. (New England's total nonagriculture industry grew during the 1969–74 period, however, because of births and expansions of firms in nonmanufacturing sectors of the economy.)

Using Dun and Bradstreet files on corporate locations, David Birch has calculated the number of closings across the country by region (see Table 3-2). His survey reveals that closings among both manufacturing and nonmanufacturing firms run at a rate comparable to the findings of Jusenius and Ledebur. In addition, he found that the Northeast, with 24 percent of the nation's population, experienced about 39 percent of all manufacturing plant closings in the country during the 1969–79 period, a fact largely explained by the high proportion of manufacturing firms in the Northeast (37 percent in 1969).

Of course, plant closings, in and of themselves, give rise to job losses, hundreds of thousands of them, a social problem at the center of the empirical work surveyed in Chapter 2. Although the competitive market process is admittedly by its very nature destructive, the destruction is "creative destruction," to use a favorite phrase of the late Harvard economist Joseph Schumpeter. As some firms go under, they release their resources to other, more cost-effective firms that offer consumers more of what they want at more attractive prices. Many proponents of restrictions cry "foul": such a process is still unfair to the losers. In fact, however, the process offers everyone an equal opportunity to compete, survive, and win.

The protection and security offered employees and communities by the market system principally resides in the opportunity it affords everyone to *meet the competition on equal legal terms.* To survive the competitive struggle, all employees have to do is keep their wages and productivity in line with their market competition; all communities have to do is keep their taxes and the quality of their services in line with their local government competition. "Build a better mousetrap" is the motto of the free-market system. Competition separates

2. Carol L. Jusenius and Larry C. Ledebur, "Where Have All the Firms Gone? An Analysis of the New England Economy," *Economic Development Research Report* (Washington: U.S. Department of Commerce, September 1977); reprinted in Richard B. McKenzie, ed., *Plant Closings: Public or Private Choices?* (Washington: Cato Institute, 1982), p. 85.

Table 3-2. Number of Closings by December 31, 1976, of Manufacturing Plants in Existence on December 31, 1969, with More than 100 Employees at that Time, by Region.

	Region			Manufacturing Plants with More than 100 Employees in 1969			
Name	Number of States	Percent of U.S. Population		Number of Plants in 1969	Number Closed by 1976	Probability of Closing by 1976, Given Existence in 1969	Interregional Percent Distribution of Closings
Northeast	9	24.1		4,576	1,437	.31	38.6
North Central	12	27.8		3,617	904	.25	24.2
South	16	31.0		3,101	1,042	.34	28.0
West	13	17.1		1,155	344	.30	9.2
Total	50	100.0		12,449	3,727	.30	100.0

Source: David L. Birch, *The Job Generation Process* (Cambridge, Mass.: M.I.T. Program on Neighborhood and Regional Change, 1979), Appendix D. Based on Dun and Bradstreet Corporation records. Note, as we have indicated in the text, that D&B's counts of business establishment closings ("deaths") include an unverifiable number of short-term movers, which have relocated with the U.S. but which D&B could/did not keep track of, as well as establishments that were moved outside the country altogether (population statistics are from *1970 Census of Population*).

the firms that are unwilling or unable to build the better mousetraps from those that are. In the process, firms go out of business, but the interests of people who want the best products they can get for their money are served.

Many people lose their jobs when plants are closed, but their loss does not necessarily mean that they are somehow worse off. Workers unemployed because their plants close are also beneficiaries of the competitive process (involving closings and openings) in other markets, which yields higher quality goods at lower prices. Workers unemployed because of their firms' failures can sometimes find other jobs in expanding sectors of the economy—in those firms that are winning the competitive struggle. Furthermore, workers unemployed by plant closings are often compensated in advance for their expected loss in income when their plants do close. Where the risk of plant closing is high, the supply of labor is often restricted (who would prefer to work where the loss of employment is highly probable or imminent?). As a result, in those risky jobs wages are comparatively high, with the wage differential providing a form of prepaid compensation for the risk of unemployment.

THE ECONOMIC CONSEQUENCES OF RELOCATION RESTRICTIONS

Economic Development

Contrary to the beliefs of the proponents of restrictions on business closings, disinvestment, and movements, such restrictions can, in an otherwise free economy, retard economic development in all regions of the country. People trade with one another in part because of the comparative advantages they have in production. A person who is relatively more efficient in the production of a good will give up less in producing that good than someone else. In other words, a person with a comparative advantage in the production of a good can produce that good more cheaply than others. If people produce those goods in which they have a comparative advantage and trade them for other goods they want, production costs will be lower than if all people try to be self-sufficient. Since costs are reduced by specialization and exchanges, more output than otherwise can be produced with the resources available to the community.

When evaluating the economic consequences of closing and relocation rules, we must keep two points in mind. First, people in different parts of the country have comparative advantages in different goods, and trade occurs between people in different parts of the country when they find that they can gain from trade. People receive a "better deal" (as they define the term) by trading with others than by trying to produce all the goods they want by themselves. They benefit by the exchanges they make, and they benefit because specialization results in reduced production costs and expanded output.

Second, the comparative advantages of people in different regions continually change because the conditions of production—that is, the availability of resources, technology, and consumer preferences for work and goods—continually changes. Changes in comparative advantage spell changes in relative costs. What was once relatively less costly to produce in the North can—because of, for example, a change in production technology—become less costly to produce in the South. By moving from the North to the South, a firm can lower its production costs.

Regional shifts in comparative advantage may occur because a strategic resource used in making product A becomes relatively more scarce in one region than in another, and therefore the cost of producing good A in the region rises above the cost of producing it in another region. Additionally, increases in workers' education level or the discovery of more abundant supplies of a given resource may cause a region to initiate production of good B. Again, a shift in production within the region from A to B can keep the costs of production below what they would otherwise be. The industry that expands as a result of beneficial cost changes begins to impinge on the resources available to industries that once dominated the region. The costs of producing A in that region go up, and, as a consequence, the producer of A moves someplace else. Finally, the preferences of people in a region can change. For example, an increase in the demand for services within a particular region may induce resources like labor to move from the manufacturing sector into the service sector, causing the wages and production costs in the manufacturing sector to rise. One result may be that some manufacturing plants close or relocate, releasing their labor to a growing economic sector.

Describing the causes of changes in regional economic structures is difficult under the best of circumstances because costs are based on subjective evaluations of goods, and those evaluations cannot be *directly* observed in the market process.[3] Over recent decades, however, the comparative advantages enjoyed by many sections of the North have changed for several reasons. First, the demand for services in the North has increased more rapidly than in other parts of the country. Second, environmental legislation has placed more severe restrictions on production in the congested northern region than in many other parts of the country and has increased the relative cost of production in the North.

Bruce Yandle has found solid statistical evidence to show that the environmental laws of the 1970s have diverted expansion capital into pollution abatement equipment, reducing the growth of those industries, like steel, that may be termed "polluting industries." He has also been able to show that environmental laws have diverted expansion capital from the heavily industrialized areas of the North, where "pollution rights" are relatively scarce, to the South and West, where "pollution rights" are relatively abundant. Such laws are necessarily driving some firms out of business ("The Effects of Investment in Pollution Control on Industry Output and Regional Development," Clemson, South Carolina: Economics Department, Clemson University, 1981). Yandle also has some preliminary evidence indicating that environmental laws, by restricting entry and driving out marginal firms, are increasing the profits of surviving firms ("Polluters' Profits": An Empirical Note," Clemson, South Carolina: Economics Department, Clemson University, 1981).

The unavailability of "pollution rights" has caused many firms to choose southern, less polluted locations. According to one report, a major reason Volkswagen chose Pennsylvania as the site of its first United States plant is that the state of Pennsylvania agreed to reduce pollution from road construction by using a more expensive paving process in order that Volkswagen might have the pollution rights to start up production.[4]

If the environmental restrictions that affect a region's comparative advantage are ill-conceived, the region's income will be reduced by them and appropriate changes in environmental laws may be called for. If ill-conceived environmental laws cannot be changed, however, the solution to a region's economic woes is not to restrict business migration. Given the existing environmental legislation, keeping some

3. James M. Buchanan, *Costs and Choice* (New York: Markham Publishers, 1969).

4. T. Bruce Yandle, "The Emerging Market in Air Pollution Rights," *Regulation* (July/August 1978): 21–29.

businesses from closing down and moving out will only cause the costs of production to be higher than they would otherwise be, and the region's income will be restricted.

If the comparative advantage of a region changes, for whatever reason, a restriction on business migration will keep resources tied up in that comparatively inefficient sector. The sector that should be expanding (given its comparative advantage) will be restricted from doing so because resources will not be released as quickly. Firms will be forced to retain employees and other resources that could be moved to the expanding sector.

In summary, governmental rules that impede the movement of manufacturing industry (by actual relocations or by a process of "deaths and births" of firms) out of one region will retard not only the development of the manufacturing industry in the South but the development of, for example, the expanding service sector in the North. Furthermore, restrictions on business closings and mobility will cause production costs to be higher than they would otherwise be, and, to that extent, will reduce national production and income.

Job Movement

Many see closing restrictions as a means of keeping northern firms from moving south or west. We showed in Chapter 2 that relocations account for a small fraction of all northern employment losses. Nonetheless, even if existing manufacturing firms in the North are restricted from moving to the South by legislation, the movement of manufacturing jobs to the South will be impeded but not stopped. Firms are willing to incur the costs of relocation because moving will enable the firms to protect their competitive positions or to gain competitive advantages over their rivals because the cost of production is lower in the new location than in the old. If firms are unable to move to new, more profitable southern locations, profitable opportunities are left to be exploited by others. Restrictions on business mobility will cause other firms to spring up in the new southern locations and existing southern firms to expand more than they otherwise would. Because their costs of production are lower, emerging and expanding firms in new locations will be able to undersell firms in old locations. Firms in the old locations will eventually be forced to contract their operations or go out of business. Because of births of new firms and deaths of old ones, the employment structure of regional economies will shift in the long run in spite of the relocation statutes. Such laws will only slow the adjustment process and, because new firms are required to form, increase the cost of adjustment.

Under the 1976 version of the National Employment Priorities Act, the Secretary of Labor, with the advice of the National Employment Relocation Advisory Council, is empowered to keep a firm from relocating if the move is without "adequate justification." Presumably this means that if a firm is deemed to be making a "fair rate of return on its investment," then it can be prevented from moving. We have noted, however, that an expanded output in new locations will reduce the profitability in old ones, and therefore even firms in old locations that are not at first able to provide "adequate justification" for a move will eventually be able to present the needed justification. What was once a move for so-called economic greed will soon become a move for economic necessity. Eventually, the government will find itself subsidizing these firms that it wants to see remain in their old locations.

Power of Unions

Unions are interested in improving wages and benefits for their members. They know, however, that their ability to do so is restricted by the threat of relocation. If businesses are prevented from moving, the *immediate* threat of job loss is removed and, as a consequence, unions can be expected to increase their demands on employers. The result will be even higher production costs in the old locations; the benefits of relocation rules can be reaped in the short-run income of union members. (More will be said later on the role of unions in the political struggle for closing restrictions.)

Worker Wages

Wages in many nonunionized labor markets will tend to fall (relative to what they would have been) because of restrictions on business mobility. The supply of labor in any market is dependent on a number of factors: skill and education required, location, climate, risk of injury, and social prestige. Since such factors affect the supply of labor in individual markets, they influence the wage rate. Steeplejacks tend to make more than janitors because the skills required are more difficult to acquire (which restricts the number of people who are *able* to do the job) and because there are risks associated with working on metal beams in high places. Ph.D. accountants teaching in universities tend to make less money than their counterparts in private industry, but they receive the nonpecuniary benefits of flexibility in scheduling their time and tenured employment, which has been described as a one-way, lifetime contract.

As noted above, the supply of labor in any labor market is also affected by any expectation that the firms will close down altogether or move elsewhere. Generally, the greater the threat that an industry's firms will move, the higher the wage employees with given skills will demand before accepting employment in that industry. Restrictions on business closings propose to reduce the threat many workers now face in losing their jobs. In the short run the effect will be to increase the relative attractiveness of employment and, hence, the supply of labor in markets from which firms might otherwise move. To the extent that those markets are competitive, the wage rates will fall. If firms are forced to give severance pay to employees they leave behind, the same thing will happen: in competitive labor markets, the relative attractiveness of employment and the supply of labor will increase, pushing the wage rates down. On the other hand, closing requirements increase the relative cost of labor, depress the demand for labor, and cause a substitution on the marginal of capital for labor.

Of course, markets are not perfectly competitive, and they do not always fully adjust to changes in the economic environment. The general tendency, however, is clear. Wages will tend to be depressed by labor and capital supply responses. Wages may be observed rising in spite of closing laws on the books. The point of this section is that they will not rise by as much as they otherwise would because more people will want to work in those areas where the threat of employment loss in the near term is reduced. Workers who were once willing to accept the risk of losing their jobs in order to receive the higher wage will no longer have that opportunity; their real income will be reduced.

In the long run, new labor market equilibrium will be achieved as regional employment structures change to what they would have been in the absence of the relocation rules. On balance, however, the country will be poorer: closing rules cause resources to be inefficiently allocated among regions, and fewer goods and services will be produced. The per capita income of the country, in other words, will be restricted; if it grows, it will grow by less than otherwise because of the relocation rules.

Before we move on to another topic, a few comments need to be added regarding relative labor costs, a particularly troublesome part of the North-South, Frostbelt-Sunbelt controversy. An added inducement to this alleged southward flight of capital, it is often argued, is the "wage attraction" of the South. It is more illuminating, however, to assess the impact of "wage push" in the North. From the wage-attraction perspective, it may appear that low-paid workers in the South are "stealing" business from and causing economic harm to the North. But the wage-push perspective suggests that wages in the North are higher and on the rise for such classical economic reasons as competition for workers from the developing service sector in the North. In other words, manufacturers are forced to pay higher wages or risk losing their labor force to more rapidly expanding sectors of the economy. Firms that move south are pushed south, having been outbid for labor resources in the North. From this perspective, industrial movements to the South are a consequence of gains made by many workers in the North—and the "runaway plant phenomenon" is a positive force in the dynamic and growth economy, South *and* North.

WEALTH TRANSFERS

Restrictions on closing will cause wealth transfers and losses. When people invest in business, they are actually buying a bundle of legal rights whose market value is equal to the present value of the future income that can be received from those rights. Many people have invested in businesses (either directly through the purchase of plant and equipment or indirectly through the purchase of stocks and bonds) on the assumption that they were purchasing not only the right to operate the business but also the right to move the business to any location they perceive to be more profitable. Because they thought they had the right to move their business, they paid more for the business (or the stock) than they otherwise might have.

Restrictions on closing propose to take the right of closure away from business owners. Such restrictions thus in effect reduce the income stream of the business and the wealth of business owners. Under the National Employment Priorities Act, as well as under any one of the many proposed state laws, businesses cannot move without having government and labor consent, so the demand for the assets of a firm that would otherwise choose to move will be reduced.

When employees secure legally recognized rights to prevent a plant from closing, which can lead to continued company losses, the employees effectively secure a strong legal position to negotiate their plant's closing. To avoid losses, the company should be willing to "buy off" the workers, a payment that adds to severance pay, giving them some portion of their capital in exchange for an agreement from labor that labor will not oppose (either through specially established labor commissions or the courts) the plant's closing.[5] In this way and to this extent, closing laws transfer ownership rights from investors to workers. Accordingly, the value of the owners' portfolio of rights is reduced—because the portfolio then contains fewer rights. The implied transfer of wealth from investors to workers will *in the short run* show up in reduced prices for the stocks of companies that are prevented from closing. The wealth gained by the workers, however, will not equal the wealth lost by firms prevented from closing. A part of that wealth transfer given up by the firms prevented from closing will go to owners of companies in other places, such as the South, that are able to emerge or expand and to survive more profitably because other businesses have found their movements impeded. A portion of the wealth lost by northern firms with restricted mobility will simply be a deadweight loss because of the subsequent decrease in production efficiency. A part of the wealth transfers will be picked up by government agencies that will be expanded for the purpose of increasing government supervision over business decisions. *In the long run* the wealth transfer will be partially reversed as wages drop to account for the instituted closing costs.

Although transferring wealth from one group to another may be a socially desirable goal, closing rules seem like a particularly clumsy way of achieving it, especially since the rules amount to a negative-sum game. However, when those closing rights were effectively

5. Under a number of proposed state and federal bills, the closing laws will be enforced only if a certain percentage of the employees or a union protests the company's closing decision.

bought by investors and could be purchased by labor by an appropriate reduction in other employment, one must ask if imposed closing restrictions are not a form of legalized theft. Furthermore, the resulting shifts in rights or wealth are rather haphazard, with unexpected and unintended consequences. Many people who will lose wealth in the transfer process are, of course, high income investors; but many losers are likely to be on low incomes from retirement plans tied to the market prices of various stocks. If the value of these stocks goes down, then the prospective income from retirement programs will also fall. In short, it is doubtful that any analysis has been made by proponents of restrictions to determine who will be harmed by the proposed legislation and by how much each person will be hurt.

COMPETITIVE GOVERNMENTS

Restrictions on business closings will increase the short-run monopoly power of state and local governments. The framers of the Constitution attempted to place restraints on government by sharply defining the role of government and by introducing market principles into its organization. The founding fathers believed that the power of government could be constrained in part by *competition among governments.* A government, operating in a world of many governments, would face market constraints similar to those faced by private companies. If a company raises its price or lowers the quality of its product, it can expect to lose customers to competing firms that hold prices down or maintain quality or both. Similarly, a government that raises taxes or reduces the quantity and/or quality of its public services can expect to lose people and its tax base to other (competing) governments. Although the degree of potential competition among governments may be less than it is among private firms, competition can still occur. To the extent that it does, the power of state and local government to raise taxes and lower the quality of services provided is restricted.

Restrictions on business mobility will hinder the short-run response of business to tax increases imposed by local governments. To the extent that this occurs, closing restrictions temporarily increase the power of governments to raise taxes and reduce the quality of the services they provide. Consequently, the enactment of relocation laws is likely to lead to higher taxes and lower-quality services in many jurisdictions—but only in the short run.

State and local governments are deluding themselves if they think they can reap hefty, long-run monopoly profits from restrictions. Restrictions on closings may suppress competition among governments during the short period of time that capital cannot be moved or depreciated away, but restrictions do not eliminate forever the tendency of governments to compete. Eventually governments will catch on to the fact that they can offset, partially or totally, the costs of closing restrictions by eliminating state and local taxes on business or by expanding services and subsidies provided to business by state and local governments. Once a few governments start competing in these ways, then most must enter the competitive game. The result will be that the costs of the closing restrictions can in large measure be passed on to the state and local citizens in the form of higher taxes. Again, someone must pay the costs of the closing restrictions. Closing restrictions are a means of forcing people who do not benefit from them to pay a part of the tab. To the extent that that happens, we should expect a misallocation of resources in the economy.

CORPORATE SOCIAL RESPONSIBILITY

Backers of restrictive legislation fervently contend that firms have a social responsibility to their workers and to the communities in which they exist. They point to the social disruption caused by plant closings: the loss of tax base, the idle workers and plants, the impairment of community services because of lower tax revenues, and the higher taxes imposed on others because of higher unemployment and social welfare expenditures.[6] Dayton, a medium-sized manufacturing city in western Ohio, is to these proponents an excellent example of what plant closings can mean. In early 1980, three companies, including Dayton Tire Company, a subsidiary of Firestone, announced their intentions to close. Eighteen hundred jobs were lost at the Dayton Tire plant alone. Workers and town officials interviewed for television recounted the personal hardship the closings had imposed

---

6. See Jeanne Prial Gondus, Paul Jarley, and Louis A. Ferman, *Plant Closings and Economic Dislocation* (Kalamazoo, Mich.: N.E. Upjohn Institute for Employment Research, 1981).

on them, their families, and the communities; several denounced the companies for giving them little notice of the closings and for being socially irresponsible.

A program on plant closings was broadcast on "The McNeil/Lehrer Report," 18 June 1980. And during the week of 18 June 1980, the "Today" program on NBC television ran a series of programs on plant closings, focusing on the closing of Ford Motor Company's Mawah, New Jersey, plant. Not all of the workers interviewed appraised the closings in the same way; a few saw the closings as an opportunity to take another job.

No one seriously contends that firms do not have a responsibility to their communities, but it is hard to accept the assumption that entrepreneurs and their management teams are any less socially responsible than their workers. If nothing else, the development of good community relationships is sensible from a profit motive. Rather than enlightening listeners and readers, claims that firms have a social responsibility only camouflage basic issues: Where does a firm's social responsibility end; who is at fault in plant closings; and what are the alternatives open to workers and communities for dealing with the problems encountered when a plant shuts down? Admittedly, plant closings create hardships for some people. The important question, however, is whether the remedy—closing restrictions—is more damaging than the disease. Furthermore, should a firm's social responsibility remain a moral obligation or be made a legal one? For any society that wishes to retain the remnants of individual freedom, a sharp but important distinction must be recognized between voluntary acceptance of social responsibility and forced compliance with a government edict.

Through wages and an array of taxes—from property to sales to income—businesses contribute to the welfare of the community. It is not at all clear, incidentally, that businesses use more community resources than they pay for. In the intense competition for plants, many communities effectively "pay" plants to locate in their areas through below-cost sewage and water facilities and interest rates. Whether or not the competition that now exists among communities is socially beneficial is a question that needs careful attention.

Through personal saving, workers can secure their own individual futures against job displacement. As noted, wages tend to reflect the risk of plant closings. Proposed restrictive legislation will, if its proponents are correct, reduce the risks of job displacement for some (but by no means all or even most) workers. The reduced risk will lead to a reduction in their wages. These workers will, in effect, be forced to buy a social insurance policy that, because of its national coverage, will not always be suitable to many of their individual needs, but may be suitable for the limited number of people orchestrating the legislative drive.

Proponents of the plant closing legislation seem to imagine that in the absence of government restrictions almost all workers will be exploited and, as a consequence, be unable to prepare for their futures. They also seem to imagine that the risk of job displacement will somehow disappear with government restrictions and that the costs of the restrictions, which are either overlooked or presumed to be trivial, will be borne fully by the "firm." For a firm like Dayton Tire, however, employing 1,800 workers and paying the average wage in Dayton in 1979, the costs of the two-year notice, plus the one-year severance pay (at 85 percent of the previous year's pay), plus the fringe benefits, plus the community payments, are anything but trivial; they can easily exceed $110 million! If the proposed National Employment Priorities Act or the Ohio closing restrictions had recently been enacted and Firestone had been prevented from closing the Dayton plant (along with four others scattered around the country), the company might have had to incur more than a half a trillion dollars in production costs and losses of upwards of $60 million over the next three years, for which it would have been unprepared. Very likely, the financial solvency of the entire company and the jobs of hundreds of other Firestone workers, which were precarious at the time, would have been placed in even greater jeopardy.[7]

To operate in a financially sound manner under such a law over the long run, a company must prepare for the eventual expenditure associated with closing: it can establish its own contingency fund or buy insurance against the risk that it must assume. Either way, the cost will be recovered either from wages that would otherwise have been paid or from higher prices charged consumers, in which case the purchasing power of the workers' incomes is reduced. Although there is no question that owners of companies will be hurt by the legislation, the point that needs emphasis is that most workers will not escape *paying* for the benefits received under the restrictions.

---

7. Bernard W. Frazier, paper presented at a symposium on plant closing legislation sponsored by the Liberty Fund, Charleston, South Carolina, 9–11 May 1982.

Instead of restricting business rights, communities could set aside funds from their taxes, and these funds could be used to alleviate social problems created by plant closings. In the absence of national or state legislation, community contingency funds could be established to meet local needs and to account for the trade-offs that people in the different communities were willing and able to make. If current tax collections were insufficient to meet community needs, then tax rates could be raised. Of course, such an increase would discourage firms from either establishing or expanding their operations. But the proposed restrictions have the same effect. They are a subtle form of business taxation that, like all taxes, would deter investment and thereby further erode growth in productivity and wages. Contrary perhaps to the good intentions of its advocates, the new restrictive legislation increases the social cost associated with business operations.

Plant closing restrictions would probably increase not decrease the number of business failures because, as noted, they raise the cost of doing business *and of staying in business.* Indeed, closing restrictions can force closing decisions. Firms must continually evaluate their future prospects, asking whether they can make it through the next six months, year, or two years. Once they announce their decision to close, their coffin can be sealed: Their employees can be expected to leave and their suppliers, buyers, and creditors can be expected to deal more cautiously with them. Because of the notification requirements, many firms will announce their intentions to close at a time when they might otherwise try to ride out what might be temporary adverse market conditions. In this respect, "plant closing laws" are laws that close plants.

MOBILITY: A KEY ECONOMIC LIBERTY

Proponents of restrictions insist that because firms draw on the resources of the communities, they have an obligation to compensate the community for the benefits the firms have received over the years. Proponents are particularly concerned when companies use the profits made in one place to expand elsewhere. Does not the company owe the community a "fair share" of any future expansions? Messrs. Bluestone and Harrison describe with some eloquence how northern firms are "disinvesting" themselves of their plants in the

North by earning a profit and then expanding their operations in the South and West.[8] A principal problem with such a line of argument is that it is perfectly applicable to employees: workers also draw on a community's services and the resources of their plant. When they decide to resign their employment and move elsewhere, do they not owe a social debt to their community, and should they not compensate their employers, as restrictive legislation proposes that firms repay their employees and communities? Through wages received and purchases made on household goods, employees send their incomes out of the community. To be consistent, should not proponents propose that the "public interest" dictates that employees spend a "fair share" of *their* incomes in the community? Should not employees (and their unions) be told how much of their incomes must be invested in their companies?

These questions are not intended to make the case for restrictions on employee earnings and expenditures. Rather, the point is that we allow individuals the freedom to do what they wish with their incomes and to move when and where they please for very good reasons. First, a worker's income is only one half of a *quid pro quo*, a contractual agreement between the employer and employee that is freely struck and presumably mutually beneficial. Second, freedom gives workers the opportunity to seek out the lowest-priced and highest-quality good compatible with their preferences; that very same freedom forces sellers to compete for the purchases of the workers and provides workers with the security of having a choice of places to work and buy goods.

Third, but foremost, there is the firm belief—call it faith—that people are indeed created with certain inalienable rights. Individuals know, within tolerable limits, what is best for them in their individual circumstances, and they are the ones best qualified to say what they should do and where they should live and how and where they should invest their resources, labor, *and* financial capital. The right of entrepreneurs to use their capital assets is basic to a truly free society; the centralization of authority to determine where and under what circumstances firms should invest leads to the concentration of

8. Barry Bluestone and Bennett Harrison, *Capital and Communities: The Causes and Consequences of Private Disinvestment* (Washington, D.C.: The Progressive Alliance, 1980), chapter 8; or *The Deindustrialization of America: Plant Closings, Community Abandonment, and the Dismanteling of Basic Industries* (New York: Basic Books, Inc., 1982), chapters 4–6.

economic power in the hands of the people who run government. Private rights to move, to invest, to buy, to sell are social devices for the dispersion of economic power.

There are those who believe that the case made against this restrictive legislation is obviously an apology for the "corporate giant." Not so. Embedded in the proposed federal legislation are provisions that effectively institutionalize the Chrysler bailout of 1979 and 1980. The government is given broad discretionary authority to provide unspecified forms of aid to companies that go bankrupt.[9] This type of bill could effectively swing the doors of the federal treasury wide open to any firm sufficiently large and with sufficient political muscle to enlist the attention and sympathies of the Secretary of Labor. The bill destroys, in part, the incentive firms now have to watch their costs and avoid bankruptcy. Because votes are what count in politics, under the proposed law the incentive firms have to avoid losses diminishes as the size of the firm (meaning number of employees) grows.

Large rather than small companies will be most likely to secure access to the discretionary authority of government. Chrysler was bailed out in 1979 not because it was the only firm that went broke that year (there were hundreds of thousands of others), but because it was large and had—through its employees, stockholders, and suppliers—the necessary political clout. Of course, the taxes of many smaller businesses will help finance these subsidies for their larger competitors. The marginal firms will be forced to close because of the extra tax burden. We can only imagine what such a bill portends.

Businesses, like their workers, do not always like to compete or to worry about someone else outproducing or underpricing them. Many businesses actively seek government bailouts, subsidies, and buyouts. For these reasons alone, we should be cautious in interpreting the consequences of restrictions, no matter what their stated intentions. Restrictions on plant exits from are also restrictions on entry into competitive markets. They keep competition out of local markets by restricting the ability of businesses to move from other areas of the country, and they discourage the emergence of new businesses, meaning both new investment and new competitors. Thus, such laws can protect some established wealth by protecting established busi-

9. United States Congress, House, "National Employment Priorities Act of 1979," H.R. 5040 (96th Congress, 1st Session), pp. 34–36.

nesses with market-proven products from potential competitors with goods untried in the market. Northerners can be assured that the southern textile industry, for example, does not look kindly upon northern businesses expanding into their low-wage markets.

THE VISIBLE AND INVISIBLE EFFECTS OF RESTRICTION

Supporters of the restrictive legislation frequently point to the emotional and physical difficulties of those who suffer job displacement. These problems can be serious; there is no debate on that point. However, the political attractiveness of restrictive legislation can be appraised by the *visibility* of the harm done by plant closings and the *invisibility* of the harm done by restrictions on closings. The hardship associated with closings is easily observed. The media can take pictures of idle plants and interview unemployed workers; researchers can identify and study the psychological effects of job displacement.[10] *On the other hand, restrictions on plant closings are also restrictions on plant openings.* They reduce the competitive drive of business, deter investment, and reduce the growth in productive employment, in generally retarding the efficiency of the economy. However, it is impossible for the media to photograph plants not opened because of the restrictions on plant closings, or to interview workers not able to find employment (who, as a consequence of unemployment, develop hypertension, peptic ulcers, and severe depression) because of the inability (or lack of incentive) of firms to open or expand plants.

Proponents contend that they support both the "little person," the low-income, uneducated worker, who may otherwise be exploited by the system, as well as the relatively highly paid, skilled worker. The fact of the matter is that the proposed protective legislation will work to the detriment of some of the lower-income, uneducated workers. The legislation imposes a severe penalty on entrepreneurs who seek to establish production facilities whose chance of success is slim. Plants that would otherwise be built will, with this law, not be constructed, and therefore the law would work to the detriment of workers in low-income neighborhoods in the inner cities because that is where the chance of success is often

10. See Bluestone and Harrison, *The Deindustrialization of America*, chapter 3.

lowest. Furthermore, if the law were enacted, it would freeze in place for a period of time many of the production facilities of the country. Relatively depressed areas like Dayton, Ohio, would lose one of their best opportunities for recovering from the recent loss of jobs: the recruitment of plants from other parts of the country.

Television coverage often fails to consider the widespread economic growth occurring over time in a particular area. Dayton Tire shut down in 1980; manufacturing employment in the Dayton area was down slightly from what it was in 1970. These are the facts we hear repeatedly. What we do not hear is that, as recounted in Chapter 2, total employment in Dayton and in Ohio *rose* during the 1970s by 10 and 16 percent, respectively, and that the average weekly wage in Dayton is 50 percent higher than what it is in Greenville, South Carolina;[11] and that earnings during the 1970s, after adjusting for inflation, rose modestly but several times faster than the earnings in the rest of the country. These are the positive results brought about, to a significant extent, by the ability of firms to adjust—by closings and openings—to changing economic circumstances.

It is difficult to measure the value of goods that are never produced because of the greater (government imposed) cost of capital. Nonetheless, if restrictive legislation is passed, goods will go unproduced, and many of the goods produced will be goods consumers do not want. Firestone closed Dayton Tire because it produced bias-ply tires. Only months prior to the announced closing of Dayton Tire, the tire market had turned down dramatically; domestic car sales has plummeted because of higher automobile prices (brought on partially by safety and environmental regulations), higher fuel prices, and the shift in consumer tastes to smaller, imported cars. In addition, consumers revealed through their purchases that they wanted safer, more fuel-efficient, and more reliable radial tires. If Firestone had been required to keep the Dayton plant open, along with five others scheduled for closing, Firestone would have been forced to produce tires that consumers did not buy and consumers would have been forced to purchase bias tires that they did not want.

There are costs associated with tying up an entire economy for even short periods of time, and people will bear those costs. The residents of Gary, Indiana, may reason that closing restrictions will keep factories in place and that therefore their employment opportunities

---

11. Greenville, South Carolina, is a city near a plant opened by one of the firms that left Dayton.

will be improved. What they may fail to see is that restrictions on plant closings across the state or nation will retain firms in other cities and prevent those firms from moving to Gary, denying Gary in the process the opportunity to make use of its comparative advantages in production and to establish a strong, viable employment base for the future. Proponents of restrictions argue that "free marketeers" ignore the human costs of unfettered markets, but such a position requires that its advocates, for no other reason than consistency of argument, take account of the human costs of a "fettered" economy, especially one with restraints as extensive as those proposed.

If a plant closing law is ever passed, its victims will be largely invisible. Disenchanted consumers and unemployed workers may very well not realize they have been victimized; and if they do realize it, they will probably be unable to determine who is at fault. Therein lies the political appeal of restrictive legislation; Congressman Ford and others can champion this cause of the political left without ever confronting those harmed by it.

Ford, Bluestone, Harrison, and others dislike the fact that in the American economic system, businesses strive for profit. They fear that without government rules and regulations, employees and communities will be left without protection. They seem to imagine businesses as giant, voracious octopuses, totally unconcerned about their community and workers and willing to do anything for a buck. To Ford and his supporters, profit is a four letter word. Although it is hard to argue that businesses are any less socially concerned than the government bureaucrats who run control programs, we must acknowledge that profit is the basic driving force behind the business system—*and it should be.* It is the motivating force that gives rise to competition, to new and better products for consumers, and to cost savings. The drive for profits provides workers and communities with the primary means of keeping the businesses they have and expanding their business tax base. By holding taxes and wages in line with the competition, workers and communities can induce firms to stay and expand—to buy out and to put back in operation those plants that are closed. Contrary to what is so often written and heard, profit provides protection.[12] Unfortunately, many of the advocates

12. On "The McNeil/Lehrer Report" workers expressed dismay that Firestone was asking $20 million for a plant it felt compelled to close. Actually, the workers should have been elated with the "high" price tag. A high asking price tends to indicate that the plant

of the restrictive legislation, including unions, do not want to meet the competition. Bluestone and Harrison say as much:

> Trade unionists are especially concerned with how firms use capital mobility to keep labor off guard, to play off workers in one region against those in another, and how the threat of capital relocation is used to weaken labor's ability to resist corporate attacks on the social wage itself.[13]

What advocates of restrictions seem to want is protection from competition and from threat of pricing themselves out of the market. Consumers and taxpayers should be gravely concerned about plant closing restrictions. As bills are now written, proposed closing restrictions endow unions with the additional power to price labor out of the market, to turn a profitable concern into a money-losing one and then give them access to the coffers of the federal government for a bailout or buyout.

PLANT CLOSINGS AND FAMILY PROBLEMS

In defending closing restrictions, some medical researchers point to the high incidence of child beating among laid off workers and implicitly ask if government does not have a role in protecting children from abuse.[14] The preferences of children are not always adequately "internalized" (that is, considered) in market transactions. As Lewis Margolis writes in a comment on an article of mine,

> Professor McKenzie contends that free mobility of corporations and workers will minimize the general societal costs of unemployment. However, reliance on free mobility alone denies the needs and the rights of individuals—such as children—who are unable to avail themselves of that freedom.
>
> In his argument, Professor McKenzie inappropriately draws an analogy between corporate and individual responsibility to the community. . . . A more appropriate analogy would be between the company's responsibility to the community and the primary wage earner's responsibility to his family. An individual worker may indeed include the risks of ulcers, depression, or suicide in calculating whether to opt for higher wages available in a company

---

has a market value, an alternative use to some other firm willing to pay the price for the facility. A selling price approximating zero would tend to indicate that the plant has no alternative use and that the plant and workers would tend to remain idle.

13. Bluestone and Harrison, *Capital and Communities*, p. 7.

14. Bluestone and Harrison, *Capital and Communities*, introduction.

unencumbered by restrictions on its movement of capital. However, the mere fact of involuntary termination probably affects the children detrimentally. ... Throughout 1980, approximately 500,000 men with children involuntarily lost their jobs.

To cite just one—but particularly cruel—cost of involuntary work loss, the children of terminated workers are at substantially increased risk of suffering physical abuse at the hands of their parents. ... Are not these children entitled to some protection through attempting to prevent that abuse instead of the equivocally effective treatment which variably follows child abuse? What of the battered children who remain undiscovered and thus bear an invisible cost of parental work loss?[15]

Granted, few people can remain unmoved by the sight of badly abused children. The relevant question is not whether an important social problem, child battering, exists, but whether the proposed remedies (i.e., plant closing laws) will relieve or aggravate the problem. Proponents see the legislation as a direct means of reducing unemployment and, thereby, family problems. Opponents, on the other hand, believe the regulation will at best affect the timing of the unemployment. At worst, they believe regulation will, in the long run, impair worker employment and income opportunities. (Again, restrictions on plant closings are restrictions on plant openings.) The people who are unable to find jobs and remain unemployed because new plants do not open or old plants do not expand can, if the studies are correct, take out their frustration on their children. The children abused by these parents, *because of plant closing restrictions*, should be no less a concern of the state than the children abused because of plant closings.

Similarly, we might all agree that plant closings lead to divorces, hypertension, and suicide. However, to prove the moral superiority of their position, it would appear encumbent on proponents of restrictions to show that their legislative proposals will, *on balance*, ameliorate marital and family problems. *That has not been shown.* Until it is, we must all look askance at any listing of how many peptic ulcers, suicides, and child abuse cases are *associated* with (but not necessarily *caused* by) plant closings.

15. Lewis H. Margolis, "Plant Closures," *Policy Review* (Fall 1981): 10–11.

CONCLUDING COMMENTS

Advocates of restrictions chide supporters of a market economy for their opposition to restrictions, claiming their arguments are based on models of a perfect economy that are never duplicated in the real world. Real world markets, so the argument goes, are fraught with imperfections in the form of restrictions on the mobility of labor and the ability of prices and wages to adjust to new market conditions, such as changes in income and tastes.[16] Such a criticism is totally misdirected. Economists who understand their models have never seen them as "descriptive reality," but as means — methods or theoretical tools — designed to accomplish one objective, to make correct predictions concerning the impact of public policy changes. The usefulness of such theories must accordingly be judged in terms of that objective.

Descriptively speaking, the case for a free market is strengthened by a recognition of its imperfections. People, including state government officials, know little of what others want and how those wants can best be satisfied. We need some social means by which information on people's preferences is revealed to others. The free play of individual actions, resulting in millions of daily exchanges organized through business firms is what we call "the market." However, the market must be understood as more than the sum of what individuals do, for through the forces of competition the market generates critically important information on individuals' preferences and relative costs of production that cannot effectively be generated in any other way. Competition forces people to reveal what they are willing to accept for the labor and other resources they have to offer. One of the more important bits of information passed around by the market is where the most cost-effective production locations are. If firms are denied the right to move to less costly areas of production, those firms can be certain that other firms will emerge to take advantage of the unexploited cost savings and to outproduce and underprice firms held in place by plant closing laws. Inevitably, plant closing laws will be transformed into firm shut-down laws.

Many of the arguments of the proponents of restrictions amount to the simple proposition that not all people want to compete, which

16. Bluestone and Harrison, *Capital and Communities*, introduction.

is to a degree understandable. That is basically what is implied when advocates of restrictions deride "cheap labor" in the South (as if highly paid workers in the North, for example, have an inherent right to demand whatever they want in the form of wages and fringe benefits, no matter what other people are willing to do, and to deny by way of government restrictions workers in the South "higher" paying jobs).

Competition is a hard taskmaster, but it is also the glory of the free market system. It is the social process that insures that, on balance, the incomes earned in the North or South or West have significant purchasing power in terms of prices and qualities of goods and services. We must question whether restrictions on plant closings actually improve on the imperfect competitiveness of the market system or simply make the system more imperfect. Opponents of restrictions suggest the latter is the case.

Chapter 4

CLOSING PROFITABLE PLANTS

The plant closing bills introduced in Congress and state legislatures are supported by a variety of arguments, the most important of which is that firms are inclined to close "profitable" plants. In introducing his original plant closing bill in Congress in 1974, Congressman William Ford (D–Mich.) offered the following caveats:

> My own congressional district suffered the effects of the runaway plant in 1972 when the Garwood plant in Wayne [Michigan] moved and left 600 unemployed workers behind. ... Mr. Speaker, the reason these firms are moving away is not economic necessity but economic greed. For instance, the Federal Mogul Co. in Detroit signed a contract in 1971 with the United Auto Workers and six months later announced it would be moving to Alabama. A spokesman for the company was quoted as saying they were moving "not because we are not making money in Detroit, but because we can make more money in Alabama."[1]

Ford s concern that firms are closing profitable plants has been echoed repeatedly by proponents of restrictions on private disinvestment. Such an assertion serves two functions: It suggests that private firms are behaving not only irresponsibly but irrationally, even according to a major criterion (profitability) of the market system;

---

1. U.S. House of Representatives, *Congressional Record*, 94th Congress, 1st Session, 10 June 1974, p. 18559.

second, the claim shifts responsibility for plant closings to management-capitalists and away from workers. After all, shouldn't productive workers be protected from disinvestment moves that are inefficient, if not downright stupid? That is the sort of question-begging implied in Congressman Ford's remarks.

This chapter analyzes the economic and political case for plant-closing restrictions by examining three central contentions of its proponents. First, firms are closing profitable plants. Second, firms are ruining otherwise profitable plants by using them as "cash cows" (the meaning of which will become apparent). Third, the modern wave of industry conglomeration has reduced the ties of firms to the communities in which their plants are located and led to the closing of plants that would otherwise have remained viable businesses.

PROFIT AND LOSS

The profit motive is held in considerable disrepute by radical socialists. Profit itself is often characterized as an unnecessary money grab on the part of capitalists, a form of surplus value extracted from the sweat of labor, which may be viewed as the sole source of value of all goods and services produced and traded in a market system. Capital (at least the assets of basic industries) must be controlled by the state to avert the exploitation of labor by capitalists, who presumably can coerce workers to produce a total product value that is in excess of worker wages. Marxism expounds this view of profit.

Social reformers, even those who profess faith in the free-enterprise system but who are disenchanted with what they believe to be the excesses of an unfettered economy, seem to look on profit *up to a point* as a necessary evil, a kind of compensation for the capitalists' frugality and investment wisdom. This type of profit is judged more by its morality than its incentive effects. Profit beyond the (generally unspecified) moral limit is, however, not only unfair but unnecessary in the sense that it does not affect the distribution and efficient use of resources. To one extent or another and in one form or other, these perceptions of profit undergird proposals for plant-closing restrictions, as the comments of Barry Bluestone and Bennett Harrison show:

> In our kind of so-called free enterprise system, workers as a class neither own nor control capital to any significant degree. The people who do have every

incentive to exercise their control with the objective of making as much profit as they can and, in the process, accumulating as much wealth as possible. To meet this objective, employers must keep their cost of production down, which requires them to coax as much productivity out of their employees as available technological conditions will allow. The entire process is handled, in all but the very smallest shops, by a cadre of professional managers hired by the owners of the capital.[2]

According to this view, production is driven to a more or less fixed level by the coercion implicit in ownership of physical capital; profit is the cream that capitalists skim by force from a more or less fixed output; any business relocation that is made based on profit is a zero-sum move (meaning that what the capitalists receive in profit is extracted from "highly exploitable labor")[3] at best and a negative-sum move at worst because the accompanying conflict between labor and management, as well as competition among firms for market shares and among workers for jobs and wages, must divert resources from productive uses.

The controversy over plant-closing restrictions is thus in part a conflict over the social role of profit. To advocates of an economy relatively free of governmental restrictions, profit, what remains on the proverbial "bottom line" after accounting expenses have been deducted from sales, is partly a form of compensation, like wages, that must be paid to owners of capital for the services of capital: it is a necessary price, like wages, that is ultimately established by competitive forces. This minimum profit level (viewed by economists as a normal production cost, again like wages) is no more or less ethically corrupt than the wages of workers who are paid for the use of the "human capital" contained in their skills. Profit is what it is — necessary compensation, which cannot be determined outside of some market process in which people can reveal what they are willing to do, that is, how much or how little they are willing to accept as minimum compensation for the services of the resources at their disposal.

Profit over and above this minimum level, the common notion of profit, serves another important function: it directs the use of resources to their most productive and valuable uses. Although profit

2. Barry Bluestone and Bennett Harrison, *Capital and Communities: The Causes and Consequences of Private Disinvestment* (Washington, D.C.: The Progressive Alliance, 1980), pp. 3–4.
3. Ibid., p. 7.

above the minimum level is unnecessary in the sense of being more than enough, it is profit of this kind that everyone, capitalists and workers alike, seeks. Profit above the minimum level is, indeed, what most economists mean by profit. It, too, is a necessary part of the strategic incentive and information system that a free society, through free markets, must maintain to remain free.

Of course, proponents of restrictions are not impressed with this allocative role of profit because they do not wish to maintain an open and free system—for everyone, that is. They believe that somehow the political process can be organized to constrict the freedom of some without in the long run constricting the freedom of all, including themselves. They seem to think that profit can be politically suppressed or, better, diverted to workers and that capitalists will not exploit an open political arena to achieve their own end—more profit. Again, the view that making profit is a "grab" by capitalists comes through in the often-voiced delusion that profit can actually be redistributed (which implies that it will not be destroyed in the attempt. An underlying presumption is that profit exists, like rocks on the Appalachian Trail, independent of the competitive market process in which it is created and can be collected by anyone, under almost any political arrangement, for distribution to the masses. Proponents of restrictions fail to appreciate the extent to which profit is *created* in the process of being sought. The search for and attainment of profit cannot be conceptually or objectively separated from the competitive market process.[4]

The contention that money-grubbing capitalists will sacrifice truly profitable plants is a blatant contradiction. Of course, there are times when the bottom line of a firm's income statement for a soon-to-be-closed plant will be written in black ink. But, the plant may be closed for the same reason that workers quit: the compensation reported on the bottom line is below what is required to keep the plant open. The plant that closes because its profits are below the "minimum" is in a sense not covering all of its production costs, including the legitimate cost of rewarding the owners of capital; it is, in effect, incurring losses. Requiring such firms to keep their capital in place when they would otherwise move it is tantamount to requiring workers to stay in their jobs when higher rewards exist elsewhere.

4. For a complete statement of the view of the competitive market process and profit being touched here, see Israel Kirzner, *Competition and Entrepreneurship* (Chicago: University of Chicago Press, 1975).

At other times, firms may appear to be in the black when they are actually in the red, that is, not covering ali of their out-of-pocket expenses. Modern inflation misleads people into thinking that businesses are more profitable than they in fact are. Because the costs of plant and equipment appearing on profit and loss statements tend to be based on their historical prices, and not their higher replacement prices, and because revenues are computed from current sales at current prices, the profit of businesses tends to be substantially overstated, perhaps by as much as 30 or 40 percent, during prolonged periods of double-digit inflation. Some businesses reporting profit during recent inflationary times in the United States are actually losing money (but are paying taxes on their accounting "profit").[5] They are not covering the costs of doing business and what Peter Drucker calls the costs of "staying in business."[6]

Then there are times when accounting techniques employed by multiplant firms distort their profitability. At the time of its closing in 1980, the Dayton [Ohio] Tire Company (a subsidiary of Firestone Tire and Rubber Company) was, showing a profit on paper. Using an accounting system common among large corporations, Firestone, on paper, "bought" tires from its Dayton plant at a price above plant costs. The plant, accordingly, showed a "profit." However, after the costs of warehousing and marketing incurred by other divisions of Firestone were added, the total cost of the bias-ply tires produced at Dayton exceeded the price that could be charged in the market.[7] In short, the production of tires at Dayton was not profitable.

Firms must always keep an eye on their competition and must constantly look to the future. At times, a firm may close a plant

5. This theme is developed more completely in Richard B. McKenzie, "What We Have Learned from Inflation: Ten Short Lessons" (Clemson, S.C.: Economics Department, Clemson University, 1980).

6. Peter Drucker, *Managing in Turbulent Times* (New York: Basic Books, 1979). The replacement cost of plant and equipment in current prices is greater than what is set aside in the form of depreciation allowance for existing plant and equipment computed on historical purchase prices. The cost of using existing plant and equipment is therefore higher than what is allowed; profits are lower than what is allowed on accounting statements, meaning that taxes, if they are paid, are higher than they "should be." In such inflationary times the government is actually confiscating the capital of firms, not just their "profits."

7. From a telephone conversation with Bernard Frazier, director of governmental relations, Firestone Tire and Rubber Company, June 1980. One test of whether or not the Dayton plant was profitable was to ask if the workers, or anyone else, were willing to buy the plant and equipment and continue its operation as a tire company. After all, the buyer would then be beneficiary of the profits. Although the facility was offered for sale, it was eventually closed for lack of a buyer.

because of greater cost savings at another location. It knows that if it does not take advantage of lower production costs elsewhere, someone else surely will, and this someone else will be able to undersell and outcompete other producers. To be truly profitable, a plant must be able to cover the very real costs associated with absorbing the risks of keeping its capital in place.

Why would a firm interested in profits close a profitable plant? That is the central question for proponents of restrictions. The typical answer is superficial: "The firm can make more money elsewhere." Such a retort contradicts logic; the firm could even make more money elsewhere *and* keep the "profitable plants" (subject to closure) open. That is known as expansion. Proponents of such an illogical view must believe that firms that close profitable plants have extensive control over prices and that any extension of their firms' supplies, by way of firm expansions of the number of plants, will lead to price and profit reductions.

Monopoly power requires barriers to entry into markets. However, the very existence of more profitable opportunities elsewhere means that the firm's markets are, unless guarded by government fiat, open and can and will be invaded by other profit-hungry firms. Such a circumstance is hardly descriptive of a monopolized industry; the barriers do not exist. The so-called monopoly firms must adjust their production to the less costly, more profitable locations or see their profit eroded by competition.

Any attempt by government to restrict firms from removing, by relocation or disinvestment and reinvestment, their capital from its current employment will be at best a short-lived palliative. Plant-closing restrictions that truly save jobs in the long run must be accompanied by entry restrictions, which is a certain way of monopolizing industries and enabling industries to obtain the monopoly profits they seek.

"CASH COWS"

In *Capital Flight*, Bluestone and Harrison, along with Lawrence Baker, continue the attack on corporate America they began in *Capital and Communities*:

> Another more subtle form of disinvestment which often occurs is the severe reduction of operations at an old facility by a multi-branch corporation,

which then gradually shifts machinery, skilled labor, managers, or marketing responsibilities to newer facilities elsewhere. Such a multi-branch corporation may also leave an older plant's capital stock in place but simply reallocate the plant's profits to another, newer facility. This "milking" of a profitable plant is especially common among conglomerates (where the term "cash cow" is sometimes used to describe the object of such a profit drain) and is responsible for ruining many sound companies. In fact, this last management technique . . . is one facet of an amazing corporate activity which occurs not infrequently: the shutting down of healthy, profitable plants—not just money-losers.[8]

The "milk" (cash flow) a firm secures from a "cash cow" is obtained directly from a plant's profits and indirectly from the depreciation allowance subtracted from sales, along with its expenses, to determine profits. Recorded profits are reduced by the depreciation allowance, but the firm still has access to the untaxed revenue (which can be reinvested in the firm's other plants or in the acquisition of other companies or product lines). Because the existing plant and equipment are not replaced, the productive ability of the "cash cow" plant deteriorates until, finally, it must be closed.

Does this milking of cash cows shorten the life of or otherwise ruin profitable plants? Certainly, firms make mistakes; for example, they may conclude incorrectly that a production facility cannot maintain its competitive market share when in fact the contrary is the case. Mistakes are to be expected in all social systems, however, and the relevant question is whether or not the market system intentionally seeks to drain firms of their productive capacity and whether or not corrective adjustments can be expected. When profit is the assumed motivating force, which is the assumption of advocates of restrictions, no plant will be intentionally "depreciated away" if, in the long run, its operation is expected to be profitable. A truly profitable plant is one in which the income stream exceeds the cost of operation, including the cost of replacing the firm's plant and equipment. A firm that milks a profitable cash cow will receive investment funds, but it could generate even more investment funds by keeping it in operation: it could reinvest the depreciation allowance *and* the profit. By simply milking the supposed cash cow, the firm has only the depreciation to reinvest.

8. Barry Bluestone, Bennett Harrison, and Lawrence Baker, *Capital Flight* (Washington, D.C.: The Progressive Alliance. 1981), p. 14.

Plants are allowed to depreciate for one overriding reason: replacement of buildings and equipment at current prices and continued operations will mean future company losses. From this perspective, a company that operates a cash cow is, if anything, extending the life of the plant, *not* cutting it short. The company is using the buildings and equipment (both of which are scarce resources) to their fullest— the economical thing to do. From a social perspective is it better to have plants and equipment, which are no longer economical to replace, sit idle or be used only until they are no longer productive?

Furthermore, if a firm mistakenly begins to milk a profitable plant, other profit-hungry entrepreneurs could be expected to move in to buy it at a price roughly approximating the present discounted value of the depreciation allowance and operate it *at a profit*. The company's workers or their union might be willing to make an offer. To assume that a profitable plant would be closed when such resale prospects exist is tantamount to assuming that everyone who is free to enter the market and purchase the firm would make the same mistake in assessing the future profitability of the plant. In short, the logic of the cash cow argument is mind-boggling.

As proponents of restrictions contend, taxes do affect investment decisions. No argument on that score is possible. The North, without question, is having its growth rate marginally reduced by the progressive income tax system used by the federal government and its generally higher state and local tax rates. The average income tax rate is marginally lower in the South, where incomes are lower, than in the North.[9] However, contrary to what is heard from defenders of restrictions,[10] the tax code can prop up and extend the life of many failing firms. A failing firm is often recording losses because of its depreciation allowance.

The tax advantage of purchasing a failing firm stems from three principal sources: (1) the reported losses can be deducted from the profits of the acquiring firm, reducing the tax liability of the acquiring firm (as a general rule, the greater the losses of the acquired

9. See C.L. Jusenius and L.C. Ledebur, *A Myth in the Making: Southern Economic Challenge and Northern Economic Decline* (Washington, D.C.: Department of Commerce, Economic Development Administration, November 1976) for a discussion of the average tax rates of states and regions. See also, Richard B. McKenzie, *Restrictions on Business Mobility: A Study in Political Rhetoric and Economic Reality* (Washington, D.C.: American Enterprise Institute, 1979), pp. 26–30, for a summary of Jusenius and Ledebur's work on taxes.

10. William Ford, *Congressional Record*, p. 18559.

firm resulting from depreciation allowances, the greater the tax benefits to the acquiring firm); (2) the failing firm can be purchased at a price depressed by its losses; (3) the acquiring firm can secure the cash flow from the depreciation allowance, which is nontaxable revenue. The reduced taxes on the profits of the acquiring firm and the depreciation allowance can spell profit for the acquiring firm (a flow of funds in excess of the purchase price). Again, however, the life of the firm that is acquired is extended, not shortened, *because of the tax system.*

This analysis does not mean that the tax system contributes to economic efficiency. On the contrary, other firms might suffer because of the tax code. Because capital will be directed into the milking of "losers," funds will be more expensive to otherwise profitable firms, especially new, potentially profitable firms. Ironically, high tax rates on corporate income provide a subsidy to workers and owners of failing firms: they increase the resale value of the firm and extend the job tenure of its workers.

PLANT DESTRUCTION BY CONGLOMERATES

The case for plant-closing restrictions becomes most noticeably confused over the issue of the so-called destructive consequences of corporate giants. On the one hand, advocates contend that technical changes in production processes have

> ...both promoted, and have in turn been promoted by, what is without question the most fundamental characteristics of capitalist economic development: the tendency toward the concentration of economic power and control of larger and larger multi-plant, multi-regional, and finally, even multi-national corporations whose everyday activities shape and reshape the political-economic environment and even to some extent the cultural boundaries of the whole society. In the past, this power was used to concentrate production in units of ever-greater scale, the inefficiencies from which helped to promote even further concentration of control in each industry in the hands of a smaller and smaller number of leading firms.[11]

Such corporate giants are supposed to be able to secure for themselves the monopoly profits described in the lectures of every teaching economist in the country; they are supposed to be able to accom-

---

11. Bluestone and Harrison, *Capital and Communities*, p. 156.

plish this end by pitting worker groups across the globe against one another for the social wage and by restricting supply, and, ergo, the motivation for plant closures. On the other hand, "competition between the largest international corporations [for labor and market shares] has reached an unparalleled intensity."[12] We must wonder how these giants become so big if they are everywhere and at all times exploiting labor with low wages (why would labor work for them?) and consumers with high prices (why would consumers buy from them?).

Similar faulty logic is revealed in the charge that the growth of conglomerates is necessarily an important cause of plant closures because of the remoteness of conglomerate control of local plants:

> Large corporations—and conglomerates in particular—*will* and frequently *do* close profitable plants of previously acquired businesses for a variety of reasons directly related to the nature of centralized management and control. In other cases, the "remote control" of operations by a home office far removed from the production site, or unfamiliar with the industry in which a subsidiary is competing, actually *creates* the unprofitability of the plant or subsidiary which then leads to an eventual shut-down.[13]

The inefficiencies of remote control supposedly stem from several sources:

1. Requirements that new acquisitions "carry additional management staff sent from headquarters, personnel not previously needed by the subsidiary . . ."[14]
2. Requirements that subsidiaries pay fees to their parent companies for "management services"[15]
3. Rules that force subsidiaries to purchase inputs from "distant providers, even if the subsidiary's managers know where they can cut costs by purchasing locally"[16]
4. The clumsiness of the headquarter's interference with the "local managers who know the situation best"[17]

12. Ibid., p. 157.
13. Ibid., p. 199.
14. Ibid., p. 206.
15. Ibid., p. 207.
16. Ibid., p. 208.
17. Ibid., p. 208.

In general, although conventional wisdom stresses the efficiency of mass production, "mounting evidence . . . points to the opposite conclusion: that the managers of giant corporations and conglomerates often create inefficiency through 'over-managing' their subsidiaries, milking them of their profit, subjecting them to at best strenuous and sometimes impossible performance standards, interfering with local decisions about which the parent's managers are poorly informed, and quickly closing the subsidiaries down when other more profitable opportunities appear."[18]

If conglomerates are so destructive of newly acquired subsidiaries, how can they secure the funds to out-price other local bidders for their subsidiaries, and how they can be induced to hang on to their subsidiaries when they are running them into the ground and when others could turn them into going concerns? If capitalists are truly profit mongers, will they invest in conglomerates that intentionally destroy profitable plants? After all, conglomerates must pay competitive prices for their acquisitions, and such prices approximate the present discounted value of the future profit stream. To destroy such profit intentionally would mean that the conglomerate had embarked on an irrational course: paying for the profit (in terms of the purchase price) and then proceeding to destroy the profit and the resale value of the plant. Proponents of restrictions may retort that conglomerates can outbid other local buyers because they have the funds (from profits and capital markets), but the wholesale destruction of profit would mean that they would not have the profit and could not find willing investors in the capital markets. One must wonder how a conglomerate (starting out small as almost all businesses must) could become a conglomerate if it pursued such a course.

If the conglomerate's headquarters were intentionally to impose unnecessary costs on its subsidiaries, making them unprofitable and subjecting them to closure, it would appear that local buyers would be able to buy the firm from the conglomerate. The conglomerate should be willing to sell at a price reflecting its computed profits, which should be less the profits that would supposedly exist when the unnecessary costs of the conglomerate were eliminated by local ownership.

Actually, logic suggests that conglomerate ownership, with its broad base of operations, should lead to the continued operation of

18. Ibid., p. 210.

many plants that would have to close under local ownership. Many firms are subject to seasonal and cyclical swings in sales, revenues, and profits. A business might continue a facility's operation in spite of current losses because its sights were on the long-run profitability of the company. A locally-owned firm, with limited access to capital market and without the cushion of profits from other product lines on a different business cycle, might be forced to close a temporarily unprofitable plant because of lack of funds to carry it through its financial storm. A conglomerate would solve such problems. It would reduce the risk of investment by spreading the investment over a number of varied ventures and increasing its access to financial capital, enabling it to "subsidize" temporarily unprofitable plants and adding a measure of stability to worker jobs.[19]

This does not mean that conglomerates will not close profitable plants; mistakes can always be expected in an imperfect and uncertain world. It simply means that systematic plant closings by conglomerates should not be expected. A disproportionate share of plant closures (or large plant closures) may be associated with conglomerate ownership, but that does not mean that conglomerate ownership, in the final days of a plant's life, was the cause of its dissolution. Many conglomerates can be in the business of acquiring firms that would otherwise fail, hoping that their management services and access to financial markets will enable them to revive a sufficiently large percentage of the failing firms to make the whole salvage effort worthwhile. In such cases, the lives of all of the plants are extended, some for very short periods, others indefinitely.

Proponents of restrictions on closings suggest that conglomerate owners, far removed from the community in which the plant is located, do not have the welfare of the workers in their "utility functions"—which, translated, means that conglomerate owners care less about worker welfare than do local owners of plants. The argument is pure supposition. Both in-town and out-of-town owners have to meet the competition; both groups are pushed by the forces of competition to operate in very much the same way. If, for example, owners in Philadelphia were willing to accept a lower rate of return because of the satisfaction of having done something good for the home town, then it would appear that Philadelphia investors could

---

19. I am indebted to Yale Brozen for making this point evident to me (personal correspondence, 27 December 1981).

and would outbid nonresident conglomerates for control of Philadelphia firms.

CONCLUDING COMMENTS

When examined in the light of common sense, the economic case for restrictions on plant closings discussed here is inconsistent and contradictory, based largely on a contemporary version of Marxian historical determinism and beliefs about the exploitation of labor that have been discredited by the rise of workers' wages. The bottom line is simple: no profit-maximizing firm would close profitable plants. They would sell them first.

As noted in Chapter 1, a number of proposals to augment disinvestment decisions of private firms authorize someone, e.g., the Secretary of Labor, to provide financial aid to displaced employees who would like to buy a closed plant and continue its operations. Such a provision is based on the assumption that many profitable plants are closed. If that were true, then employees would not need the aid; private investors should be willing to provide the necessary financial capital. Indeed, employees and their unions should be able to raise the necessary money among themselves. After all, working people do save and invest. Private pension funds have hundreds of billions of dollars in assets, and a profitable plant should be a good investment.[20]

Many of the proponents of restrictions seem to think that businesses are almost totally owned by higher-income groups, not people of the working classes, and that the costs of the restrictions borne by businesses will inevitably be imposed on higher-income groups. However, although it is true that high-income groups own a disproportion of the country's corporate stock, workers and unions, through the investments of their savings and pension funds, have a substantial stake (up to one-third of the financial control) in the profitability of businesses. Restrictions on plant closings could seriously affect the retirement of present and future members of all income classes.

If funds could not be raised privately, it would appear that the plant was not profitable, and taxpayers, who would then have to

20. Peter F. Drucker, "Pension Fund 'Socialism,'" *Public Interest* (Winter 1976): 3–46.

foot the bill for the purchase, would be taken for another welfare ride.

Furthermore, without government aid, the proposed restrictions on firms very likely will reduce the chance that employee-owned and managed businesses can be financially successful. If a plant-closing law is in force, the employees — as owners — will then have to assume the risks and costs that the proposed restrictions impose on the firm. *They* will be the ones who will be responsible for giving, say, a one- or two-year notice of a planned plant closing, fifty-two weeks of severance pay, and the restitution payments to the community. *They* will be the ones to see their savings go up in the smoke of company losses that may be incurred during the extended period of time the firm must wait before it can close its doors.

The chances, for example, of the Dayton Tire workers converting their plant into a profitable concern were slim at best, especially without the management skills, the licenses and patents, the ware-housing and distribution capabilities, and the marketing talents that would probably not be sold along with the plant but retained by Firestone. If the workers owned the plant, they would have to look squarely and soberly at the stark facts of the bias-ply market faced by Firestone and ask whether they were willing to take the implied market- and government-imposed risks. With the proposed restrictions on the books, it appears that without government aid the employees will be less willing to put their money where their hearts are. Certainly, if they take time to reflect on other job opportunities, many will have second thoughts over investing in their own firm. That is why workers should carefully consider proposals for government aid to failing businesses. Such aid means that taxpayers — workers included — will be investing in businesses in which they would not voluntarily invest and over which they will secure no ownership rights.

Chapter 5

PLANT CLOSING RESTRICTIONS IN LABOR LAW[1]

Union support of plant closing restrictions is self-evident.[2] Many of the arguments offered in support of closing restrictions and evaluated in detail in earlier chapters are found in union-supported publications. Although the rationale for union support of legislative restrictions on industrial mobility may appear obvious, it is worth examining in detail. First, it is in the perceived interest of an incumbent union, especially in those industries such as automobiles and steel (which have secured "monopoly rents" in the form of higher wages, have been badly buffeted by competition, and have suffered consequent declines in their employment), to seek to prevent or delay cessations of operations. Plant closure laws can accomplish this by elaborate provisions for advance notice and compensation of employees and communities. The threat of the imposition of these heavy costs may delay the implementation of a management decision to close a failing operation or (in a less drastic case) to move an operation to a better economic environment. Plant closure laws, in short, can hold plants "hostage"—at least for a time. Second, unions may perceive the legislative approach as "cost free," in that

1. This chapter is a condensation of a much longer study, Francis A. O'Connell, Jr. and Richard B. McKenzie, *The Politics and Economics of Barriers to Plant Closures: Unions, NLRB, and the Courts*, (Clemson, S.C.: Economics Department, Clemson University, 1983).
2. Union support for plant closing laws is further analyzed in Appendix C.

workers do not have to trade anything (as they would in collective bargaining) for the restrictions on management's freedom to move, and the social and (long-range) economic costs are distributed to others.

The legislative process, however, can be slow and costly and sometimes unsuccessful, so labor sees the need for other more immediate means for blocking removals and closures. Understandably, labor may look for relief from problems associated with plant closings to the administrative/judicial process, specifically the decisions of the National Labor Relations Board (NLRB) and the federal courts that interpret and apply the National Labor Relations Act (originally known popularly as, and hereafter called, the Wagner Act), as amended.[3] Significant impediments to industrial mobility—far beyond anything state legislatures and Congress have enacted—have been created by the NLRB, frequently with the approval of the federal appellant judiciary, including the Supreme Court of the United States.

This chapter examines the restrictions embodied in NLRB and court decisions in order to clarify (1) the uses for unions of this form of attack on the "capital flight" problem, and (2) the limitations and uncertainties of this approach. This review of NLRB and court cases shows where the labor law appears to stand on plant closings, but the review has another objective as well. It will also help explain continuing union support for the legislative attack on plant closure at both federal and state levels. More specifically, a central argument of the chapter is that unions seek, through legislated plant closing laws, to impose restrictions on the closing in the nonunion sector similar to the restrictions that have been imposed on the union sector by way of NLRB and court decision. Such legislated restrictions, if enacted across all states, will tend to impede the flow of capital from the union to the nonunion sector and enhance the bargaining positions of unions.

LABOR LAW

In order to understand how NLRB and court decisions aid unions in blocking or stalling plant closings, two key provisions of the Wagner

---

3. *Labor-Management Relations Act* (Taft-Hartley Act), *Statutes at Large* 61, Section 8(a)(3) (1947), *U.S. Code*, vol. 39 (1952).

Act (Section 8 (a) (3) and Section 8 (a) (5)) need to be examined. Section 8 (a) (3) defines an unfair labor practice as "discrimination in regard to hire or tenure of employment . . . to encourage or discourage membership in any labor organization."[4] For a plant closing to be held to be an unfair labor practice under this provision, the employer must both discriminate and act for the purpose of discouraging union membership. That he is discriminating in a broad, nonlegal sense (that is, acting in a manner detrimental to the job interests of the workers involved) when he closes a plant is fairly obvious; not so obvious is the *intention* of the employer to discourage union membership or, in the jargon of labor law, to have acted with an "antiunion animus."

Section 8 (a) (5) gets at the problem of plant closings from a different angle — the employer's duty to bargain. This section makes it an unfair labor practice for an employer to refuse to bargain with a union over conditions of employment. This section has been interpreted to go beyond working conditions on the job and to include the basic question of whether or not the job shall exist at all or continue to exist. The duty to bargain is spelled out in detail in Section 8 (d) of the Act:

> For the purpose of this section, to bargain collectively is the performance of the mutual obligation of the employer and the representatives of the employees to meet at reasonable times and confer in good faith with respect to *wages, hours, and other terms and conditions of employment*, or the negotiation of an agreement, or any question arising thereunder, and the execution of a written contract incorporating any agreement reached if requested by either party, but such obligation does not compel either party to agree to a proposal or require the making of a concession [emphasis added].[5]

Both Section 8 (a) (3) and 8 (a) (5) have been utilized by unions in plant closing situations. Charges have been filed under those sections in order to impede or reverse an employer's action. Although for the employer the effect of impeding or reversing his decision is much the same, the conditions under which one section or the other is invoked are frequently quite different, as are the remedies prescribed by the NLRB. Accordingly, the employer who proposes to close or move a plant needs to be aware of *both* of these sources of possible union challenge, backed by the NLRB, to his or her right

4. Ibid.
5. Ibid., Section 8 (a) (5).

to shut down. To that end, a brief review of the legal bases and the circumstances under which unions are able to invoke these statutory countermeasures is worthwhile.

Antiunion Animus

The plant closure cases decided under Section 8 (a) (3) of the Wagner Act have generally arisen after (1) an employer decided to close a plant whose employees were represented by a union and the union alleged that the purpose of the closure was to get rid of the union, (this is the classic case of the "runaway shop") and (2) a union that has been seeking to represent employees charged that the shutdown was intended either to deter employees from joining the union or to punish them for having done so. Property rights are important in both circumstances. Does an employer have an absolute right to close his plant (i.e., to go out of business at that location) or can that right be abridged by the NLRB? If the right can be abridged, does it make a difference whether the union actually had representation rights prior to the shutdown?

In the traditional runaway shop case, the union has been in place (often for an extended period of time), and the employer decides to move, either to escape the union or for other business reasons or for some combination of the two. It was of the essence for this runaway shop case that the employer was not going out of business but simply changing the site of the operation, and it has long been accepted that where the purpose of the move was to rid himself of the union (and of the employees who had joined the union), and to set up new (presumably nonunion) operations in a different locale, the NLRB would intervene either to prevent the move, or, if the move had already taken place, to order compensation to the employees left behind. But what if, instead of moving the plant, the employer simply closes it? Is there not an absolute right, inherent in the ownership of a business, to take that action, regardless of motive? Or, if his motive is to avoid doing business with the union, is his property right abridged by the labor law?

One of the most significant cases involving Section 8 (a) (3), the financial burden of which was only recently resolved, was *Textile Workers Union* v. *Darlington.*[6] In a 1957 ruling (which was reversed

---

6. *Textile Workers Union of America* v. *Darlington Manufacturing Company, et al.,* 267 U.S. 37 (1965).

by the Fourth Circuit Court of Appeals but confirmed by the Supreme Court) the NLRB found Darlington in violation of Section 8 (a) (3) because its president, Roger Milliken, had exhibited an antiunion animus in the closing of its one and only plant in Darlington, South Carolina. In March 1956 prior to the plant's closing, the Textile Workers Union initiated a campaign to organize Darlington's workers that was "resisted vigorously" by Darlington.[7] The company's resistance apparently included threats that if unionized the plant would be closed. Shortly after the workers voted in the union in September 1956, Roger Milliken called a meeting of the company's board of directors, which approved closure and liquidation of the plant, a process completed by the end of the year. The union filed charges with the NLRB claiming the plant was closed because of Roger Milliken's personal antiunion animus, and Darlington was ordered to provide back pay and to pay the Darlington workers until they obtained equivalent employment at other Deering Milliken plants. The ruling was predicated on the finding that Darlington, although legally independent of Deering Milliken Inc., was effectively one of twenty-seven plants operated by Deering Milliken; hence, the closing of the Darlington plant was interpreted as a "partial closing" of operations, not a total cessation of business.

In reviewing the lower court's reversal of NLRB's action, the Supreme Court ruled in 1965 that "an employer has an absolute right to terminate his entire business for any reason he pleases [including an antiunion animus]," but disagreed with the Court of Appeals "that such a right includes the ability to close part of a business no matter what the reason. We conclude that the case must be remanded to the Board for further proceedings" [a process finally concluded in 1981 with a determination of the amount of back pay the employees or their heirs would receive].[8]

Why does a firm have an "absolute right" to close all but not part of its operations? In the opinion of the Supreme Court, delivered by Justice Harlan, three basic reasons justified the legal distinction between complete and partial closings. First, "a proposition that a single businessman cannot go out of business if he wants to would represent such a startling innovation that it should not be entertained without the clearest manifestation of legislative intent or unequivo-

7. Ibid., p. 265.
8. Ibid., p. 268.

cal judicial precedent so construing the Labor Relations Act."[9] Harlan agreed with the reasoning of other courts that the complete cessation of a business would remove an employer from future coverage by the Wagner Act and that act "does not compel a person to become or remain an employee. It does not compel one to become or remain an employer. Either may withdraw from that status with immunity, so long as the obligations of any employment contract have been met."[10]

Second, the Supreme Court reasoned that a complete closing would mean that the employer, imbued or not with an antiunion animus, could not benefit monetarily from his decision. The closure could not affect the willingness of other company employees to seek unionization or, if unionized, higher pay and fringe benefits. A complete closing of the firm means there would then be no other company employees. However, the employer could, as it was thought to be the case in *Darlington*, benefit from the partial closing of a plant, effected just after a successful union campaign. Harlan wrote that "Darlington's action was similar to a discriminatory lockout," which is prohibited "because [it is] designed to frustrate organizational efforts, to destroy or undermine bargaining representation, or to evade the duty to bargain. One of the purposes of the Labor Relations Act is to prohibit the discriminatory use of economic weapons in an effort to obtain future benefits. The discriminatory lockout designed to destroy a union, like a 'runaway shop,' is a lever which has been used to discourage collective employee activities."[11] The court ruled that the partial closing of a business would have a "chilling" effect on unionism at other Milliken plants. Hence, Roger Milliken himself, a major owner of the textile holding company, could benefit directly and monetarily from the exercise of his antiunion animus.

Third, when a firm goes totally out of business, one of the principal remedies used by the NLRB is unavailable: the discharged workers cannot be reinstated, whereas they can be if other plants continue operation.[12]

9. Ibid., p. 270.
10. Ibid., p. 271; cited from the Court of Appeals.
11. Ibid., pp. 271–72.
12. Ibid., p. 273.

How broadly did the Court think its decision applied? The Court's answer was reasonably straightforward:

> If the persons exercising control over a plant that is being closed for anti-union reasons (1) have an interest in another business, whether or not affiliated with or engaged in the same line of commercial activity as the closed plant, of sufficient substantiality to give promise of their reaping a benefit from the discouragement of unionization in that business; (2) act to close their plant with the purpose of producing such a result; and (3) occupy a relationship to the other business which makes it realistically foreseeable that its employees will fear that such business will also be closed down if they persist in organizational activities. We think that an unfair labor practice has been made out.[13]

Admittedly, the decision in *Darlington* may be more restricted than it appears on the surface. First, the decision applies only in cases of partial closings. Second, the burden of proof of the antiunion animus is on the unions. Third, the antiunion animus must be stated relatively clearly. As Professor Gorman has noted, " . . . the Court held in *Darlington* there must be a specific showing that the shutdown was purposefully designed to chill unionism at the other plants [not in the plant that is closed].[14] To this Professor Thomas Haggard has added, "and unless that showing of an antiunion animus is by direct evidence or statements of such an intention, a mere circumstantial inference of union animus can usually be refuted if the employer can, in fact, show economic justification for the closure."[15] Presumably, if a plant is closed because of antiunion animus but the closing does not "chill" unionism at other plants, the plant in question can still be closed.

Still, we must conclude from *Darlington* that unionized, multiplant firms probably face a closing cost not faced by nonunion firms. Employers have to be concerned about how the closing of a unionized plant will affect unionization efforts and union stability in other plants. They must also be concerned with how the courts will interpret those effects. Because the requirement to bargain over the *effects* of a closing, as opposed to the decision itself, has remained a

13. Ibid., pp. 275–76.

14. As quoted in Thomas R. Haggard, "Plant Closure and Relocation: The Legal Issues" (Columbia, S.C.: Law School, University of South Carolina, discussion paper presented at a Liberty Fund Symposium on plant closing legislation May 9–11, 1982), p. 10.

15. Ibid., p. 11.

matter of legal conflict, court decisions and the NLRB view have been to require firms to bargain over partial closings in almost all cases. As John Irving, a former general counsel of the NLRB, has commented, "Otherwise, employers would run the risk of a later adverse finding by the NLRB or a court, which could be very costly indeed."[16]

Section 8 (a) (3) has also been applied to the partial closing of a single plant's operations. In 1977 the NLRB found that Ethyl Corporation was in violation of the section when it transferred a product line from a plant that had only recently been unionized to a non-union plant in a different city.[17] Similarly, the section has been applied to the subcontracting of work. For example, when Beacon Industries, an engine manufacturer, acquired Smith Manufacturing Company, a unionized producer of bookbinding machinery, Smith had defaulted on loans.[18] During the following year, the profitability of the company apparently had been turned around. Nonetheless, the bookbinding operations were subcontracted to another firm. The NLRB found that Beacon had exhibited a "hostile" attitude toward its union by firing one or more union committeemen and that Beacon had closed the Smith plant to discourage unionism. Beacon was ordered to reinstate the laid-off workers and to provide back pay.

Unions may understandably see in Section 8 (a) (3) an effective means of forestalling the closing of plants: ensure that the closing of a plant is made at the same time an organizing campaign is underway either at the plant slated for closing or at another plant operated by the same firm. The National Labor Law Center, a legal arm of unions, advises unions that

> [A] 8 (a) (3) violation is generally found only in the context of an organizing campaign, either at the closed plant, or at another plant of the same employer. *As a result, the possibility that a plant might be closed may become an incentive to workers of that plant either to start an organization campaign or to assist a campaign at another plant* [emphasis added].[19]

---

16. John S. Irving, Jr., "Closing and Sale of Business: A Settled Area?" *Labor Law Journal* (April 1982), p. 220.

17. *Ethyl Corp.*, 231 NLRB 431 (1977).

18. *Smith Manufacturing Co./Beacon Industries*, 247 NLRB 164, 103 LRRM 1432 (1980).

19. National Lawyers Guild, *Plant Closings and Runaway Industries: Strategies for Labor* (Washington, D.C.: National Labor Law Center, 1981), p. 5.

The Duty to Bargain

Firms that fail to notify their union representatives of any intentions to close a plant run the risk of being charged with a failure to bargain, a violation of Section 8 (a) (5) of the Wagner Act. The board found Fibreboard Paper Products in violation of that section in 1961,[20] a decision that was upheld all the way to the Supreme Court. In 1959, Fibreboard had a contract with its maintenance workers, represented by the United Steelworkers, that was to expire in July. Although the union indicated a willingness to negotiate a new contract in May, the company refused to meet until four days before the expiration of the contract, at which time the company informed the union that substantial savings could be effected by subcontracting the work to Fluor Maintenance, Inc., and wrote the union, "In these circumstances, we are sure you will realize that negotiation of a new contract would be pointless."[21] The company was charged with failure to "confer in good faith with respect to wages, hours, and other terms and conditions of employment." When the case was first considered, the board held that employment itself could not be a "condition of employment" and that Congress never intended "to compel bargaining concerning basic management decisions, such as whether and to what extent to risk capital and managerial effort."[22] When the case was reconsidered with Kennedy appointees on the board, however, *Fibreboard* was reversed, with the board holding that the company had violated its obligation under the act by not having engaged in decision-bargaining (as opposed to effects-bargaining) before contracting out its maintenance services.[23] The Supreme Court gave several reasons for upholding the Board on the reconsidered *Fibreboard* case. First, "[o]ne of the primary purposes of the act is to promote the peaceful settlement of industrial disputes by subjecting labor-management controversies to the mediatory influences of negotiation. The act was framed with an awareness that refusals to confer and negotiate had been one of the most prolific causes of industrial strife."[24]

20. *Fibreboard Paper Products Corp.*, 130 NLRB 1558 (1961). The case was before the board twice, as discussed below.

21. Ibid., p. 1560.

22. Ibid., p. 1561.

23. *Fibreboard Paper Products Corp.*, 138 NLRB 550 (1962).

24. *Fibreboard Paper Products Corp. v. National Labor Relations Board, et al.*, 263 U.S. 14 (1964).

Second, experience had indicated that the issue of subcontracting work had been "brought, widely and successfully, within the collective bargaining framework," a claim supported by "numerous" collective bargaining agreements that addressed the issue.[25]

Third, the subcontracting of work resulted in a reduction of the firm's work force, an issue that had also been dealt with in many collective bargaining agreements. All that was required of the firm was that it "discuss" the issue of subcontracting with the union. As the Court of Appeals found, "[i]t is not necessary that it be likely or probable that the union will yield or supply a feasible solution but rather that the union be afforded an opportunity to meet management's legitimate complaints that its maintenance was unduly costly."[26] Although bargaining in good faith may not be interpreted to mean that the company has to make concessions, unions and the NLRB interpret the requirement to mean that company records used in making the closing decision must be disclosed and the closing can be forestalled.[27] Further, as cases show, if a firm refuses to bargain, it runs the risks of being required to reestablish operations, rehire released workers, and provide back pay.

FROM FIBREBOARD TO FIRST NATIONAL MAINTENANCE

The subsequent history of decision-bargaining offers little basis for management confidence that a closing decision is not a mandatory subject of bargaining. The board has consistently held to the philosophy expounded in *Fibreboard* (as well as in *Town & Country Mfg. Co. Inc.*)[28] that, when a management decision will put jobs at stake, the employer has a mandatory duty to bargain over the decision. In short, according to the board, employee bargaining rights tend to transcend management property rights.[29] The board's hard line on decision-bargaining has by no means found universal favor in the federal appellate courts, however. Courts of appeals have generally re-

25. Ibid.

26. Ibid., p. 24.

27. National Lawyers Guild, *Plant Closings and Runaway Industries*, pp. 9–10.

28. *Town & Country Mfg., Inc.*, 136 NLRB 1022 (1962).

29. See *Ozark Trailers, Inc.*, 63 LRRM 1264 (1966), for the Board's elaboration of this line of argument.

fused to take that view, and in so doing have relied heavily on limitations of *Fibreboard* spelled out by Justice Stewart in his concurring opinion in *Fibreboard*.

In *Adams Dairy*, which arose soon after *Town & Country*, the company decided to change its method of operation from delivery of its products by its own drivers to delivery by an independent contractor, a change roughly analogous to a partial discontinuance of operations.[30] The board issued a *Fibreboard*-like order (reinstate operations and provide employees with back pay), but the Court of Appeals for the Eighth Circuit refused to enforce it.[31] The board appealed to the Supreme Court, which remanded the case to the Court of Appeals with instructions to reconsider the case in the light of the Supreme Court's intervening decision in *Fibreboard*.[32] The Eighth Circuit did so, but hewed firmly to its original views,[33] arguing, *inter alia*, that the case did not involve a mere substitution of one set of employees for another (as did *Fibreboard*), but a basic change in operations, a kind of partial liquidation, and a change in capital structure and investment. The Eighth Circuit even found support in the opinion of Chief Justice Warren in *Fibreboard*, noting that to require bargaining here would "significantly abridge [Adams'] freedom to manage its own affairs," a result that the Supreme Court had found lacking in *Fibreboard*.

Not long afterward, the same court reached a similar result in a quite different case, one involving not subcontracting but a decision to close a branch operation because of total loss of its customers.[34] Among other services, the Burns Agency provides security guards for plants and institutions. The union had been certified as labor's bargaining representative in February 1963. Before negotiations could commence, however, Burns lost its last contract for guard services in the Omaha area, and it so advised the union in April, adding that, under the circumstances (no contract for services, no need for guards, no justification for a branch office), there seemed to be "no practical reason for meeting" to discuss a contract to cover the defunct operation.[35]

---

30. *Adams Dairy Co.*, 137 NLRB 815 (1962).
31. *NLRB v. Adams Dairy, Inc.*, 322 F.2d 553 (CA8, 1963).
32. *NLRB v. Adams Dairy, Inc.*, 379 U.S. 644 (1965).
33. *NLRB v. Adams Dairy, Inc.*, 350 F.2d 108 (CA8, 1965).
34. *Wm. J. Burns Intl. Detective Agency*, 346 F.2d 897 (CA8, 1965).
35. Ibid., 900.

After some preliminary confusion as to how to proceed against Burns, the board settled on refusal to bargain over the termination of the contract between Burns and its customer, Creighton University. The court held that there had been no improper failure to bargain, because, unlike *Fibreboard*, Burns "completely discontinued" its Omaha operation; no kind of contracting out was involved.[36] Justice Stewart is quoted at length concerning the "narrower concept" of "conditions of employment" for which he had argued in *Fibreboard*, and his language holding that not every decision that may affect job security is thereby a subject of compulsory collective bargaining is set forth at length, as is his strong affirmation of the right of management to be free of an obligation to bargain over managerial decisions "which lie at the core of entrepreneurial control."

The motivation or animus element was also important to the court of appeals in this case, and the absence of antiunion animus was significant in its reasoning. Citing *Darlington*, the court said that the teaching of that case is that "partial closing of one's business is not an unfair labor practice in the absence of a showing of motivation which is aimed at achieving a prohibited result." And the Court put *Darlington* and decision-bargaining together in these words:

> Under *Darlington*, the finding of lack of antiunion motivation in closing the Omaha division for economic reasons precludes a finding of unfair labor practice in refusing to bargain . . .[37]

This intermingling of *Darlington* and *Fibreboard*, the hanging of a bargaining order (or not) on whether there was antiunion animus (or not) is puzzling. There was no decision-bargaining issue in *Darlington*, and no antiunion animus issue in *Fibreboard*, yet the interplay of the two ideas runs through a number of cases. In any case, the courts can hardly be blamed for taking their cue from the board and, in some cases, ruling against an order to bargain over a management shutdown decision on the ground, among others, that there was no antiunion animus. *Wm. J. Burns* was one such case, and *Morrison Cafeterias*, also an Eighth Court of Appeals case, another.[38]

In the *Morrison* case the union won an election at the Little Rock cafeteria, and that evening Little Rock employees were informed that they all would be offered employment elsewhere; a few days

---

36. Ibid., 901–2.
37. Ibid.
38. *Morrison Cafeterias Consolidated, Inc. v. NLRB*, 431 F.2d 254 (CA8, 1970).

later, they were. Neither the shutdown nor the offer of other employment was negotiated with the union, although, in between the two actions, the union demanded negotiations concerning the "purpose and details" of the shutdown.

At first the Board proceeded on the basis of Section 8 (a) (3), but the Eighth Court of Appeals remanded the case for reconsideration in light of *Darlington*'s principles. On remand, the board's trial examiner saw the case as involving both *Darlington* and *Fibreboard*.[39] On the *Darlington* issue, the trial examiner found that the employer, like *Darlington*, had shut down to avoid doing business with the union, but, going on to apply the *Darlington* principle, he exonerated Morrison on the ground that, unlike *Darlington*, the "partial closing" was not motivated by an intention to "chill unionism" in the other parts of the operation. On the *Fibreboard* issue, he found that *Morrison* had violated Section 8 (a) (5) by failing to notify the union and failing to bargain over both the decision and the effects of the closing. The Eighth Circuit refused to enforce the Board's decision-bargaining order, citing *Darlington* again. It did, however, require bargaining over the *effects* of the decision to close. And it acknowledged that its decision was, to that extent, interfering with the exercise of the right to shut down, but said it *"recognizes the need to balance employer and employee rights."*[40]

In 1965, the same year in which the Eighth Circuit decided *Adams* and *Burns*, the Court of Appeals for the Third Circuit had before it *Royal Planting & Polishing Co.*[41] The company's decision (not bargained about) to shut down one of its two plants called forth a board order to revoke the action, reinstate the employees, and bargain over the decision and its impact on the employees. The Third Court of Appeals refused to enforce the decision-bargaining order, holding that the decision to shut down was an investment decision, involving a change in economic direction. That being so, the decision was not subject to bargaining because (in the words of Justice Stewart from *Fibreboard*) it lay "at the core of entrepreneurial control." The Board also fared badly in the Ninth Court of Appeals two years later[42] and in the Tenth Circuit two years after that.[43]

39. As reported in the opinion of the Court of Appeals.
40. *Morrison Cafeterias Consolidated, Inc.*, 269.
41. *NLRB v. Royal Plating & Polishing Co.*, 350 F.2d 191 (CA3, 1965).
42. *NLRB v. Transmarine Navigation Corp.*, 380 F.2d 933 (CA9, 1967).
43. *NLRB v. Thompson Transport Co., Inc.*, 406 F.2d 698 (CA 10, 1969).

This phase of our discussion concludes with the case that seems to represent to the board's proponents and opponents alike the high-water mark of the campaign to establish the board's philosophy with respect to the scope of the employer's duty to bargain. The case, *Ozark Trailers, Inc.*, is significant not so much for what it holds, but rather for the philosophy set forth in the board's opinion.[44]

Building further on the *Fibreboard* decision, the Board found that Ozark Trailers, Inc., a manufacturer of refrigerated truck bodies, was a part of a single firm referred to in the case as "Ozark, Hutco, and Mobilefreeze" and that the closing of Ozark's one and only plant in 1964 was tantamount to a partial closing. The union complained that Ozark, Hutco, and Mobilefreeze had refused to bargain over the closing. The firm, on the other hand, contended that the union had never requested a bargaining session, to which the union replied that the firm had misled workers into believing that the closing was a temporary layoff, "due to lack of business." Consequently, the union did not know that it should or could request negotiations over the closing of the plant. In the decision, the NLRB effectively defined the ownership rights of workers to their jobs as equal to the ownership rights of investors to their capital:

> With all respect to the Court of Appeals for the Third and Eighth Circuit, we do not believe that the question whether a particular management decision must be bargained about should turn on whether the decision involves the commitment of investment capital, or on whether it may be characterized as involving [a] "major" or "basic" change in the nature of the employer's business. True it is that decisions of this nature are, by definition, of significance for the employer. It is equally true, however, and ought not be lost sight of, that an employer's decision to make a "major" change in the nature of his business, such as the termination of a portion thereof, is also of significance to those employees whose jobs will be lost by the termination. For just as the employer has invested capital in the business, so the employee has invested years of his working life, accumulating seniority, accruing pension rights, and developing skills that may or may not be salable to another employer. And, just as the employer's interest in the protection of his capital investment is entitled to consideration in our interpretation of the Act, so too is the employee's interest in the protection of his livelihood.[45]

44. *Ozark Trailers, Inc.*, 161 NLRB 561, 63 LRRM 1264 (1966).
45. Ibid., 566.

The board reiterated its position that the employer's obligation to bargain "does not include the obligation to agree, but solely to engage in a full and frank discussion . . . in which a *bona fide* effort will be made to explore possible alternatives." The board concluded that while the requirement to bargain was an intrusion on the rights of management to run its business, it was "no significant intrusion to require that an employer—once he has reached the point of thinking seriously about taking such an extraordinary step as relocating or terminating a portion of its business—discuss that step with the bargaining representative of the employees."[46] Still, decision-bargaining and the remedies imposed for a failure to bargain in good faith represent costs faced by unionized firms *not* also confronted by nonunionized firms.

FIRST NATIONAL MAINTENANCE

The NLRB expanded the coverage in 1979 of Section 8 (a) (5) in its ruling on First National Maintenance Corporation, a firm doing housecleaning work for a number of other firms.[47] In 1977, First National had a contract with Greenpark Care Center, a nursing home in Brooklyn, to do its housecleaning, but because of "lack of efficiency," Greenpark gave the required thirty days notice that its contract with First National would not be renewed. The termination notice caused First National to accept a lower fee, one which ultimately meant that the operations were unprofitable. After asking Greenpark to restore the original fee and being turned down, First National terminated its operations at Greenpark and the thirty-five workers employed there. First National was charged by its union for failure to negotiate the termination of its employees at Greenpark, a violation of 8 (a) (5) supported by the board. The Court of Appeals for the Second Circuit enforced the board's order, but employed a different rationale.[48] Rejecting the board's theory of a bargaining duty, the Court of Appeals held that Section 8 (d) of the act creates a "presumption in favor of mandatory bargaining," which is, however, rebutted by showing that the purpose of the statute would not be furthered by such bargaining (for example, where bar-

---

46. Ibid., 568.
47. *First National Maintenance Corp.*, 242 NLRB 462 (1979).
48. *NLRB v. First National Maintenance Corp.*, 627 F.2d 596 (CA 2, 1980).

gaining would be futile or where there were "emergency financial circumstances").[49]

In a seven-to-two decision, the Supreme Court in 1981 handed down what may eventually be construed as a landmark decision.[50] It reversed the judgment of the Court of Appeals on *First National*, contending that the particular facts of the *First National* case distinguished it from *Fibreboard* and remanded the case to the Court of Appeals for revision in line with the Supreme Court's opinion. Justice Blackmun, who authored the majority opinion, remarked at the outset on the conflict in the cases on decision-bargaining, stating that the Second Circuit "appears to be at odds with decisions of other courts of appeals."[51] Justice Blackmun noted that several appellate courts held that bargaining is not required over any management decision involving "a major commitment of capital investment" or a "basic operational change," while others held that there is no bargaining duty unless "antiunion animus" and a Section 8 (a) (3) violation are involved.[52] He also noted some inconsistency in the board's own rulings and stated that the Supreme Court had taken the case "because of the importance of the issue and the continuing disagreement between and among the board and the courts of appeals."[53]

Clearly the case was intended to clarify the state of law, and clearly all the necessary elements were present: the issue of management's duty to bargain over (1) the decision to cease operations, and (2) the effects of that decision. The issue of balancing the managerial need for freedom in decision making against the interests of the employees in their jobs, and the extent to which the act abridges the former to serve the latter, were also present. Whether or not Justice Blackmun was altogether successful in settling these issues is less clear.

In particular, the Supreme Court argued that the fee Greenpark paid First National was outside the "authority" of First National and that First National "had no intentions to replace the discharged employees or to move that operation elsewhere." The company's sole purpose was to reduce its losses. In addition, the Court con-

49. Ibid., 601–2.
50. *First National Maintenance Corp. v. NLRB*, 452 US (1981).
51. Ibid., 672.
52. Ibid., 673.
53. Ibid., 674.

cluded that (1) business "must have some degree of certainty beforehand as to when it may proceed to reach decisions without fear of
later evaluations labeling its conduct as an unfair labor practice";
(2) management has a "great need for speed, flexibility, and secrecy
in meeting business opportunities and exigencies"; (3) "publicity
incident to the normal process of bargaining may injure the possibility of a successful transition or increase the economic damage to the
business"; and (4) the union is protected from unfair dealings by
management by Section 8 (a) (3), which "prohibits partial closings
motivated by antiunion animus." [54]

Moreover, the Court concluded that "the harm likely to be done
to an employer's need to operate freely in deciding whether to shut
down part of its business purely for economic reasons outweighs the
incremental benefit that might be gained through the union's participation in making the decision, and we hold that the decision itself
is not part of 8 (d)'s 'terms and conditions' . . . over which Congress
has mandated bargaining." [55] The Court contended that "[t]he decision to halt work at this specific location represented a significant
change in [the] petitioner's operations, a change not unlike opening
a new line of business or going out of business entirely." [56]

Finally, the Court declared, contrary to past rulings, that the "pre-
sumptive analysis [in favor of decision-bargaining] adopted by the
Court of Appeals seems ill-suited to advance harmonious relations
between employer and employee. An employer would have difficulty
determining beforehand whether it was faced with a situation requiring bargaining or one that involved economic necessity sufficiently
compelling to obviate the duty to bargain." [57]

The direction the Supreme Court will now take in future cases
involving partial or total firm closures is not completely clear. On the
one hand, the *First National* decision appears to be a strong denunci-
ation of previous positions, namely, that the economics of partial
and total plant closures can be distinguished and that negotiations
over partial plant closures are necessary to promote industrial har-
mony; indeed, they may promote disharmony and increase economic
inefficiency. On the other hand, the Court was careful to distinguish
the facts of the *First National* case from *Fibreboard*. Fibreboard had

54. Ibid., 678–83.
55. Ibid., 683.
56. Ibid., 688.
57. Ibid., 684.

direct control over its maintenance workers, who had been terminated because its maintenance work could be subcontracted to another firm, whereas First National did not have the same degree of control over its fee received from Greenpark Care Center.

Furthermore, the decision in *First National* clearly was one based not so much on legal principle as on the particular presumed costs and benefits of the case. Writing for the Court, Justice Blackmun said as much: "Nonetheless, in view of an employer's need for unencumbered decisionmaking, bargaining over management decisions that have a substantial impact on the continued availability of employment should be required only if the benefit, for labor-management relations and the collective bargaining process, outweighs the burden placed on the conduct of the business."[58] While the Court denied that the partial closing of the operations of First National at Greenpark came under the "terms and conditions of employment" open to bargaining, we cannot at this point be sure that the NLRB, the courts of appeals, and the Supreme Court will see the costs and benefits of requiring bargaining in the same way that the Supreme Court saw them in *First National.* Other courts may agree with Justices Brennan and Marshall, who stressed in their dissent that the Court's reversal of the NLRB's decision is based on "pure speculation."

The Court reasoned that if the problem faced by First National was low profitability brought about by excessive wages and given market conditions, management would have a definite incentive to negotiate those wages down. In *First National*, the problem was the fee paid by the nursing home, which could not be changed by First National through bargaining with its employees. At least, there is much room for interpretation over the breath of the *First National* ruling.

Finally, it is important to note that it appears that the current general counsel to the NLRB, William Lubbers, has chosen to interpret the *First National* decision very narrowly.[59] In *First National*, the Court made the practical suggestion that, even where decision-bargaining ought not to be required owing to the exigencies of busi-

---

58. Ibid., 679.

59. William A. Lubbers, Office of the General Counsel, National Labor Relations Board, "Guidelines of NLRB General Counsel under First National Maintenance" (Memorandum to all regional directors, November 30, 1981) *Daily Labor Report*, No. 10 (January 15, 1982), pp. E1–E2.

ness, etc., effects-bargaining could accomplish many, perhaps most, of the objectives that a union may legitimately entertain when confronted with a plant closure. However, Lubber's memorandum suggests that the NLRB will continue to be devoted to mandatory decision-bargaining on a wide scale. Seizing upon the Court's disclaimer to the effect that "we of course intimate no view as to other types of managerial decisions,"[60] General Counsel Lubbers proceeds to advise the board's field officers in a 1981 memorandum that the decision "expressly left open" such decisions as to (1) relocating a plant; (2) subcontracting work; (3) eliminating bargaining unit jobs through automation; and (4) consolidating operations.[61] Lubbers instructs the board's regional offices to apply the Court's balancing test, weighing the burden of bargaining against its benefits. But, he adds, in doing so they are to "focus on whether the employer's decision was based on labor costs or other factors that would be amenable to resolution through the collective bargaining process."[62] In order to blunt or turn aside the apparent anti-decision-bargaining thrust of *First National*, the general counsel argues that *First National* is a case involving "going-out-of-business," and its doctrine has application only to cases similarly involving some degree of going-out-of-business. Thus, referring to the Court's lists of excepted decisions (that is, decisions to which balancing and possibly decision-bargaining will apply), Lubbers says in a footnote:

> To be sure, some of these decisions may result in the closing of a plant. However, it does not follow that the employer is not obligated to bargain about the decision. The issue in *First National Maintenance* was whether a decision to go partially out of *business* is a mandatory subject, not whether a decision to close a plant is a mandatory subject.[63]

After evaluating the current general counsel's interpretation of the *First National* decision for NLRB, former General Counsel John Irving writes, "And what, then, is the state of law of decision-bargaining today, at least as seen by the General Counsel? As a practical matter, it is right back to square one; it is back to the Second Circuit's 'presumption' in favor of bargaining, because if the General Counsel is right, in all but the *clearest* closing and sale cases, the em-

60. Ibid., p. E-1.
61. Ibid.
62. Ibid.
63. Ibid., note 11.

ployer must engage in decision-bargaining. What is worse, in most cases the law reverts to the pre-*First National* uncertainties about which the Supreme Court was so critical and concerned. . . . However, one thing will be certain: if the employer wants to avoid litigation, he had better have a crystal clear case which does not hang on credibility determinations. If not he can be sure that litigation will ensue if the union chooses to file a charge with the NLRB General Counsel."[64]

The correctness of the general counsel's interpretation of *First National* is a matter of considerable intrinsic importance. For our purposes, however, it is sufficient to note that the general counsel's insistence on decision-bargaining, in spite of the *First National* ruling, continues to impede the closing of unionized plants that is not, to the same extent, imposed on the nonunionized ones.

THE MILWAUKEE SPRING CASE

The NLRB decided the *Milwaukee Spring* case in the fall of 1982, a year after *First National Maintenance* and six months after the general counsel's memorandum.[65] It is an interesting case for three reasons:

First, it involved both plant removal (work was shifted from one plant to another) and an attempt by the employer to get the union to engage in so-called concession-bargaining.

Second, although the employer engaged in decision-bargaining and was willing to engage in effects-bargaining, the board nevertheless found that he had failed in his bargaining duty because, when the move was finally made, it was made without the union's consent.

Third, in addition to the Section 8 (a) (5) bargaining violation, the board held the employer guilty of violating Section 8 (a) (3) (discouragement of union activity—the *Darlington* Issue), although both the board's general counsel and the union stipulated that there was no antiunion animus.

Milwaukee Spring Division is one of four companies making up Illinois Coil Spring Company. For some years, Milwaukee Spring had had contractual relations with the United Auto Workers (UAW). In

64. Irving, "Closing and Sale of Business," p. 226.

65. *Milwaukee Spring Div. of Illinois Coil Spring* 265 NLRB 28 (1982), as reported in *Daily Labor Reporter* (10 October 1982), pp. D-1 – D-5.

January 1981 the company sought to engage in "concession-bargaining" with the union, requesting that it forgo a wage increase scheduled for April and also asking for other improvements in the union contract, requests that the union ultimately rejected. On March 12 the employer informed the union that the economic situation was worse than it had originally estimated, owing, among other things, to the loss of a contract that meant $200,000 a month in revenue. The company proposed moving its assembly operations to one of the parent company's other plants. This plant was not unionized, and the hourly wage rates and fringe costs were substantially lower than those called for by the UAW contract at Milwaukee Spring.

On March 22 the company informed the UAW that it was willing to bargain over alternatives to relocating its assembly operations, and it also advised the union that it needed relief if it was to avoid moving its moulding operations. The next day the employer was told that the union membership had voted against accepting the reductions of $4.50 in wages and $1.50 in fringe benefits, but was willing to have discussions continue. On March 29 the employer gave the union a memorandum of the terms upon which it would keep the assembly operations in Milwaukee. After the union rejected contract concessions, the plant was closed. The facts of the case specified that the relocation thereafter undertaken by Milwaukee Spring was "due solely to the comparatively higher labor costs" under the UAW agreement and that the decision was "economically motivated and not the result of antiunion animus." The parties further stipulated and agreed that Milwaukee Spring "had bargained with the union over the decision to relocate the assembly operations" and "has been willing to engage in effects-bargaining with the union." [66]

The union and the board's general counsel contended that Milwaukee Spring violated both Section 8 (a) (3) and Section 8 (a) (5) of the Wagner Act by its decision to make the move *during the term* of the labor agreement, without the union's consent, and solely on the ground of the labor costs under that agreement. This position was based fundamentally on the bargaining duty as defined in Section 8 (d) of the act, and the argument that the move contemplated a "modification of the terms and conditions" of the UAW contract within the meaning of Section 8 (d). Because the contract between the UAW and *Milwaukee Spring* still had some time to run, the board held that the union was under no obligation to negotiate or to yield

66. Ibid., p. D–2.

and, under those circumstances, the employer was prohibited from taking any action without the consent of the union. The board argued that, in defining the duty to bargain, Section 8 (d) specifically affirms that *where there is in effect an agreement* for a fixed period, neither party is required "to discuss or agree to any modification of the terms and conditions" contained therein.[67]

Thus we are introduced to a major qualification of the decision-bargaining rationale. It now appears that it is not sufficient for an employer to be willing to engage in decision-bargaining when faced with the need to close or move a plant. If he has a contract with a union and it has some time to run, then the employer, in the board's view, is immobilized by Section 8 (d), absent the consent of the union. The employer's only avenue in this situation lies in obtaining the consent of the union, which may take one or the other of two forms: (1) the union agrees to engage in bargaining over the move, or (2) the union has earlier agreed, in negotiations, to language that authorizes the employer to make the move without further consultation with the union.

In arguing the latter in *Milwaukee Spring*, the board based its position on two separate parts of the UAW agreement: the "recognition clause" and the "management rights clause."[68] The company's argument on the inclusion of the clause was simply that its language confined the applicability of the contract to the operations at Milwaukee and that, when those operations moved away from Milwaukee, the contract no longer had anything to operate on. Thus, the argument ran, the contract was not "modified" by the move; it was rendered nugatory.

The recognition clause in the UAW contract stipulated that the union was recognized for the "production and maintenance employees in the company's plant in Milwaukee." The purpose of such a clause is twofold. First, from the union's standpoint, it reaffirms, by agreement of the employer, the union's representative status, and it defines the bargaining unit that the union represents. Second, from the management's standpoint, the clause defines and limits the bargaining unit and the operations or facility covered by the agreement. The board, however, dismissed the employer's interpretation of the recognition clause, stating that it was merely the "descriptive recita-

67. Ibid., p. D–3.
68. Ibid.

tion of the physical location of the facilities at the time of the contract's negotiation."[69]

The board then addressed itself to the contract's management rights clause. Among other things, that clause provided that "the Company shall have the *exclusive* right to manage the plant and business and direct the working forces" [emphasis added]. The management clause goes on to specify some of the rights embraced within the foregoing general statement of the "exclusive" rights of management. It mentions the right "to determine the operations or services to be performed in or at the plant . . . to introduce new and improved methods, materials, or facilities, or to change existing methods, materials, or facilities." The issue at stake was the extent to which this language preserves management's flexibility and mobility. The board found that "we find nothing in this clause which expressly grants [the] respondent the right to move, transfer, or change the location of part of its operations from its Milwaukee facility to another facility."[70]

An extended exegesis of the contrast between the language of the contract and the board's interpretation of it is not our purpose. Suffice it to observe that, at the very least, the language seems open to interpretation pursuant to the company's right to "manage the plant and business" and to "control operations," and to make decisions to "introduce new . . . facilities" or to "change existing . . . facilities." Nevertheless, the board concluded that there is "nothing giving the company the right to move" and that the company was in violation of Section 8 (a) (3) even though there was no antiunion animus. The remedy was to rescind the removal decision, to require Milwaukee Springs to reinstate its operations at Milwaukee, and to offer reinstatement and back pay to employees laid off in consequence of the removal decision.

Although a case can be made that Milkwaukee Springs had reason to believe from previous NLRB and court interpretation of labor contracts that it retained in its labor contract the right to shift the allocation of work among plants, the lesson from the *Milwaukee Springs* case is straightforward: prudence would require that in contract negotiations management must seek to obtain language that is as firm and explicit as possible on the right to discontinue or relocate

69. Ibid.
70. Ibid., pp. D–3 – D–4.

operations. In the absence of explicit wording to the contrary, decisions to relocate work apparently now require, in the NLRB's view, the consent of the union. In the words of the NLRB, "Contractual waiver of statutory right must be clear and unmistakable."[71] This does not necessarily mean that companies cannot move while a union contract is in force. It simply means that the company may have to "buy out" the union from its contract and that the benefits of the move to a new location may be largely absorbed by the union for the remaining term of the union contract. Right or wrong, the growing tendency of the courts and the board to thwart company moves during the term of a union contract translates into greater costs for capital in the unionized sectors of the economy.

WORKERS' RIGHTS TO THEIR JOBS

Submerged in the policy debate over plant closing restrictions is the question of the legally protected rights workers have to their jobs.[72] The fundamental legal issue is, do workers have rights in the event of a plant closing or relocation of work, and, if they do, what are they? For example, do they have the right to stop a plant from closing, to continued employment, to severance pay or advance notice of a shutdown, or even to participate in a decision about closing?

The question of workers' rights to their jobs can be addressed initially from the same perspective as all other rights issues are addressed in the courts: the rights depend on the terms of the contract. A contract can be negotiated between an employer and employee that spells out the rights workers have to severance pay, advanced notice, and decision participation. Of course, worker rights are generally not acquired free of charge; employers generally require an inducement such as a wage reduction to incur the cost of the worker rights.

Workers enter employment negotiations with the right to refrain from working, if nothing else. In exchange for giving up the rights

71. Ibid., p. D-3.

72. For extended discussions of the issue of worker rights to their jobs, see Eirik G. Furubotn, *The Rights of Workers to Their Jobs: An Analysis of the Changing Nature of the Employment Relations* (Arlington, Tex.: Economics Department, University of Texas-Arlington, a monograph under development for a conference on "Worker Rights to Their Jobs" to be sponsored by the Liberty Fund, Inc., 1983), Simon Rottenberg, "Property in Work," *Industrial and Labor Relations Review* (January 1963): 279–88.

to his or her time to the employer (or for investing in job-related skills), the worker receives other rights, which amount to inducements to work — wages, fringe benefits, and even closing rights. Like the employer, the employee can forgo closing rights, but only for benefits, e.g., higher wages than he or she could otherwise secure. Clearly, if employers are (as proponents of closing restrictions fervently argue) profit maximizing and if workers value closing rights, a mutually beneficial exchange of rights and wages can be arranged. Just as clearly, when these deals are struck, the courts (or agencies such as the NLRB) must assume their legitimate economic role of enforcing the terms of the contract. If they do not do so, labor may be exploited by *short-sighted* employers who negotiate contracts that include an exchange of closing rights for lower pay or for reduced fringe benefits and then close the plant without compensating workers for the wages forgone. The role of the courts in such labor contracts is no different from their role in enforcing the terms of a car loan: to ensure that contracts are obeyed. (We emphasize the phrase short-sighted because employers who renege on labor contracts and stay in business will find that their wage bill will rise to reflect the fact that workers will tend to view their closing provisions as worthless and demand higher wages).

The *Milwaukee Springs* case exposes difficulties inherent in contract enforcement. If at the time the contract was negotiated management and labor understood the contract to mean that the company did in fact retain the right to close and relocate work, then it seems reasonable to conclude that the right to close and relocate work would have been offset by higher wages for labor. The decision reached by the board thus gave labor a form of double compensation — higher wages from the negotiated contract and continued employment and back pay from the NLRB's remedy. If the imprecise wording of the contract meant that management had forgone the right to relocate without the consent of the union, in exchange for lower pay, then the remedy developed by the board was nothing more than a means of asserting that management had to live up to its contract or gain the consent of the union by providing compensation prior to closing its plant and relocating work. The remedy in effect meant management would have to buy out the remaining portion of its contract, which in turn meant, in part, paying back the benefits workers had given up. We have already suggested a solution to these problems: management must be forthright in declaring its retained rights, meaning it must stand ready to compensate labor for retaining flexibility and plant mobility.

The issue of worker rights, however, becomes even more untidy when we recognize that all contingencies in employer–employee relationships cannot always be fully specified in contracts. As Professor Armen Alchian has noted, employers sometimes ask workers to invest their own funds and time in developing skills that are specific to a given job but useless elsewhere.[73] Although nothing may be written down, the workers may willingly invest in their job-related skills because of an implied commitment by the employer to advance notice, severance pay, or continued employment in another plant if the workers' plant is closed. When job skills are useful to a number of employers, the problem employees face in receiving compensation for their job-related investment can be solved by market forces. Employers will bid among themselves for workers with the needed skills, adding a premium to the wage that will tend, over time, to compensate workers for their investment. If the workers' plant closes under these market conditions, a worker will lose little or nothing because he or she can shift employment to one of the several other firms and still receive the going market wage rate.

When the skills are specific to an employer, however, what economists call "quasi-monopoly rent" is received by employees who make the needed investment in skills. By their very definition, quasi-rents are the short-term employment benefits that are over and above the wage that can be received elsewhere. Quasi-rents induce workers to invest in job-related skills unusable elsewhere. Of course, workers should be reluctant to make the needed investment without some guarantee of compensation. The worker who has adjusted his (or her) skills at his (or her) own expense, with the knowledge that he (or she) has acquired rights to severance pay or advanced notice, can be in a precarious market position in the absence of legal protection. The worker may have the remaining value of his investment expropriated by the employer who, on closing or threatening to close a plant and in violation of unwritten parts of his labor contract, offers little notice or severance benefits. Granted, when worker skills are job-specific, we would expect to see employers paying for the training (because workers would want to be protected against the

---

73. Armen A. Alchian, "Decision Sharing and Expropriable Specific Quasi-Rents: A Theory of *First National Maintenance Corporation v. NLRB*," *Supreme Court Economic Review* (forthcoming).

possibility of their investment being expropriated). Nevertheless, the courts and the NLRB will from time to time have to settle disputes over unwritten commitments by employers to their employees. That is (or rather should be) their *raison d'etre.* (For that matter, the courts and the NLRB will have to settle disputes over unwritten com- mitments of employees to their employers.) In these instances, when unwritten commitments have been made, negotiation over a plant closing can be nothing more than a means of ensuring that workers' investment in their jobs, which at the time of the closing may not be fully compensated, are not expropriated by the employer.

The legal questions that arise include (1) whether or not labor has actually invested in job-specific skills; (2) whether or not labor has been compensated through wages or other benefits for its investment; and (3) whether or not the benefits from the investment have been subject to expropriation. We concur with Professor Alchian that no evidence was offered in *First National* that would suggest that the workers had made a material investment in skills specific to house- cleaning work at the nursing home, the benefits of which were sub- ject to expropriation. No evidence was offered indicating that First National was acting opportunistically, that is, with the intent of ex- propriating benefits from its workers. The relevant issue in *First National*, from this perspective, is not, as the Supreme Court sug- tested, one of weighing the needs of management flexibility versus the harm to labor. Management can secure its needed flexibility through contract negotiation. The issue is rather one of whether or not there was an explicit or implicit agreement that induced labor to forgo benefits in exchange for job security—or closing rights.

Finding a legal remedy for expropriated quasi-rents when plants are closed should generally be no more difficult than finding a rem- edy in the case of loss of life or limb in an automobile accident. Clearly, the court should reason that specific job-related skills were acquired by employees with some thought of compensation. Other- wise, why would the investment have been made? If it were solely interested in compensating employees, the court could compute the award as being equal to the investment cost incurred minus the added employment benefits already received by the employee at the time of the closing. Again, the remedy here is a requirement that firms live up to their contracts.

At times, businesses must fold for financial reasons and may not be able to compensate their employees fully for job-related investments. Funds may simply not be available to cover even labor-related costs, which take a high priority in liquidations. Ultimately, employees must recognize that as investors in their own "human capital," a role they cannot completely avoid, employees cannot escape the risks of investment. To protect themselves fully, employees must bargain for the employers to incur all job-related investment costs up front, which, in many situations, may be impossible to do.

Again, *Milwaukee Springs* is an example of how a firm *may have* been (but was not necessarily) attempting to expropriate benefits from its employees after the employees *may have* forgone (but did not necessarily forgo) employment benefits. Although legal precedent might suggest that the company had greater managerial flexibility than the board found, there is admittedly room for interpretation. If a bargain is struck, however, management as well as labor must be held to its terms, in spite of changes in financial exigencies. Otherwise, all exchanged benefits are subject to expropriation by one party or the other. When it settles with labor, management must recognize that the contract is binding and that risks are involved. It would seem that in settling on a union contract for a period of years, it must take account of comparative labor costs that are likely to exist among plants during the contract period. *Milwaukee Springs* teaches that such a comparative analysis is (or must be) implicitly accepted by management at the time of the contract signing. To repeat a point already made, this does not mean that the company *cannot* move. It means that explicit language should be used to ensure that management's ability to move is retained. It also means simply that when management has "sold" its managerial flexibility to labor for a reduction in other benefits going to labor, management must effectively buy its flexibility back in order to move or shift work.

Market solutions are feasible when property rights are clearly defined. When the courts and the board vary in their interpretations of labor law, however, property rights remain ill-defined, and both the risks and the costs of doing business are needlessly increased.

The requirement that all employers provide closing benefits without regard to explicit or implicit, but legally supportable, contractual arrangements has a number of unforeseen adverse consequences. Several of these have probably been felt by unions that have been able to restrict the closing of unionized plants. Such laws implicitly set standards as to the form of worker compensation that are not tradable and not applicable to all worker groups. For many worker groups, the costs of such employment restrictions can easily exceed the value of any remedy for job-related expenses incurred or benefits given up by the employees. As argued elsewhere in this book, these closing restrictions should lower the wages paid workers and will deny workers who would not otherwise have negotiated closing restrictions the right of trading closing rights for higher pay.

Such legislated restrictions tend to be nontradable, but to the extent the legislated closing rights *are* tradable, they will tend to be traded away by labor. The very fact that the closing restrictions are imposed suggests that workers would prefer the higher pay and other fringe benefits they could have in place of the closing rights (otherwise mutually beneficial trades would tend to be struck between labor and management, meaning the legislation would tend to be unnecessary). Another way of saying the same thing is that to worker groups not covered *voluntarily* by the closing restrictions, the attendant value of the higher pay and fringe benefits that would have to be forgone to secure closing restrictions tends to exceed the value of the closing rights. This implies that when workers are given, by way of legislation, closing rights that are tradable, their welfare can be improved by trading the lower-valued closing rights for the higher-valued wages and fringe benefits. Such trades, in turn, mean employers will in time tend to reacquire most if not all of their mobility—at a price, of course. (We do not mean to suggest here that all acquired closing rights will be traded away. Because of transaction costs and the initial wealth increase of workers, due to the newly acquired rights from employers, worker demand for closing rights should be marginally greater than it was before the transfer of rights. However, because wages will be adversely affected by the transfer of rights, the wealth of workers will not be increased by the transfer of rights by as much as it might appear from consideration of the rights by themselves.) The price that management must pay for the closing rights will in the long run tend to be offset by lower wages for labor. Although the initial shift in rights, which translates into a shift of wealth, may or may not be socially desirable, it does not mean that workers will end up with all of the desired job security (or wealth) in the form of the retained closing rights envisioned by the proponents of the legislation. To ensure that the campaign for worker rights does not become merely a campaign for enhanced worker wealth, legislated rights will tend to be made nontradable, although it is difficult to see how trades of rights between workers and employers can be precluded altogether.

To the extent they remain nontradable, such restrictions will also tend to reduce overall job opportunities and to affect the skill requirements for jobs and the distribution of the costs of acquiring those skills. Employers should be less concerned about establishing production processes requiring job-specific skills, since they will have to incur the costs of closing restrictions regardless of the skill requirements. In addition, the costs of acquiring job-related skills will tend to be shifted to the employees. Because of the cost of the closing restrictions, the demand for labor should be depressed, weakening the bargaining position of the workers over the issue of who bears the cost of job-specific training. In other words, legislated closing restrictions favor skilled workers at the expense of the unskilled workers, which may be a partial explanation for union support for legislated remedies for the closing problems.

Ultimately, legally mandated restrictions applicable to all workers mean that the preferences of some subgroups of workers, namely, those who have the political power to have their favored restrictions made law, will be made legal at the expense of the preferences of other workers. Again, labor must remember that such restrictions are not applicable to labor's substitutes, namely, capital and foreign labor, which means that such restrictions place labor at a competitive disadvantage with its substitutes. One must seriously doubt that such legal restrictions, because they shift employment demands the way they do, elevate "social welfare" over and above what it would have been.

Our analysis leads to another explanation for union support of legislated remedies, one that emerges directly from our review of court cases. Not all labor is covered by the court and board-imposed closing restrictions; only unionized labor has been to any significant extent covered by the restrictions — or affected by the costs they impose on firms. As a result, we should expect the history of the court and NLRB restrictions to discriminate, in the long run (after capital has had a chance to adjust to the restrictions) against those unionized workers who tend to be "protected" (albeit temporarily) by them.

Clearly, the *First National* decision represents at least a minor setback for unions wishing to use labor law as an effective means of stalling plant closings, of securing the types of restrictions on plant closings that are now being sought through state legislatures and the Congress. Just as clearly, as the position on *First National* taken by the NLRB's general counsel shows, employers have had and will probably continue to have reason to believe that their decisions to close unionized plants will be undermined by a court decision that the company had failed to bargain over the issue, or that, if it had sat down at the bargaining table with its union representatives, had failed to bargain in good faith. Employers still have to be very concerned that in the act of closing plants, they are not subject to the charge of exhibiting an antiunion animus.

UNION SUPPORT OF PLANT
CLOSING RESTRICTIONS

Why do unions support plant closing laws? One important answer has been noted: they seek to protect their jobs and their economic rents by holding their firms in place and by increasing the demand for skilled labor. Another reason suggested by our survey of recent board and court cases must be stressed: unions have been granted plant closing restrictions that have not been afforded other worker groups, that have not been in force in nonunionized sectors of the economy. Capital (as could be predicted from the imposition of legislated plant closing restrictions) has moved marginally to areas of the country not dominated by unions, such as the South.

In the 1930s, unions supported minimum wage laws for the explicit purpose of retarding the movement of capital to the South. Unions saw in minimum wage laws a method of reducing the responsiveness of employers to the demands for union labor. Unions may seek the same outcome from legislated plant closing laws uniformly applied across states (or across union and nonunion sectors of the economy), thus once again reducing the responsiveness of employers to the demands for union labor to wage increases. In other words, unions may intuitively or consciously sense that their bargaining strength has been eroded by the closing restrictions implied in union labor law. We have argued all along that capital can be expected to move away from areas where closing restrictions are in place. Unions have admitted that they are opposed to capital flight, and capital

flight from union areas can be motivated by a variety of reasons—
noncompetitive wages, featherbedding, reduced productivity, *and
judicially and contractually imposed closing restraints.*

Surely the implied closing restrictions in unionized sectors of the
economy cannot explain all of the flight of capital out of the sector,
but may it not explain a portion of the flight? To that extent, may
the implied restrictions not explain a part of organized labor's interest in legislated closing restrictions? Closing restrictions can enhance,
albeit marginally, a union's bargaining position above what it otherwise would have been. The whole of the argument against "capital
flight" developed by Barry Bluestone and Bennett Harrison can be
construed as making these basic points.[74]

CONCLUDING COMMENTS

Our review of NLRB and court decisions indicates that unionized
plants are beset with closing restrictions not fully applicable to nonunionized plants.

First, in closing a plant, employers of unionized workers must
be careful that they are not charged with exhibiting an antiunion
animus.

Second, they must be careful that the partial closing of operations
does not chill unionism in other parts of the company.

Third, they must be aware that if they refuse to bargain over the
closing decision or the effects of the closing on workers, they may be
found in violation of labor law that requires bargaining over the
terms and conditions of employment and may be required to reestablish operations after a closing has been completed or to provide alternative employment for the affected workers and to provide back
pay. Even if bargaining is undertaken, employers run the risk of
being charged with failing to bargain in good faith.

Fourth, while a union contract is in force, employers may not be
able to move or close without the consent of the union.

Fifth, when a decision to close has been made and bargaining over
the decision or the effects of the decision is undertaken, employers

---

74. Barry Bluestone and Bennett Harrison, *The Deindustrialization of America: Plant
Closings, Community Abandonment, and the Dismantling of Basic Industry* (New York:
Basic Books, 1982), chapter 6.

may be required to provide their unions with considerable information from records concerning the basis for the closing.

Although the law on these issues is in some dispute and unsettled, employers must interpret these restrictions as expected costs not incurred fully in the operations of nonunionized plants. We may or may not agree on what the law *should* be but still agree on the economic consequences of such restrictions and their attendant costs.

Union support for plant closing restrictions is strong. In spite of the Supreme Court's decision in *First National Maintenance*, unions may still eventually be able to obtain the type of closing restrictions that are now being proposed in state legislatures. As a result of NLRB and court decisions, restrictions on closing unionized plants were gradually being tightened. Admittedly, during the 1970s the costs imposed on businesses by those restrictions may not have been as severe as proposed legislative remedies. But they were not inconsequential either, and the NLRB and the courts during the 1970s gave every indication that the costs of closing unionized plants would become more severe. In other words, expected closing costs of operating union plants were clearly rising. In those *expected* costs may lie a hidden reason for union support of plant closing legislation. Because investment is tied to future income and costs, capital flows across sectors of the economy must respond to expected costs as well as income. Those NLRB and court decisions—and the added business costs implied in them—were an added inducement for business to seek out nonunion areas of the country. The resulting capital flight may then have led unions to support plant closing restrictions. At least, this is a thesis that cannot be summarily dismissed.

The *First National* Decision and the NLRB general counsel's reaction to it muddy the legal waters on plant closing restrictions embodied in labor law. If *First National* is a reversal of previous trends in legal decisions, it would appear that capital flight from unionized sectors will, in the future, moderate.

Chapter 6

COMMUNITY BARGAINING OVER PLANT CLOSINGS
Reindustrialization Boon or Bane?

Before the 1960s most major industrial firms feared that public disclosure of their ongoing location searches would inflate real estate prices. When Walt Disney sought in the early 1960s to buy 43 square miles (27,443 acres) of orange groves in central Florida for his planned Disney World, the land was actually purchased by several different law firms, most of whom did not know Disney was the buyer. These diversionary tactics were justified on the grounds that if the landowners knew a single buyer was involved and the buyer was Disney, they might withhold strategic pieces of property and inflate their prices.[1]

Many firms still hold their expansion plans close to their corporate chests; however, beginning most noticeably in the mid-1960s, a sizable number of firms began to change their strategy. In contrast to keeping their plans quiet, many firms—especially very large ones—began announcing their expansion intentions to political leaders within selected communities. While the professed purpose may have been to find the most advantageous industrial site, a hidden motivation for these announcements has always been to pit communities against one another in a competitive struggle for the jobs and tax

1. Edward L. Prizer, "The Disney Decade," *Orlando Land*, October 1981, pp. 29–63. Disney ended up buying the acreage at an average price of $200 an acre. Once it was known that Disney had bought the Disney World tract, prices of surrounding land jumped six to seven times the previous selling price.

bases that are at stake. Communities and states have responded to the competitive challenge by offering a wide range of industrial inducements: the issuance of industrial development bonds, which ultimately means the purchase or lease prices of the land and plants involved are subsidized by government; the making of federal, state, and local government grants that cover the installation costs of roads and interstate interchanges and of sewer, water, and gas lines; and the exemption of the industrial property from local property taxes for several years. State and local government development boards have even built plants and leased them to firms at nominal rents, all in the interest of securing industrial jobs and a greater tax base.

When Teledyne, Inc., planned the construction of a new plant in South Carolina in 1981, it considered locations in Oconee, Anderson, Pickens, and Laurens counties. Oconee County got the plant, which in full operation will employ 500 workers. It won the competition, however, only by agreeing to build the plant and then lease it back to Teledyne at favorable rates—a concession the other counties were unwilling to offer.[2]

After acquiring its first American plant to produce Rabbits, Volkswagen found that it did not have the necessary "pollution rights" to operate its Pennsylvania plant. Because hydrocarbon pollution in the area of the VW plant had reached the legal ceiling, a hydrocarbon "offset" had to be made in another production process before VW could start production. In order to keep VW, the state agreed to keep the area's overall pollution level within legal limits by shifting to a less polluting but more expensive asphalt processing and road paving method.[3]

In the early 1980s another industrial strategy began to emerge. Rather than pit communities against one another over the location of new plants, firms began to announce plans to close one or more plants, giving the communities affected an opportunity to bargain over their closing.[4] In 1980 General Motors announced that it

2. Interview with Trey Senn, executive director of the Anderson County Planning and Development Board, Anderson County, South Carolina, 9 September 1982.

3. See Bruce Yandle, "The Emerging Market in Pollution Rights," *Regulation* (July/August 1978): 21–29.

4. The extent of the new plant closing strategy is not known. The examples here are intended to illustrate the problems posed by such a strategy and recognized by advocates of closing restrictions as a cause of plant closings. See Barry Bluestone and Bennett Harrison, *The Deindustrialization of America: Plant Closings, Community Abandonment, and the Dismantling of Basic Industries* (New York: Basic Books, Inc., 1982), chapter 6.

planned to close two outmoded Fisher Body plants and replace them with a new $800 million Cadillac plant that might eventually employ as many as 6,000 workers. It informed the city of Detroit that, unless a suitably large land tract (500 acres) could be found in the city, General Motors would have to locate its proposed new plant in another area of the country.[5] Because the proposed new plant could mean over $8.1 million a year in business tax revenue (even after a twelve-year, 50 percent property tax abatement) and $1.5 million in wage taxes, Detroit responded by offering to condemn, under its powers of eminent domain, a 250-acre section of the city known as Poletown, encompassing 3,500 mainly Polish residents, 150 businesses, and 16 churches. The city bought the land for approximately $200 million, $150 million of which came from federal sources.

In order to sell the land to General Motors (for a little more than $8 million), Detroit in the end had to remove many of the residents of Poletown forceably. At present, although the buildings of Poletown, including a Catholic church, an emotional centerpiece in the controversy, have been removed, the promised Cadillac plant is not scheduled to be in operation until sometime after 1985. Given the downward trend of automobile sales, the plant may never be built.

In 1982, because of severe financial difficulties, International Harvester began to close and consolidate several of its twenty-three heavy equipment plants. In one contemplated plant closing, Harvester informed Fort Wayne, Indiana, and Springfield, Ohio, that one of the cities would see its plant closed, asking at the same time that each consider buying its plant and leasing it back to Harvester.[6] Harvester saw in the sale-leaseback plan a means of securing capital that it could not obtain from private markets because of its heavy indebtedness and the looming threat of bankruptcy. By September 1982, each city had offered to buy its respective plant for $30 million or above, using a combination of public and private monies.[7] Because

---

5. See "The Rape of Poletown," *Inquiry* (August 3 and 24, 1981): 11–12.

6. See "Springfield-Worker: 'We'd Just Like to Have Some Answers' " and "Fort Wayne: Community Spirit Evident, But May Not Be Enough," Dayton, Ohio, *Journal Herald*, 14 August 1982, p. 1; and "Indiana City Offers Deal to Keep Harvest Plant," *Washington Post*, 11 August 1982.

7. According to a *Wall Street Journal* report, Springfield offered a $30-million sale-leaseback plan on a 15-year-old plant at a time when Fort Wayne had put together a $9-million offer on a 60-year-old plant. Fort Wayne later countered, however, with a $31 million sale-leaseback offer. "Two Towns Fight to Keep Harvester Plants, Knowing That Only One Will Remain Open," *Wall Street Journal*, 8 September 1982, p. 35.

they involved the potential continued employment of more than 7,500 workers in cities that were suffering substantially higher unemployment rates than the national average, the sale-leaseback arrangements were eagerly supported by community leaders. In October 1982, the Fort Wayne plant was selected for closing.[8] Why Fort Wayne was selected is much less important than the fact that officials of two cities, set in competition with one another, were willing to pay more for their respective factories than the market would have allowed. If that were not the case, Harvester need not have gone to the governments of Fort Wayne and Springfield in search of a sale-leaseback contract.

Harvester also announced in 1982 that it was closing its plant in Louisville, Kentucky. At approximately the same time, Harvester told Rock Island, Illinois, that it would transfer its terminated rear-end transmission operations at Louisville to Rock Island if Rock Island and the State of Illinois would cover part or all of the $10 million cost of transporting equipment from Louisville to Rock Island and of installing the equipment in Harvester's Rock Island plant.[9] Since the relocation of the transmission works would add approximately 550 jobs to the community's employment base, Rock Island (which, like Fort Wayne and Springfield, was experiencing heavy unemployment) agreed in September 1982 to pay $6 million of the transfer expenses. The State of Illinois also agreed to funnel a $1 million grant into Rock Island for retraining Harvester workers who would take the jobs at its expanded facility. Crucial to the negotiations was the city's belief that the 800 workers then on indefinite furlough at the Rock Island plant (which at its peak in 1979 employed 3,500) might never be rehired if the local government aid were not forthcoming.

Concession-bargaining over closure has not been restricted to basic industries in the private sector. It is a growing phenomenon in professional sports and even government. In 1982 the Federal Aviation Administration began consolidating many of its field offices around the country. In order to attract the consolidated regional offices, communities have been competing for the regional offices by offering to lease office space to the FAA at nominal annual rates. Anderson County, South Carolina, offered in the summer of 1982 to lease

8. "Ohio Wins Bid for Harvester over Old Fort Wayne Plant," *New York Times*, 28 September 1982, p. D–5.

9. Telephone interview with Neal Nielson, City Manager of Rock Island, Illinois, August 16, 1982.

the FAA office space for $1 a year at the county airport, currently being used as a field office. Trey Senn, Executive Director of the Anderson County Planning and Development Board, remarked, "We may not get the regional office, but surely no one will undercut us on price."[10]

The owners of the Washington Capitals, a hockey team that plays its games in Maryland, just outside the nation's capital, threatened in June 1982 to take their franchise elsewhere unless four conditions were met by local fans and governments by the end of August 1982. The conditions were (1) the sale of 7,500 season tickets; (2) sellouts for the first seven home games; (3) a reduction in the rent on the coliseum; and (4) a reduction in the entertainment tax on tickets from 10 to one-half of one percent.[11] All conditions were met in an eleventh-hour campaign, and the team pledged to stay another year.

Similar threats of closure are being made across the country. To keep plants open, firms have asked or demanded financial concessions by communities. There is need, therefore, to explore the economic consequences of concession-bargaining by communities (which has understandably been termed "industrial blackmail"). The overriding issue of this chapter is whether or under what circumstances concession-bargaining is a boon or bane to community reindustrialization efforts. Because community concessions on plant locations and plant closings are conceptually similar and because the former will lead, in a competitive government environment, to the latter, such an investigation must deal generally with both location and closing concessions. However, bargaining by governments, when it involves taxes imposed on the entire community and subsidies limited to a segment of the community, is conceptually distinguishable from bargains struck in private markets. For this reason, the first step in our analysis must be a restatement of fundamental market principles.

BARGAINING WITHIN PRIVATE MARKETS

Bargaining over resource prices is integral to competitive market processes. After all, bargains made subject to revision are what markets produce. Because bargains can be almost anything the trading parties

10. Interview with Trey Senn, see note 2.
11. Ken Denlinger, "What Capitals Need Is a Power Play Like Pollin's," *Washington Post*, 25 August 1982, p. D–1.

choose to make them, markets exhibit considerable flexibility, an important advantage since consumer tastes and conditions of production fluctuate. Furthermore, when made in the knowledge of alternative resource prices and with all costs and benefits considered by the trading parties, the bargains struck in markets give rise to an efficient allocation of resources. Efficiency in the allocation of resources is simply the economist's way of saying that resources have been so divided among competing uses that the value of the resulting combination of goods and services, as evaluated by those involved in the market transactions, is maximized.[12]

Market system failures to achieve maximum efficiency are fully acknowledged in economic literature. These failures stem primarily from the presence of monopoly power and the existence of external benefits and costs in production and consumption. In the interest of maximizing profits, monopolies tend to hold back on production, forcing their prices and profits upward. An inefficiency occurs in the sense that consumers would pay a price for additional units that would more than cover the additional production cost. Because the monopoly will not allow these additional units to be produced, resources migrate to other uses, giving rise to "too little" of the monopolized product and "too much" of other goods (in the sense that consumers would prefer more of the monopolized product and less of other things).

External costs are costs of production not incurred by the producers of the product and imposed on some third party not involved in the trade; external benefits are benefits of consumption not received by the buyer and received by some third party not involved in the trade. Where external costs exist and no reasonably inexpensive method is available for internalizing the external cost (meaning the full burden of production cost is imposed on the producer), the good or service will tend to be underpriced and oversold. The additional expense fishermen must incur in fishing the lakes of the country because of acid rain, which in turn is due to pollution, is a classic example of external costs. The polluters can underprice their products because a part of the production cost is imposed on the fishermen, resulting in too many of the polluters' products and too few fish being produced.

---

12. Alternatively, it may be said that an efficient market outcome occurs when resources cannot be rearranged among their alternative uses without reducing the total value of the goods and services produced.

Where external benefits exist and no way can be found to internalize the benefits (meaning sellers can charge for the benefits received by others), the good or service in question tends to be underpriced and underproduced. A classic example of an external benefit is the security people feel when criminal activity is deterred. If the government were not involved in police work, the public would individually buy less police protection than they would if they could charge for the benefits received by others. An inefficiency exists in our examples in the sense that consumers would prefer more of one thing and less of something else. Again, this result emerges because market prices do not reflect the full costs and benefits of the goods that are traded.

Outside of these cases, bargains struck within markets must reflect the considered choices of the participants, meaning that each party to the trade must weigh the costs and benefits of what he or she does. These trades increase community welfare because of the differences in relative evaluation of what is traded. Each trader has to bear the full cost of what he does, meaning simply that he acts (trades) on the basis of a comparative analysis of the value of what is forgone with the value of what is received. Presumably, trades occur only when the benefits to each exceed the costs to each. Of course, when people seek to maximize their own individual welfares, they may be inclined to impose as many of the costs of their trades as they can on others. When they are successful in doing so, resource allocations are misdirected trades, and overproduction is encouraged. As long as people are denied the benefits of their efforts, potential mutually beneficial trades will be left unexploited; when all benefits are not received by the person who has to incur the costs of production, it stands to reason that fewer costs will be incurred, fewer trades will occur.

JUSTIFYING GOVERNMENT SUBSIDIES

The foregoing discussion is relevant for one simple reason: subsidies to sway industry location or closure decisions are often justified from an economic (as opposed to a political or ethical) perspective on what are thought to be "externality" grounds. "The whole community benefits" is an often heard refrain. After all, when a new plant moves in, the number of jobs in the community increases, wages of workers rise along with the competition for labor, real estate prices go up, and the tax base expands. When a plant is subsidized under threat of closure, the argument retains its essential character: when the subsidies work, jobs are saved, wages and real estate prices are kept from falling, and the tax base is held intact. As the argument is developed, the location inducements can have a multiplying effect within the community: the workers directly affected by the subsidy will tend to spend a sizable share of their income on locally produced goods and services, the producers of which will buy from others in the communities, and so forth. All of them will pay into the tax coffers.

Admittedly there may be losers as well as winners. For example, many people who do not share in the growth in personal income may suffer higher rents (because of inflated property values). However, proponents of this economic development policy (often referred to as "industrialization" or "reindustrialization policy") may reason that over the course of many such inducements, almost all in the affected community will *on balance* benefit.

Although they may affect few jobs directly, government subsidies of sports facilities, such as enclosed stadiums, are also justified on externality grounds. The fans who attend the games and concerts gain directly: they can see events that they would not otherwise have a chance to attend (or could attend only at considerable expense), and they see them at reduced, subsidized prices. However, others also gain (there are externalities), or so the argument goes. Because of the stadium, others benefit by knowing they could attend if they ever decided to attend; an increase in the range of entertainment options may be construed as a form of wealth increase by individuals. Also, the community-financed sports (and fine arts) facility will act as a magnet, attracting more visitors and more firms and giving rise to on jobs, incomes, and taxes, as noted above.

Any subsidy can be viewed by community leaders as an investment that is recouped by way of greater incomes and taxes in the community. Residents may have to pay higher taxes to cover the subsidy, but they have higher incomes from which they can pay their taxes. Indeed, if the subsidies are planned carefully, some special industrial location inducements will even lower the average tax rates of the citizens. The greater tax base may permit a spreading of the community's tax burden. Mention was made above that the proposed Cadillac plant in Poletown would return approximately $10 million in local tax revenue each year on a local government investment of $50 million (plus cost of services to the GM plant, if it were ever built).

Empirical analysis of the actual profitability of this form of community investment produces mixed results. A number of studies have found that few firms make their location decisions on the basis of community concessions.[13] When community inducements are more or less decisive, they tend to affect the choice among communities within a given state or region of the country; state and local government inducements, in other words, affect in a very minor way interregional location decisions,[14] largely because the concessions tend to be widespread, as would be expected in a competitive government environment, and tend to be offsetting. Other analysts have argued that for the communities involved inducements can provide a rather hefty annual rate of return on the investment, extending up to 87 percent.[15] This statistical debate is largely a side issue for the purposes of this discussion, however, in which the central concern is whether or not community locational and anticlosing subsidies to businesses tend to promote efficiency (that is, avert market externalities) or promote inefficiency (create externalities of their own).

AN ASSESSMENT OF THE ARGUMENT

There is some truth to the statement that industries that move into a community do give rise to "externalities" (although not necessarily externalities of the pure problematic kind, known among economists as "technological externalities"). "Technological externalities" are contrasted in economic literature with "pecuniary externalities." The former arise because of some basic defect in the market's ability to internalize all costs and benefits without government intervention. The latter are financial costs imposed on others in the market *because of the operation of the market as a pricing system*. When demand rises because more buyers enter the market, prices will rise,

---

13. For a survey of the literature on the effectiveness of industrial development bonds, see Thomas L. Martin, "Tax-Exempt Development Bonds: Arguments and Evidence Concerning Their Effect on Business Mobility" (Clemson, S.C.: Economics Department, Clemson University, 1982), especially Section III.

14. Ibid.

15. James R. Rinehart, "Rates of Return on Municipal Subsidies to Industry," *Southern Economic Review* 29 (1961): 297–306.

imposing in the process a greater financial or pecuniary burden on buyers who were in the market prior to the demand increases and who still want to buy the good at the higher price. Technological externalities result in misleading pricing signals and consequent misallocation of resources. Pecuniary externalities, on the other hand, are the pricing signals that give market directions to resources.

Local government subsidies can and often do give rise to jobs, which in turn may give rise to other employment opportunities within the community. The problem is that this is only part of the story. A complete assessment of subsidies in any form and for any purpose requires a look at the costs of community development strategies.

Local government subsidies to attract or retain industrial plants must come out of the pockets of people, either as taxes or borrowed funds. The drain on these pockets will also have multiplying effects, but in the opposite direction of the subsidies. The relevant questions are whether the subsidies *on balance* give rise to more jobs within the community; whether the costs and benefits of the program are in time equally distributed among the residents and, if they are, whether taking from Peter to give to Paul can be justified on ethical or community welfare grounds; and which level or levels of government are best suited for funding industrialization or reindustrialization programs. All of these issues come down to the highly normative, but politically sensitive question of whether governments as a matter of organizational prerogative should be allowed to compete for industries by providing specially targeted benefits for prospective or distressed firms within communities. The analysis relates directly to the issue of the appropriate regulation *of* government (not *by* government).

As a matter of national policy, federal efforts to encourage plant openings or discourage plant closings with federally financed concessions through industrial development bonds and economic development grants must be seriously questioned. To see the validity of this point of view, consider first the position of the individual, "very small" local government. For this local government the "employment and tax base multiplier" justification for opening and closure concessions has (depending on the size of the locality and how other communities respond) a measure of validity.

Especially for very small communities, taxes that are collected from local residents would largely have been spent on goods and services imported from elsewhere. While some jobs may be lost initially in the community because of a decrease in local purchases by the citizens who must pay the subsidy bill, more jobs *can be*, but not necessarily will be, added than lost. In this idealized small community, the costs of the industrial subsidies will, by the virtue of the community's size, tend to be paid by the beneficiaries of the subsidies (there will tend to be few externalities on the tax or subsidy side of the industrial concession). The subsidy will therefore tend to be evaluated by the voting residents, as all efficient economic decisions should be, in light of the *full* costs and benefits of the proposal. It should furthermore be noted that the emerging competition among many small local governments can result in lower tax rates and higher quality local government services. These lower tax rates and improved services can stimulate investment.

Under small local government competition, a discriminatory tax and service policy (one that differentially benefits one group of businesses at the expense of other residents and businesses) will be difficult to maintain. Those local firms and residents who feel they are discriminated against in the taxes they pay or the services they receive retain the option to move elsewhere. The smallness of the political units ensures the existence of location options.

If the concessions do not result in lower taxes and higher quality services, then the concessions will tend not to be made. As economist Charles Tiebout has persuasively argued,[16] concessions in the "small government" political environment tend to be a part of a positive-sum game because concessions that are unproductive on balance will reduce the overall competitiveness of the community and thus become counterproductive; the local government would then have to make concessions to offset its relatively higher taxes, thereby prompting the exodus of firms and residents. Any differences that exist in the way local governments treat firms in such a competitive government environment must reflect differences in the costs of collecting taxes or providing services to different types and sizes of businesses. To reemphasize a fundamental point, if a "small" local community attempts on balance to help one business group at the expense of another, the group that is penalized will move elsewhere, saddling those who are the beneficiaries of the concessions with the entire tax burden.

---

16. Charles M. Tiebout, "A Pure Theory of Local Expenditures," *Journal of Political Economy* (1956): 416–24.

When small governments make concessions, externalities of a sort tend to exist.[17] The governments that make the business concessions force other governments to make similar concessions. These "externalities" are market signals like prices, however; they induce governments to operate efficiently and aid in allocating public resources among competing uses.

As a community becomes larger and more inclusive, concession-bargaining becomes progressively more questionable from both efficiency and equity perspectives for the community that makes the concessions. In a very large community—for example, a country the size of the United States—the funds for the concession will be drawn from people who would have spent most of their income within the community. Any concession, then, tends to result not in an increase in the tax or employment base for the community (i.e., the country), but a locational shift in the tax and employment base within the community. Although a shift in the tax and employment base may be a legitimate objective of government, the point here is that as the community becomes larger the multiplier argument developed above tends to lose its relevance. The concession may have a positive multiplier effect within individual sectors of the community, but the taxes will tend to have a negative offsetting multiplier effect within other sectors of the larger community. Given these conclusions, critical questions abound when any reindustrialization proposal is tendered at the federal level. For example, why would a country the size of the United States be interested in funding concessions that would divert jobs from cities and towns in Kentucky or Idaho to cities and towns in Michigan? What is the market failure involved? Indeed, the movement of firms from Michigan to Kentucky may be a clear indication that the market is working well and sending out the right signals. To the extent that federal funding of concessions is not uniformly distributed, government can distort signals, giving rise to a government-imposed externality.

It is arguable that federally funded business subsidies are a means of offsetting union-imposed wages that are rigidly held above competitive levels and are standardized across the country. From this perspective, federal subsidies may be seen as a second-best policy—a means of adjusting regional pricing signals to reflect true regional comparative advantages obscured by uniform wage rates. Problems

---

17. Again, these are pecuniary externalities.

abound with this argument, however. First, federal subsidies can be a means of encouraging communities and worker groups to accept rigid wage structures. Second, since costs are largely subjective, it could be asked whether government is capable, even conceptually, of appropriately assessing the comparative advantages of different regions. Third, government subsidies will not delay the breakdown of uniform wage signals. Fourth, the policy of income redistribution implicit in such subsidies (which may very well be from the relatively poor to the relatively rich) may not be in line with social objectives expressed by an array of other government policies. If government concession funding is distributed uniformly across communities, with no implied redistribution of purchasing power, the federal funding will lead to a competitive bidding war among communities (as federal funding has)[18] with most of the funds being realized in subsidies to the owners of footloose capital (and the more mobile the capital, the greater the subsidy, other things being equal). Some investment will be stimulated by the federal funding, but some investment will be deterred by the taxes involved. And there is the question of whether subsidizing business according to the mobility of capital should be a national objective. The subsidies will certainly encourage capital mobility, which is seen as the source of major social problems by advocates of reindustrialization policies.[19]

In larger communities, business concessions have a greater potential for being a negative-sum game. One group can seek concessions, imposing its cost on the rest of the community. In the national community, people have few havens where they can escape the tax burden imposed by the concessions. Indeed, it is the people's relative inability to avoid the tax burden of redistributive programs that gives a central government the monopoly power to charge higher than competitive tax rates, to provide lower than competitive services, and to benefit one group at the expense of another group. This increasing inability of people to move as the inclusiveness of government grows has led advocates of welfare programs to contend that redistributive programs should be a function of the federal government. When applied to business location and closing decisions, however, the ethics of the redistributive objective must be raised. The concession subsidy can easily benefit the relatively high-income workers,

18. Martin, "Tax-Exempt Development Bonds."
19. See Barry Bluestone and Bennett Harrison, *The Deindustrialization of America* (New York: Basic Books, 1982), chapter 4.

managers, and stockholders of firms at the expense of the rest of the community, many of whom may have lower incomes than those who benefit from the concession. Indeed, the high, noncompetitive wages of the workers involved may often be the source of the economic difficulties of companies contemplating closure.

Furthermore, workers always have an option of attracting employers or preventing their employers from moving elsewhere simply by accepting lower wages and allowing the company to remain cost competitive. If workers cannot lower their wages sufficiently to attract or retain their jobs, then resources in the firm, including the employees, should move elsewhere. If in the absence of the concession, workers cannot regain employment at approximately the same wage, then their wage is artificially high because of restrictions on the labor market, and the concession becomes a means by which workers in the community (i.e., the country) who may be earning competitive wages are forced, because of the tax and subsidy system, to prop up the wages of other workers that are above competitive levels. The ethical content of such an arrangement must be suspect, especially since it is the relatively higher income, perhaps unionized, workers, who will tend to possess the needed political power to attract subsidies and hence be the beneficiaries of them.

In short, as a community becomes larger, concession-bargaining is likely to create problems of externalities rather than reduce them. The political decisions made to subsidize one set of firms will come at a cost that is "externalized" by way of the tax system to the rest of the population. If all groups enter the concession game, asking to be treated like other groups with special government programs, then more resources will be spent in the *political arena* attempt to shift community resources from one group to another, and fewer resources will be spent and less income will be generated in the private sector.

MARGINAL AND INFRAMARGINAL CONCESSIONS

In the highly competitive world of inter-government rivalry for industry, concessions on plant closings (such as the concessions that Detroit made for GM and Springfield made to International Harvester) are a natural, expected outgrowth of concessions on new plant locations. Knowing that a community is so eager to attract new employment opportunities and additions to its tax base that it will offer tax and benefit concessions to prospective industries, existing industries will see the value in the threat of withdrawal from that community. All other conditions being equal, a city should be at least as eager to *keep* its industrial base as it is to build on it, and it should therefore be willing to make the same concessions to existing firms as to prospective firms.

When concession subsidies are initially provided, they may indeed be expected to affect marginally the level as well as the distribution of industrial investment. But with the passage of time, the concession benefits will become more generous and/or the quantitative and distributional impact of any given funding level on investment will begin to dissipate as all firms contemplating a location decision learn how to take advantage of concession bargaining and as existing firms that may not be contemplating an expansion or a move learn that concession bargaining over expansions can be applied to concession bargaining over closings. Accordingly, over time, funds intended to affect marginal investment decisions will be soaked up by what would have remained, in the absence of the concessions, inframarginal investment decisions. Alternately, the budget for concessions can be expected to escalate as both inframarginal and marginal business location decisions are subsidized.

LARGE VERSUS SMALL FIRMS

The problem with concessions stems from the monopoly power assumed by governments (which arises because of the cost of relocation). The concessions can be discriminatory in the sense that the tax burden they generate is imposed on one group of residents at the expense of another group. The groups that benefit are likely to be those having the political clout to redistribute income in their own favor. These groups are likely to represent large-scale employers whose employees represent a voting bloc and whose departure may cause severe hardship for the community. International Harvester's proposal to Fort Wayne and Springfield that those communities buy and then lease out Harvester's plants attracted the attention of community leaders not because Harvester was the only firm about to leave those cities in 1982 but because it controlled a substantial block of jobs, voters, and a tax base.

The uneven distribution of economic and political power among employers means that the fundamental tax principle that equals should be treated equally will be violated. The larger employers will receive favorable tax treatment independent of the cost of providing the services or collecting the taxes. In addition, subsidies that tend to favor large firms will in themselves encourage larger firms than cost and technology conditions would dictate, generating a market inefficiency of its own.[20]

CONCLUDING COMMENTS

The significant changes in industrial location strategies in recent decades have lent an element of validity to arguments for plant closing restrictions. These changes have occurred partly in response to the willingness of federal, state, and local governments to use taxpayer monies to subsidize industries. A central argument of this chapter has been that subsidies intended for industrial expansions will eventually be used to prevent plant closings because firms will sooner or later learn that communities willing to subsidize to attract new industries should be just as willing to subsidize to retain existing ones.

Federal government involvement in industrial location decisions, by way of tax-exempt industrial development bonds and economic development grants issued by local and state governments, has escalated dramatically over the past two decades. In 1960 the dollar volume of industrial development bonds (IDBs) amounted to only $46 million (double that of 1957); by 1967 the dollar volume had reached $1.5 billion; by 1981 the dollar volume was $10 billion.[21]

20. If subsidies are concentrated on firms that are failing, larger firms will be able to shift the sources of their revenues among plants in different communities, "justifying" subsidies in a way that smaller firms with only one location cannot.

21. Many of these bonds were used to finance investment projects of a number of relatively large companies. In 1978–1979 Mobil Oil received IDB financing to the tune of $63 million; Atlantic Richfield, $61 million; General Mills, $26 million; and Standard Oil of Ohio, a whopping $675 million. See James T. Bennett and Thomas J. Dilorenzo, "The Political Economy of Corporate Welfare: Industrial Revenue Bonds," *Cato Journal* (Fall 1982): 607–16.

Federal economic regional development grants from the Commerce Department to states have risen equally dramatically from $127 million in 1969 to $500 million in 1981, and a substantial portion of these grants (how much cannot be calculated with precision) has been used to aid communities in financing industrial concessions. (Additional economic development funds are no doubt included in the budgets of other federal departments.) This rapid increase in IDBs and federal grants is symptomatic of a tendency of competing communities to make use of all inducements at their disposal to attract industry. It also reflects the attitudes of communities interested in ensuring that they do not lose their competitive position and their existing tax bases.

These figures on IDBs and economic development grants also represent a redistribution of the tax burden that is difficult to justify on efficiency or welfare grounds. It is time that centralized—specifically federal—efforts to affect business expansion and closing decisions be reevaluated. Given that subsidies for expansions will inevitably be converted to subsidies to prevent closings, it follows that such subsidies will be granted to large, politically powerful firms. It is difficult to understand why the federal government, especially, should as a matter of economic development policy become involved in redirecting the flow of jobs from those communities and workers who are willing to remain competitive to others who must be subsidized to compete.

Chapter 7

SOLUTIONS TO PLANT CLOSINGS

As this study was being completed, the *Washington Post* carried a report about the Exxon Corporation's withdrawal from its shale oil business.[1] Exxon's pullout meant closing down a mining project near Parachute, Colorado, in which it had invested $400 million "re-arranging the mountainside above this one-stoplight town."[2] The article vividly captured the emotions surrounding plant closings and spoke, albeit indirectly, of the appeal of plant closing restrictions.

The Exxon story had all of the important elements of a great human interest report: a picture of a recently unemployed worker loading his van, an aerial view of a town that obviously had been hastily expanded to accommodate the anticipated boom in the shale oil business (given the high prices of gasoline in the late 1970s), and interviews with several of the 2,100 workers at the project who had been or would be terminated and who were understandably distressed by the few prospects they had for reemployment in Parachute. The report told of one family that had recently bought a $35,000 home and of parents who had left their children in Wilkes-Barre, Pennsylvania, and borrowed $1,500 to make the trip to Parachute "with the promise of a job," only to arrive two days after the announcement of the closing.

It is difficult for anyone to read such a report (and, admittedly, it is one that has been written time and time again across the United

1. "Busted Boomtown: Parachute Fails to Open," *Washington Post*, 7 May 1982, p. A1.
2. Ibid.

States with differing casts of characters and settings) without feeling sorry for the affected workers, without being moved to think that something should be done to prevent the harmful results of such closings. "There ought to be a law . . . " is a refrain that appears to be particularly applicable to the problem of business closings. After all, large companies are often involved, many workers are distressed, and many communities must adjust their budgets to new and sometimes harsh economic realities.

The purpose of this study has not been to deny the economic hardship caused by many, but by no means all, plant closings. Its purpose has been to argue that the proposed legal remedies, outlined in Chapter 1 and detailed in Appendix A, will probably create more social problems than they solve. Legislated restrictions on closings appear on the surface to be direct solutions to a social ill; like so many other presumably straightforward solutions, however, there are serious side-effects that, when examined in the light of logic and facts, make them no solution at all. In this concluding chapter, the central arguments of the foregoing chapters are summarized and alternative solutions for dealing with plant closings are considered.

THE ARGUMENT RESTATED

The case against plant closing restrictions developed here is not a case for unrestricted plant closings. If the market system were as "uncorked" and "irrational" as proponents of restrictions seem to suggest, then governmentally imposed remedies would certainly be in order. A basic tenet of the study, however, is that the market manifests a degree of orderliness brought about by the incentives people have to pursue their own interests and by the coordinating influence of the pricing system. The competitive market process is "destructive," as noted before. *Indeed, the history of progress is a history of the destruction of jobs and businesses.* Improvement requires replacing the "old" with the "new"—old plants with new plants, old jobs with new jobs. This isn't to say that the competitive process works perfectly. Of course, it doesn't. We live in an imperfect world. Mistakes abound. The questions strategic to the consideration of proposed remedies are whether or not one would expect the market to destroy in some irrational manner plants and jobs and whether or not one would expect the proposed restrictive legislation to improve on the imperfect market outcomes. Four themes have been evident:

- Circumstances of people and business differ. Laws applied uniformly across these different circumstances create much inefficiency and hardship.

- Costs are ultimately borne by people, not businesses, and restrictions on plant closings impose costs on people. Someone must pay those costs. The people who benefit from the restrictions will pay a part, if not a major share, of the costs, but many hidden costs will be transferred to people who do not benefit by the restrictions. The diffusion of the costs to others is one of the political attractions of the legislation.

- Because of the costs involved, restrictions on plant closings ultimately translate into restrictions on plant openings. One must wonder whether restrictions can, when considering the full context of market behavior, preserve or even lengthen the employment opportunities of workers.

- Communities or states that institute plant closing legislation will be placed at a competitive disadvantage in seeking long-term employment opportunities. National legislation will tend to make this disadvantage uniform across the country. However, enactment of national legislation means that the United States will be placed at a competitive disadvantage vis-à-vis other countries in attracting industry. Furthermore, such a national law cannot take account of the many geographical and cultural much less individual, differences that exist across the country.

Each state and region will have its preferred set of restrictions, its favored notification and severance pay requirements, for example, that may reflect the dominant political interests in the state or region. Proponents of restrictions seem to think that their preferred set of restrictions is the one that will be enacted and imposed on others, but that cannot be the case. As usual, the politically powerful will get their way in the political process.

SOLUTIONS FOR WORKERS

Notification of impending closings and severance pay when the closings occur are apparently things that many workers want. One way that workers, particularly unionized workers, can secure them is to bargain for them. As we have maintained all along, workers must be prepared to give up something in the form of forgone wages or fringe benefits in exchange for any other set of benefits. A fundamental rule in economics is that "there is no such thing as a free lunch," and that rule cannot and will not be denied in this instance. If workers are willing to pay for the benefits, much as they must be willing to pay for health and life insurance and recreation facilities, employers should be willing to make concessions, within limits. Through bargaining, workers and management can tailor their closing provisions to meet their individual circumstances—and their individual evaluations of the costs and benefits of their own closing restrictions.

There are those who contend that management has no incentive to provide notification to workers of impending closings, and we have noted the problems inherent in notification. Instances in which the market turns so abruptly against businesses that workers cannot be given reasonable notice prior to bankruptcy are inevitable. However, if workers truly want notification benefits and are willing to pay the attendant price, management's interest in profits should make management willing to establish a closing policy. An announced closing policy can make good business sense to management. If a firm announces its closing policy and workers truly value that policy, the firm's supply of workers should expand, resulting in a lower wage bill for the company. The company that has a closing policy should therefore be able to underprice its competition, inducing its competitors to follow its lead in establishing a closing policy.

Such a solution does not mean that business is left to do what it wants. Once a company announces its closing policy, it must be held legally responsible for it, meaning the policy must be seen as a part of the company's contract with its workers. A business that violates its announced closing policy must be treated legally in the same manner as others that breach their contracts are treated.

In 1982 the Singer [Sewing Machine] Company was required to place on deposit $2 million in settlement of a suit brought by its workers when it closed its plant in Elizabeth, New Jersey.[3] The money was scheduled for use in compensating workers for damages they had suffered in their plant's closing. Singer had signed a contract in 1981 that included a promise to spend $2 million to modernize its production facility in Elizabeth and to devote "attention to the procurement of defense work compatible with the plant's ma-

---

3. Bureau of National Affairs, "Scheduled Closing of Plant Prompts Damage Award against Singer Company," *Daily Labor Report* (May 25, 1982): A–1 and 2 and D–1–D–5.

chine shop capabilities. . . . "[4] In exchange, the workers gave up two floating paid holidays per year and two ten-minute rest breaks per day, and the union agreed to reduce from ten to seven the number of paid hours shop stewards could spend on union business and to change the production incentives. Five months after the contract was signed, "Singer halted any plans to restructure the plant, stopped all efforts to secure defense work, and explored the possibility of closing the plant."[5] Although the particulars of the settlement may or may not be unreasonable (and it does appear that the workers got quite a bargain), the legal principle involved deserves broad application. Firms should not be permitted to strike such deals with employees, getting concessions in the process, without being held to their end of the bargain. Workers should be encouraged to make the implied bargains as explicit as possible, if for no other reason than self-protection.

In rebuttal to the argument that plant closing policies should be rigorously structured, proponents of restrictions say that businesses have specialized information, not available to workers, on impending closings. In addition, the information cannot be provided to one worker without being provided to all, and thus, so the argument is developed, individual workers cannot bargain effectively over a closing policy; businesses must be forced by the power of government rules to reveal to their workers their specialized information. In evaluating such a position, we must keep several points in mind. First, firms have specialized information on a host of benefit programs, for example, health and retirement programs, that must be provided all workers (i.e., individual workers usually do not have complete latitude to bargain individually over the types of fringe benefits they receive), but the programs are still provided, and for good reason: employers see in such programs an incentive to provide them a greater labor pool and lower wages.

Second, information is an economic resource, if not a prime resource, undergirding most successful business enterprises. *Forcing* a firm to reveal its information on its closing intentions is tantamount to requiring the firm to give up a very valuable resource like machinery, which must be obtained at some expense. The justice of such a requirement, especially when bargaining alternatives are available, must be suspect.

4. Ibid., p. A–1.
5. Ibid.

Third, if the information is valuable to both the firm and its workers, there would often be some mutually beneficial bargain that could be struck in exchange for more information of impending closings and severance pay.

Fourth, without expecting to become fully informed on the economic health of their firm, workers can infer a great deal of information about their future employment prospects with the firm just by being on the job and observing the demands put on their time. Perhaps employees are not well suited to evaluate the information they have or can obtain on the financial solvency of their firms. Perhaps they know little about how to obtain readily available information, much less use it. After all, evaluating the financial health of a company frequently requires sophisticated financial and accounting skills. If lack of skills is the problem, then it would appear that workers, especially those in a union, can enlist (or buy) the necessary services of financial experts. There are many firms eager to do the required analysis. If workers are not willing to pay the cost of securing the information, then perhaps the workers believe that the information is not really worth the price or that they are better off without the information than with it, given the price that must be paid.

These are not the starry-eyed, academic solutions of market economists. A significant growing percentage of labor contracts contain closing provisions.[6] The unions receiving such protection paid a price—gave up something—to secure those contract provisions. Many companies realize the benefits of establishing a closing policy. General Motors, which must be concerned with how communities receive new plants, has outlined its closing policy, including the following provision: "When possible, GM will give at least six month's advance public notice of any permanent plant closing."[7] Such a public declaration should, and probably does, carry a legal responsibility. During the recession of 1980–82, workers, especially in basic industries like automobiles, tire, and steel, sought to save their jobs in the most effective way possible: offer the company some basis, some incen-

---

6. In 1966 only 5 percent of the union contracts surveyed by BNA had a provision restricting the rights of management to close and relocate. In 1979 the percentage of union contracts with such a provision was 17 percent. The very fact that not more of the contracts required a closing restriction may indicate labor's, as well as management's, assessment of the costs of such provisions. See B.R. Skelton, "Plant Closing Restrictions in Union Contracts," (Clemson, S.C.: Economics Department, Clemson University, 1983).

7. "A Balanced Policy on Plant Closings and Relocations," *General Motors Public Interest Report: 1981* (Detroit: General Motors Corporation, 1981), pp. 30–32.

tive, for staying in business by accepting reductions in the growth of wages and fringe benefits or outright reductions in wages and fringe benefits. In exchange for those concessions, they received guarantees, which again should be legally enforceable, from their companies not to move their plants. As stressed all along, if firms want to move for profit and workers really value the retention of their jobs, striking some mutually beneficial deal should often be possible.

SOLUTIONS FOR COMMUNITIES

Policy alternatives exist for communities that face the prospects of plant closings (and all communities do). One obvious remedy every community has is to actively promote its community to prospective industry. This is the approach taken by Pittsburgh in 1981 with a full-page advertisement in the *Wall Street Journal* portraying the city as "Dynamic Pittsburgh." Every time a city complains bitterly about its economic distress, it can be assured that some company decides to locate elsewhere; it can be certain that other communities elsewhere are pleased because industrial recruitment has for them been made just a little easier. Another perhaps less obvious solution is for the community to remain competitive in terms of taxes and services delivered. We have stressed that profit-maximizing firms will not allow their capital to go down the economic drain. Keeping taxes in line with the taxes paid by other companies in other communities ensures firms of an equal chance of competing in their markets.

Many communities are distressed that industries have set up operations with tax exemptions for a specified period of years. In such arrangements is the making of a legally enforceable quid pro quo. If communities allow companies to escape taxes for a time, then it would appear that a legal presumption exists that the company is getting something, tax relief, in return, for example, for a commitment to remain in operation for a period of time. Such agreements should be made explicit. According to news reports, Parke-Davis and Co. was required to pay the city of Detroit nearly $1 million in compensation in eight annual installments when it decided to leave that city.[8] Although the exact legal details and circumstances of the settlement are unclear, the legal principle behind the settlement does

8. "Firm Pays for Leaving Detroit," *Charleston Daily Mail*, 14 May 1982.

not appear to be unreasonable. Parke-Davis had moved to Detroit three years earlier with an explicit twelve-year tax abatement from the city, and there is reason to believe that Parke-Davis had not honored its part of the obligation. It would appear that similar remedies could be exacted from other companies where a quid pro quo is involved.

Through their savings, workers can provide for their own severance pay benefits. To build a private severance pay fund, equal to the required firm's payments under the typical plant closing bill, a worker would have to save less than two percent of his or her earnings, gaining the interest in the process. Communities can provide for redevelopment funds by following a similar policy: they can set aside a reserve fund from taxes, also earning interest. Such a solution spells higher taxes, a cost on the citizenry. That outcome, as we have emphasized throughout, is no different from plant closing laws. The primary difference between the legally mandated restitution payments and community savings from taxes is that the former is forced on all communities regardless of individual circumstances, while the latter is voluntary and thereby an individual community choice.

Between 1965 and 1980, manufacturing employment in Massachusetts had fallen at a compound rate of about one-half of one percent a year. The long-term trend, however, hides a reversal in the economic hopes of the state. Since 1975, manufacturing employment has risen at a compound rate of 3.3 percent. Although modest in comparison with the rate of employment in the neighboring New England states of Vermont and New Hampshire and a number of states in the West, it is significantly faster than the 2.7 percent growth rate for manufacturing employment in the South during the period.

What explains the reversal in Massachusetts manufacturing employment? Any explanation will necessarily be incomplete. A significant part of the state's manufacturing employment growth is in high technology industries, and a part of the upturn can be explained by the political efforts of the Massachusetts High Technology Council, a group of about 115 businesses interested in expanding the supply of technicians and engineers.

High technology industries were able to expand in New England during the early 1970s because of reductions in the use of engineers and technicians in defense and space industries. According to Ray Stata of Analogue Devices, Inc., however, by the late 1970s the "overhang" in supply of critical personnel had been exhausted. The High Technology Council found that its growth was being capped by a shortage of personnel, which, in turn, was being choked by high state and local taxes on worker incomes. The council turned its efforts toward reducing taxes and helped pass "Proposition 2½," a state constitutional restriction on property taxes similar to the much talked-about Proposition 13 in California.

Stata stresses that the council's main contribution to the political dialogue was getting acceptance of the concept that Massachusetts has to be competitive among states—that in the maintenance of a healthy economic base, a state must keep its taxes in line and keep a watchful eye on how education dollars are being spent. By encouraging businesses to step up their contributions to universities in support of engineering and sciences, council members have put their money where their mouths are. The public-private partnership in Massachusetts has apparently paid off. Other communities can imitate and elaborate on that approach.

CONCLUDING COMMENTS

When all is said and done, plant closing laws are difficult to justify. The case for them is replete with factual errors, distortions, and misrepresentations. The conceptual arguments undergirding them are logically flawed. And private solutions to plant closings exist in a market economy for workers and communities. Above all, plant closing laws are an affront to a people who hold individual freedom dear, who believe that meaningful social progress is made principally through individual adjustment to individual circumstances, free to the greatest extent possible from government intrusion.

APPENDIXES

APPENDIXES

Appendix A

PLANT CLOSING LAWS
Federal and State Proposals

U.S. CONGRESS OR STATE BILL OR PUBLIC LAW (YEAR PROPOSED)	U.S. CONGRESS S. 1608 and H.R. 5040 (1979)
COVERED BUSINESSES	
Minimum Size	Gross annual sales of $250,000 for entire company and with 50 employees at any single establishment (with change permanently affecting the lesser of 100 employees or 15 percent of workforce at any single establishment).
Years in Operation	None specified.
PRE-NOTIFICATION REQUIREMENT	2 years with 500 or more employees; 18 months with 100 to 499 employees; 6 months with fewer than 100 employees.
BUSINESS PAYMENTS TO EMPLOYEES	
Severance Pay	Weekly "income maintenance payment" equal to 85 percent (or 100 percent if employee is in a retraining program) of "weekly equivalent pay" (average hours worked times "highest rate of pay" in previous 2 years for the position held) for 52 weeks, not to exceed $25,000 (extended income maintenance benefits for workers 53 to 61 years old).
Fringe Benefits	Continuation of all benefit programs for as long as income maintenance payments last. (Employees who are 55 may retire with full benefits they are entitled to at 62.)
BUSINESS PAYMENTS TO LOCAL COMMUNITY OR GOVERNMENT AGENCY	85 percent of average taxes paid state and local governments during the previous 3 years for changes within U.S. (300 percent of average taxes paid for moves to locations outside the U.S.)
GOVERNMENT ASSISTANCE TO COVERED AND AFFECTED BUSINESSES	Loans, loan guarantees, interest subsidies, and the assumption of outstanding debt; technical assistance that "may include grants and contracts for research and development in connection with new production or marketing techniques which will create new employment opportunities"; and special procurement arrangements with federal government to improve employment opportunities. Loans, loan guarantees, and technical assistance may also be available to any employer or "cooperative association of employees" for expanding or acquiring an establishment.
GOVERNMENT ASSISTANCE TO AFFECTED COMMUNITIES	Grants, loans, and loan guarantees, provided local unit has suffered a "substantial decrease in income."

U.S. CONGRESS **H.R. 2847 (1983)**	**Alabama** **H. 308 (1979)**

50 employees at any single establishment (with change permanently affecting the lesser of 100 employees or 15 percent of the employees).	50 employees within entire company for any 6 of the preceding 12 months (with change permanently affecting the lesser of 250 employees of entire company or 50 percent of workforce at any single establishment).
None specified.	5 years within the state.
1 year with 100 or more employees; 6 months with fewer than 100 employees.	1 year.
Same as 1979 bill with the provision that the income maintenance payment will equal 100 percent of the average wage if the worker is participating in a training program.	"Severance benefits" equal to "average weekly wage" (including benefits) times number of years employed.
Same as 1979 bill.	Included indirectly in severance pay (above).
Same as 1979 bill.	None specified.
Same as 1979 bill with more attention given to federal aid to affected employees to cover retraining, job placement job search (up to $600), and moving to a new job.	Nothing specific. (Commissioner of Labor "may assist in maintaining and restoring the level of employment.")
Same as 1979 bill.	Nothing specific. (Commissioner of Labor "may assist in maintaining and restoring the level of employment.")

U. S. CONGRESS OR STAFF BILL OR PUBLIC LAW (YEAR PROPOSED)	California S. 1109, 1110, 1112, 1114, and 1117 (1981)
COVERED BUSINESSES	
Minimum Size	100 employees within entire company (with any "reduction in operations" permanently affecting 50 percent of workforce at any single establishment over any 2-year period and any closing or "relocation" permanently affecting 15 percent of the workforce at any single establishment).
Years in Operation	5 years within state.
PRE-NOTIFICATION REQUIREMENT	1 year.
BUSINESS PAYMENTS TO EMPLOYEES	
Severance Pay	"Discharge payment" equal to one week's pay (undefined) for each year employed.
Fringe Benefits	Continuation of health insurance for as long as employees are eligible for unemployment compensation and indefinite continuation of disability insurance. (Job retraining to be paid by employer.) 10 percent of "total annual wages" of affected workers.
BUSINESS PAYMENTS TO LOCAL COMMUNITY OR GOVERNMENT AGENCY	None specified.
GOVERNMENT ASSISTANCE TO COVERED AND AFFECTED BUSINESSES	Unspecified aid to lending institutions that are mortagees of dwellings owned by affected employees.
GOVERNMENT ASSISTANCE TO AFFECTED COMMUNITIES	Technical advice in identifying sources of state and federal readjustment funds.

Connecticut S. 333 and 334 (1979)	Hawaii H. 2345–80 and S. 2441
100 employees who are residents of Connecticut during the preceding 12 months (with change affecting 100 employees or 5 percent of all employees, whichever is larger).	Any business concern that has not less than $1 million in gross annual business or sales with change in operations affecting any establishment employing 50 people.
3 years within the state.	None specified.
30 days for any planned layoff and 90 days for any planned relocation.	1 year.
None specified.	Severance pay equal to the difference between unemployment compensation and 85 percent of full-time weekly pay for up to 52 weeks (up to 104 weeks for workers 55 and older).
None specified.	Continuation of health insurance benefits for up to one year and relocation allowance.
None specified.	None specified.
None specified.	None specified.
None specified.	Loans to "eligible organizations" for the purpose of acquiring ownership of establishment.

U.S. CONGRESS OR STATE BILL OR PUBLIC LAW (YEAR PROPOSED)	**Illinois** **H. 0954 (1981)**
COVERED BUSINESSES	
Minimum Size	None specified.
Years in Operation	None specified.
PRE-NOTIFICATION REQUIREMENT	None specified.
BUSINESS PAYMENTS TO EMPLOYEES	
Severance Pay	None specified.
Fringe Benefits	None specified.
BUSINESS PAYMENTS TO LOCAL COMMUNITY OR GOVERNMENT AGENCY	None specified.
GOVERNMENT ASSISTANCE TO COVERED AND AFFECTED BUSINESSES	Establishes the Office of Job Protection that has the power to investigate plant closings and relocations to places outside of state, to report on their economic impacts, and "to make recommendations regarding actions by state, federal and local governments to prevent or minimize the effects of the job loss."
GOVERNMENT ASSISTANCE TO AFFECTED COMMUNITIES	Officer of Job Protection is instructed to inform "communities and employees directly affected by plant closings or relocations of all resources and services . . . available to them."

Indiana
H. 1274 (1981)

100 employees within entire company (with "reduction in operations" permanently affecting 50 percent of workforce over any 2-year period and "relocation" permanently affecting 15 percent of the workforce at any single establishment).

5 years within the state.

1 year in Sec. 3 (c) [2 years in Sec. 5 (c); discrepancy unexplained].

"Lump sum payments" equal to 4 times the "average weekly wage" times the number of years employed plus 1.

Continuation of health insurance for 1 year.

None specified.

None specified.

Maine
Stat. 625–A ("Severance Pay")

100 employees at any single establishment at any time during the preceding year (with "relocation" and "terminations" resulting in a "substantial" permanent reduction in operations).

3 years within the state.

60 days.

"Severance pay" equal to "average week's pay" times the number of years employed.

None specified.

None specified.

None specified.

U. S. CONGRESS OR STAFF BILL OR PUBLIC LAW (YEAR PROPOSED)	**Massachusetts** **H. 1541 and 1946 [S. 71] (1981)**
COVERED BUSINESSES	
Minimum Size	50 employees in entire company at one time during at least 6 of the last 12 months (with "mass separation" affecting 250 workers or 50 percent of the "base employment level" at any single establishment) [100 workers in past year].
Years in Operation	5 years
PRE-NOTIFICATION REQUIREMENT	1 year [60 days].
BUSINESS PAYMENTS TO EMPLOYEES	
Severance Pay	Lump sum severance pay equal to "average weekly wage" (including all benefits) times years worked.
Fringe Benefits	Incorporated in severance pay.
BUSINESS PAYMENTS TO LOCAL COMMUNITY OR GOVERNMENT AGENCY	15 percent of total of all compensation, including all benefits, for previous 12 months (to Community Jobs Assistance Fund) to be used in part to cover unpaid severance benefits.
GOVERNMENT ASSISTANCE TO COVERED AND AFFECTED BUSINESSES	None specified.
GOVERNMENT ASSISTANCE TO AFFECTED COMMUNITIES	Economic redevelopment grants and loans to provide employment opportunities for affected workers, technical assistance, and matching funds to secure federal grants.

Michigan H. 4330 (1981)	Minnesota S.F. 294 (1981)
100 employees in the entire company at one time during 6 or more of preceding 12 months (with the minimum number of affected employees related to total employment at any single establishment).	100 employees within entire company during six or more months of preceding year.
5 years. 1 year.	5 years within the state. 2 years.
"Severance benefit" equal to "average weekly wage" times number of years employed *only if* the employer fails to provide proper notice or to provide paid leave time of up to two weeks (depending on years employed) to look for a job.	"Severance benefit" equal to "average weekly wage" times the number of years employed.
Continuation of health insurance for up to 1 year.	Health insurance to be continued for one year (plus up to 2 weeks of paid leave for searching for new employment).
None specified.	10 percent of the "total annual wage" of affected employees (paid to the Community Job Assistance Fund).
Community Service Council "may offer assistance . . . to promote operations" and to "evaluate the feasibility of a proposed employee-owned corporation."	Community Services Council may "offer assistance to the employer to promote operations."
Community Service Council may "attempt to persuade or induce state and local officials to grant emergency tax relief to an affected governmental subdivision."	Community Services Council may "provide direct financial assistance to affected employees; provide a grant or loan to affected municipality; . . . evaluate the feasibility of employee owned corporation; attempt to persuade or induce state and local officials to grant emergency tax relief to an affected municipality; apply for state and federal grants."

U.S. CONGRESS OR STATE BILL OR PUBLIC LAW (YEAR PROPOSED)	Missouri H. 775 (1981)
COVERED BUSINESSES	
Minimum Size	50 employees within entire company (affecting 15 percent of the workforce).
Years in Operation	None specified.
PRE-NOTIFICATION REQUIREMENT	1 year.
BUSINESS PAYMENTS TO EMPLOYEES	
Severance Pay	"Lump sum payment" equal to the "average weekly wage" times the number of years employed."
Fringe Benefits	Continuation of health insurance for 6 months.
BUSINESS PAYMENTS TO LOCAL COMMUNITY OR GOVERNMENT AGENCY	15 percent of the "total annual wages" of affected employees (to the Employee Protection and Community Stabilization Fund).
GOVERNMENT ASSISTANCE TO COVERED AND AFFECTED BUSINESSES	The Labor and Industrial Relations Commission may "contract to provide loans or interest subsidies to, and to guarantee or endorse the bonds, notes, contracts, or other obligations of, or otherwise assist financially" any covered business or any "development project" of other businesses in the "target area."
GOVERNMENT ASSISTANCE TO AFFECTED COMMUNITIES	The Labor and Industrial Relations Commission may "provide grants to, or contract to provide loans or interest subsidies to, or guarantee or endorse the bonds, notes, contracts, or other obligations of, or otherwise assist any "community development corporation." Similar financial assistance, plus technical assistance, in any employee-community-owned company.

Montana S. 250 (1981) [H. 339 and 842 (1981)]	New Hampshire H. 497–FN
250 employees at a single establishment (affecting at least 250 workers over any two-year period).	50 employees (with change affecting 20 percent of the employees at any single establishment).
5 years.	3 years within state.
Upon making the decision to close.	"Whenever a business concern has reason to believe that one of its establishments will or is likely to undergo" a change of operations.
"Lump sum payment" equal to "average *monthly* wage" times number of years employed, not to exceed $25,000.	"Lump sum" equal to "twice the employee's average weekly wage multiplied by the number of years" employed.
Continuation of health insurance for 6 months.	Continuation of health benefit coverage for a year.
25 percent of "annual payroll" of affected workers.	15 percent of total wages for previous 12 months of all affected employees.
Nothing specific. The Department of Labor and Industry may "develop plans for alleviating the effects of present and future closings and retrenchments." [H. 842 provides for grants to businesses of up to $1.5 million and credits against license taxes of up to $5 million for areas declared to be "severely economically impacted."]	"Grants and loans to organizations" for the "purchase and operation of establishments contemplating or undergoing" a change of operations.
Redevelopment grants to assist local governments and groups of 10 or more of the affected workers to form an employee-owned company (including the purchase of equity capital). [H. 339 broadens the definition of eminent domain to include the taking of private property "to offset the adverse economic effect of a workplace closure."]	"Emergency tax relief when the community faces substantial loss of tax receipts" and funds for community development projects "designed to minimize or prevent the loss of employment, wages, and tax revenue."

U.S. CONGRESS OR STATE BILL OR PUBLIC LAW (YEAR PROPOSED)	**New Jersey** **A. 61 (1980)**
COVERED BUSINESSES	
Minimum Size	100 employees including "parent corporation and all subsidiaries" (with change permanently affecting 15 percent of workforce at any single establishment).
Years in Operation	None specified.
PRE-NOTIFICATION REQUIREMENT	1 year.
BUSINESS PAYMENTS TO EMPLOYEES	
Severance Pay	None specified.
Fringe Benefits	None specified.
BUSINESS PAYMENTS TO LOCAL COMMUNITY OR GOVERNMENT AGENCY	None specified.
GOVERNMENT ASSISTANCE TO COVERED AND AFFECTED BUSINESSES	None specified.
GOVERNMENT ASSISTANCE TO AFFECTED COMMUNITIES	Grants (of up to 75 percent of the eligible revenue loss) for up to 3 years in unspecified forms if a closing or transfer of one or more plants causes the unemployment rate to exceed 8 percent on a seasonally adjusted basis and if there is a "substantial revenue loss."

New York A. 6351 (1981)	Ohio S. 188 and H. 968 (1980)
50 employees at any one establishment (affecting 50 or more employees).	100 employees within entire company (with "reduction in operations" permanently affecting 50 percent of workforce at any single establishment over any 2-year period and "relocation" permanently affecting 10 percent of the workforce at any single establishment).
4 years.	5 years within the state.
9 months to employees; 1 year to commissioners of labor and commerce.	2 years.
"Lump sum payment" equal to "highest weekly salary" during past 52 weeks times number of years employed (excluding workers employed for less than 2 years).	"Lump sum payments" equal to "average weekly wage" during previous 2 years times number of years worked.
None specified.	Continuation of "any" health insurance program for 6 months.
None specified. [Firm must, however, provide a feasibility study for an employee takeover of the business.]	10 percent of total annual wage of all affected workers (to Community Readjustment Funds).
Technical assistance in avoiding a closure or reduction in operations and in securing funds from Job Development Authority, the New York Business Development Corporation, the Industrial Development Agencies, or other state and federal programs.	Redevelopment projects, presumably involving local businesses, to improve employment opportunities.
None specified.	Readjustment grants to provide for reemployment opportunities of affected workers, tax relief of affected political subdivision, matching funds to secure federal redevelopment grants, redevelopment planning, and "other redevelopment projects."

U. S. CONGRESS OR STATE BILL OR PUBLIC LAW (YEAR PROPOSED)	Oregon H. 2550 (1981)
COVERED BUSINESSES	
Minimum Size	50 employees at any single establishment within state (with "layoff" or reduction in operations" affecting 15 or more employees at any single establishment for longer than 3 months).
Years in Operation	None specified.
PRE-NOTIFICATION REQUIREMENT	1 year within state.
BUSINESS PAYMENTS TO EMPLOYEES	
Severance Pay	Weekly "income maintenance payments" equal to 85 percent (or 100 percent if employee is in a retraining program) of "average weekly wage" for up to 52 weeks, not to exceed $30,000.
Fringe Benefits	Continuation of all benefit programs (plus, insure provision of home mortgage loans to relocate workers at interest rates no higher than workers paid at original location).
BUSINESS PAYMENTS TO LOCAL COMMUNITY OR GOVERNMENT AGENCY	85 percent of previous year's taxes for closures and relocations within the state; 300 percent of previous year's taxes if relocation is outside of state (plus, denial of Oregon tax credits and benefits associated with the move).
GOVERNMENT ASSISTANCE TO COVERED AND AFFECTED BUSINESSES	Nothing specific (but state can conduct "an investigation of alternatives to a reduction in operations and make recommendations").
GOVERNMENT ASSISTANCE TO AFFECTED COMMUNITIES	Economic redevelopment grants and low interest rate loans to create employment opportunities and technical assistance to employees and/or community groups interested in taking over, financing (with low interest loans from state and federal sources), and managing the business.

Pennsylvania	Washington
H. 1251 (1979)	H. 398 (1981)

50 employees at any single establishment (with "reduction in operations" permanently affecting 35 percent of the workforce at any single establishment over any 2-year period).

50 employees at any single establishment within state (with "layoff" or "reduction in operations" permanently affecting 15 or more employees at any single establishment for longer than 3 months).

None specified.

None specified.

1 year.

1 year.

"Lump sum payment" equal to "average weekly wage" times number of years worked.

Weekly "income maintenance payments" equal to 85 percent (or 100 percent if employee is in a retraining program) of "average weekly wage" for up to 52 weeks, not to exceed $30,000.

Continuation of health insurance for 6 months.

Continuation of all benefit programs (plus, insure provision of home mortgage loans to relocate workers at interest rates no higher than workers paid at original location).

15 percent of "total annual wages" of affected workers (to Employee Protection and Community Stabilization Fund).

85 percent of previous year's taxes for closures and relocations within the state; 300 percent of previous year's taxes if relocation is outside of state (plus, denial of Washington tax credits and benefits associated with the move).

Loans (not to exceed 50 percent of project) or interest subsidies, loan guarantees, contracts, or other unspecified financial assistance to *any* firm in the "target area."

Nothing specific (but state can conduct "an investigation of alternatives to a reduction in operations and make recommendations").

Same as for employers and affected businesses.

Economic redevelopment grants and low interest rate loans to create employment opportunities and technical assistance to employees and/or community groups interested in taking over, financing (with low interest loans from state and federal sources), and managing the business.

U.S. CONGRESS OR STATE BILL OR PUBLIC LAW (YEAR PROPOSED)	West Virginia S. 344 (1980)
COVERED BUSINESSES	
Minimum Size	100 employees within entire company (with "reduction in operations" permanently affecting 50 percent of workforce over any 2-year period and "relocation" permanently affecting 10 percent of the workforce at any single plant).
Years in Operation	5 years within state.
PRE-NOTIFICATION REQUIREMENT	2 years.
BUSINESS PAYMENTS TO EMPLOYEES	
Severance Pay	"Lump sum payment" equal to average weekly wage during previous two years times number of years worked.
Fringe Benefits	Continuation of health insurance for 6 months.
BUSINESS PAYMENTS TO LOCAL COMMUNITY OR GOVERNMENT AGENCY	10 percent of "average total wages" of affected workers over previous two years.
GOVERNMENT ASSISTANCE TO COVERED AND AFFECTED BUSINESSES	None specified.
GOVERNMENT ASSISTANCE TO AFFECTED COMMUNITIES	Redevelopment grants to community to provide for reemployment of affected workers and tax relief.

U.S. CONGRESS OR STATE BILL OR PUBLIC LAW (YEAR PROPOSED)	**Wisconsin** **Stat. 109.17 (1) (1975)**
COVERED BUSINESSES	
Minimum Size	100 employees in the estate.
Years in Operation	None specified.
PRE-NOTIFICATION REQUIREMENT	60 days.
BUSINESS PAYMENTS TO EMPLOYEES	
Severance Pay	None specified.
Fringe Benefits	None specified.
BUSINESS PAYMENTS TO LOCAL COMMUNITY OR GOVERNMENT AGENCY	None specified.
GOVERNMENT ASSISTANCE TO COVERED AND AFFECTED BUSINESSES	None specified.
GOVERNMENT ASSISTANCE TO AFFECTED COMMUNITIES	None specified.

Summary of the Major Provisions of the National Employment Priorities Act of 1979, H.R. 5040

A. Requires prenotification to affected employees and communities of dislocation of business concerns.
B. Provides assistance (including retraining) to:
  1. employees who suffer employment loss through the dislocation of business concerns;
  2. business concerns threatened with dislocation; and
  3. affected communities.

Brief Section-By-Section Analysis

Section 1. Short Title

Provides that the act may be cited as the "National Employment Priorities Act of 1979" (NEPA).

Section 2. Findings and Purpose

The Congress declares that:

  1. unemployment is a major economic and social problem which causes great loss to individuals, communities, and the Nation;
  2. irresponsible and unnecessary changes of operations at establishments of business concerns disrupt commerce and cause unemployment to increase drastically in local areas; and
  3. economic planning is needed to avert the dislocation of employment opportunities, and new mechanisms of public control are needed to insure that private investment decisions conform more closely to employee and community needs.

It is the purpose of this Act to prevent or minimize the harmful economic and social effects of unemployment on employees and on local governments caused when business concerns undertake changes of operations.

Section 3. Definitions

Section 4. Notice of Intent to Change Operations

Provides that if 15 percent of the employees of the establishment will suffer an employment loss as a result of the transfer or closing, an agent of the establishment must furnish the Secretary of Labor, the affected employees and the local government written notice of its intent not less than 2 years in advance of closing or transfer where the number of employees suffering an employment loss is greater than 500; 18 months where the number is between 100 and 500; and 6 months where the number is less than 100.

Section 5. Investigation of Intended Closing or Transfer

Provides that, if within 60 days after the receipt of notice of intent to close an establishment, a labor organization or 10 percent of the employees of such establishment requests an investigation of a proposed closing; or if before receipt of notice 50 percent of the employees at an establishment request such an investigation; or if the Secretary determines it would serve the purposes of this Act, the Secretary shall conduct a thorough investigation, including public hearings. The Secretary has subpoena power.

Section 6. Report of Investigation

Provides that at the conclusion of the investigation of a proposed closing or transfer, the Secretary shall prepare and publish a report containing findings with respect to:

1. the economic reasons for the intended change of operations,
2. the estimated extent of any economic or social loss to the employees affected,
3. the estimated economic or social loss to any affected unit of general local government and to local businesses,
4. the recommendations of affected labor organizations, local governments, and other interested persons,
5. the feasibility of preventing or minimizing such employment loss by the modification of product lines and production techniques, and
6. the Secretary's recommendations regarding actions to be taken in order to prevent or minimize the harmful effects which will result from the closing or transfer.

Section 7. Ineligibility of Certain Employees for Assistance

Individuals hired after notice of an intended change of operations is given, with knowledge of such notice, shall be ineligible for the assistance provided under the Act.

Section 8. Notice of Employment Status

When a business concern closes an establishment or transfers an operation and lays off or reduces the wages of its employees, it shall give the affected employees a written statement of employment status. If the statement does not assure that the employee will have his wages or employment restored within 26 weeks, the business concern shall begin making income maintenance payments immediately. If the statement contains such assurances and the business concern fails to prevent the employee's employment loss, it shall pay the employee a penalty equal to 26 weeks of income maintenance payments.

Section 9. Transitional Assistance by Business Concerns

1. Any business concern required to give notice shall pay its employees who suffer an employment loss 85 percent of their average wage, reduced by earned income, unemployment compensation and trade adjustment assistance, for a period of 52 weeks. No business concern shall be required to make total payments to an employee in excess of $25,000. No business concern shall be required to make payments to an employee who refuses a job providing wages as high as those in his old job, substantially equivalent benefits, and which utilizes substantially similar skills. No business concern shall be required to make payments to an employee who refuses to participate in or make good progress in a training or placement program provided under this Act.
2. A business concern required to give notice shall pay the relocation expenses of any employee who accepts a transfer to an establishment of the business concern which is beyond reasonable commuting distance.
3. Older workers shall be entitled to extended benefit payments, for which the business concern shall be reimbursed by the Secretary.
4. When a business concern fails to make a payment required by this section, the amount becomes a debt to the United States and the Secretary shall make the payment at the employee's request.

Section 10. Secondary Liability

Provides that a business concern which transfers ownership of an establishment to avoid liability under this Act shall be liable to the United States to the extent the new owners of the establishment fail to make any payment required under this Act.

Section 11. Transfer of Employees

Any business concern required to give notice shall offer to each employee suffering an employment loss employment that becomes available at any establishment of such business concern for a period of 3 years. The employment shall offer wages as high as and benefits substantially equivalent to those received at the employee's old job.

Section 12. Employee Benefit Plans

1. Whenever a business concern is required to pay weekly benefits to an employee it shall also continue to provide and make contributions to any employee benefit plan with respect to such employee.
2. Employees shall accrue credits for any week in which they receive income maintenance payments.
3. If an employee suffers an employment loss at an establishment required to give notice and has at least 5 years of vesting service in a pension plan, his rights in such plan shall vest completely and nonforfeitably.
4. Any employee who attains 55 years of age before suffering an employment loss shall be eligible to receive retirement benefits at age 62 if the normal retirement age under his plan is greater than 62.

Section 13. Federal Assistance to Employees

1. Directs the Secretary to implement a comprehensive program of assistance to employees who suffer or may suffer an employment loss, including: training programs, job placement services, job search expenses and relocation expenses.
2. To the extent practicable, the assistance shall be made available before the employment loss and shall be made available through existing programs.
3. The Secretary shall consult with the affected business concern and labor organizations before devising any retraining plan.

Section 14. Related Retraining Assistance to Employees

The Secretary may develop a special program to retrain employees for new jobs created at their establishment pursuant to an alternative production plan developed under Section 15(b)(2) of this Act.

Section 15. Eligibility of Business Concerns for Assistance

A business concern required to give notice shall be eligible for assistance if: a substantial number of employees will suffer an employment loss; the business concern will make every reasonable effort to avoid such employment loss; and assistance will enable the business concern to operate without closing or transferring its operations from the establishment.

Section 16. Assistance to Business Concerns

1. The Secretary may provide financial assistance to eligible business concerns including loans, loan guarantees, interest subsidies, and the assumption of outstanding debt.
2. The Secretary may provide technical assistance, including grants and contracts for research and development in connection with new production and marketing techniques which will create new employment opportunities at the affected establishment.

Section 17. Targeted Federal Procurement

Provides that the Secretary may issue to eligible concerns a credit requiring federal contracting agencies to treat the business concern's contract bid as if it were 95 percent of the amount stated in the bid.

Section 18. Eligibility of Local Governments for Assistance

Local governments are eligible for assistance if the chief executive officer of the state certifies that such government has or will suffer as a result of a closing or transfer of operations:

1. a substantial decrease in tax revenues;
2. a substantial increase in demand for social services; or
3. a substantial increase in the number of unemployed individuals residing within the local government's jurisdiction.

Section 19. *Assistance to Local Governments*

Eligible units of local government may receive grants, loans and loan guarantees to:

1. provide additional social services; or
2. implement a public works project.

Priority for funding shall be given to projects that will provide an efficient means to increase employment opportunities over the long term and will further other national goals.

Section 20. *Eligibility of Employers and Employee Cooperative Associations for Assistance*

Eligibility shall be determined on the basis of an employer or employee cooperative's ability to create or expand lasting employment opportunities and the unavailability of equivalent assistance from any other source.

Section 21. *Assistance to Employers and Employee Cooperative Associations*

The Secretary may provide loans, loan guarantees and technical assistance for the purpose of:

1. expanding operations at or acquiring ownership of an establishment;
2. constructing new establishments; or
3. undertaking research and development projects to identify new markets and employment opportunities.

Section 22. *Priority for Providing Assistance*

Priority in providing assistance under Sections 16, 19, and 21 shall be given where such assistance will enable employees at an affected establishment to continue to perform operations at such establishments.

Section 23. *Liability for Loss of Revenue*

1. A business concern shall pay to each unit of local government to which it was liable for taxes with respect to an establish-

ment which it closes or from which it transfers operations, an amount equal to 85 percent of 1 year's tax revenues lost as a result of such transfer or closing.

2. If a business concern fails to make such payment, the Secretary shall pay it and such amount shall be a debt owed by the business concern to the United States.

3. If a business concern transfers operations to an establishment located outside the United States when an economically viable alternative exists, it shall be liable to the United States for a sum equal to 300 percent of any tax revenues lost to the United States as a result of the transfer.

Section 24. Criminal Violations and Penalties

1. Provides a maximum $1,000 fine and 1-year prison term for knowingly making false statements or failing to disclose material facts for the purpose of obtaining payments or assistance under this Act.

2. Provides a maximum $10,000 fine and 5-year imprisonment for making false statements or failing to disclose material facts required to be disclosed under Section 4.

Section 25. Civil Violations and Penalties

Provides that it shall be unlawful for a business concern to fail to give the notice required in Section 4; to provide assistance required in Section 9; or to pay debts owed to the United States under this Act within 180 days. The Secretary shall assess penalties for such violations not to exceed the sum of:

1. any depreciation claimed for equipment transferred, disposed of or abandoned as a result of the closing or transfer;

2. any investment tax credit claimed for such equipment;

3. any business expense deduction directly related to such transfer or closing;

4. any economic benefit paid by a foreign government to induce the business concern to relocate outside the United States; and

5. 1 year's savings to the business concern in wages and unemployment taxes as a result of transferring its operation outside the United States.

Section 26. Violations of Employees' Rights

It shall be unlawful for any business concern:

1. to fail to offer an employee a transfer as provided in Section 11 (1); or
2. to discriminate against an employee because she sought to vindicate a right guaranteed by this Act;
3. provides a remedy for violations of this section.

Section 27. Recovery of Overpayments

Section 28. Reserves; Recording Requirements Relating to Loans

Section 29. Congressional Disapproval of Rules

Provides a two-house veto of any rule promulgated by the Secretary for purposes of carrying out this Act.

Section 30. Reports; Legislative Proposals

1. After any program initiated by the Secretary under this Act has been in operation for 3 years, the Secretary shall evaluate its effectiveness and issue a report to Congress.
2. The Secretary shall propose legislation:
   a. to provide appropriate assistance to eligible units of local government; and
   b. to require business concerns to report employment opportunities for inclusion in the nationwide computerized job bank created by CETA.

Section 31. General Powers of Secretary

Section 32. Implementation of Employment Policies Through National Employment Priorities Administration

Section 33. National Employment Priorities Administration

Provides for the establishment of an administration within the Department of Labor, headed by an administrator appointed by the President and approved by the Senate. In addition to performing any powers and functions delegated by the Secretary, the Administrator:

1. may conduct research projects relating to any relationship between unemployment and closings or transfers of establishments; and

2. shall identify alternative services and products which a business concern required to give notice could profitably provide if given assistance under Section 16.

The Administrator shall establish appropriate regional offices of the Administration.

Section 34. National Employment Priorities Advisory Council

Establishes a council composed of 15 members, including the Secretary of Labor, the Administrator of the Environmental Protection Agency, the Director of the National Commission for Employment Policy, the Secretary of Commerce, the Secretary of H.E.W., four representatives of the general public, three representatives of labor organizations and three representatives of business.

The duties of the council shall be:

1. to advise and assist the Secretary with respect to this Act,
2. to review and evaluate the effectiveness of programs carried out under this Act,
3. to study and report on areas of economic activity where the United States may in the future operate at a competitive disadvantage with other countries and where large economic dislocations may occur, and
4. to research and prepare new programs to assist employees and communities affected by closings and transfers and to assist business concerns to expand or create new employment opportunities.

Section 35. Amendments to Other Laws

Section 36. Authorization of Appropriations

There are authorized to be appropriated such sums as may be necessary to carry out the provisions of this Act.

Appendix B

EMPLOYMENT GROWTH BY STATE

Table B-1. Compound Growth Rates for Total Employment and Manufacturing Employment for States and District of Columbia, 1965-1980 and 1976-1980.

State	1965-1980		1976-1980	
	Total Employment	*Manufacturing Employment*	*Total Employment*	*Manufacturing Employment*
Northeast	1.07	-1.34	2.33	2.41
New England	1.81	-0.34	3.63	3.46
Maine	2.29	-0.33	2.89	2.79
New Hampshire	3.81	1.20	5.38	5.68
Vermont	3.11	1.07	4.54	6.02
Massachusetts	1.52	-0.46	3.61	3.92
Rhode Island	1.39	0.23	2.12	1.12
Connecticut	1.72	-0.80	3.73	2.83
Mid-Atlantic	.82	-1.72	1.87	1.97
New York	.27	-2.20	1.69	0.46
New Jersey	1.80	-1.84	2.83	0.92
Pennsylvania	1.80	-1.84	1.56	0.23
North Central	1.94	-0.02	2.33	0.68
East North Central	1.65	-0.34	2.07	0.18
Ohio	1.63	-0.41	1.87	-0.18
Indiana	1.81	-0.20	1.64	-0.48
Illinois	1.20	-0.91	2.30	0.64
Michigan	1.80	-0.27	1.68	-0.55
Wisconsin	2.50	0.92	3.22	2.34
West North Central	2.69	1.27	2.97	2.53
Minnesota	3.20	1.70	4.10	4.16
Iowa	2.64	1.47	1.88	1.46
Missouri	1.82	0.01	2.61	1.11
North Dakota	4.06	5.56	3.70	0.25
South Dakota	3.27	4.94	2.29	4.69
Nebraska	2.94	1.71	2.48	2.82
Kansas	3.16	2.76	3.34	4.13
South	3.70	1.93	4.42	2.60
South Atlantic	3.54	1.36	4.35	2.31
Delaware	2.11	-0.16	2.60	1.16
Maryland	2.95	-1.29	3.64	0.80
District of Columbia	-0.82	-2.65	1.95	0.46
Virginia	3.99	1.43	4.07	1.62
West Virginia	2.15	-0.54	2.36	-0.97
North Carolina	3.35	1.82	3.75	2.21
South Carolina	3.76	1.77	3.59	1.59
Georgia	3.52	1.33	4.30	2.40
Florida	5.36	3.19	6.65	6.08

Table B-1. continued

	1965–1980		1976–1980	
State	*Total Employment*	*Manufacturing Employment*	*Total Employment*	*Manufacturing Employment*
East South Central	3.24	1.82	2.92	1.04
Kentucky	3.27	1.94	2.51	0.64
Tennessee	3.12	1.47	2.81	0.99
Alabama	3.04	1.68	3.08	1.80
Mississippi	3.83	2.74	3.54	0.48
West South Central	4.28	3.28	5.41	4.56
Arkansas	3.47	2.45	3.10	1.76
Louisiana	3.65	1.81	4.73	2.15
Oklahoma	3.70	3.80	5.28	5.44
Texas	4.70	3.61	5.95	5.56
West	3.98	1.99	5.40	5.54
Mountains	5.41	4.46	8.45	8.41
Montana	3.39	0.80	2.90	1.15
Idaho	5.07	3.85	3.46	1.24
Wyoming	6.18	3.00	7.78	5.85
Colorado	5.39	4.63	7.10	6.72
New Mexico	4.45	5.53	4.63	3.33
Arizona	6.71	4.90	8.00	10.56
Utah	4.39	4.40	4.69	5.99
Nevada	7.22	9.40	9.72	10.53
Pacific	3.55	1.65	5.25	5.37
Washington	3.54	0.88	6.28	6.23
Oregon	3.90	2.21	4.70	3.12
California	3.44	1.57	5.05	5.50
Alaska	7.68	5.59	-0.01	6.99
Hawaii	4.04	-0.32	3.95	0.85

Figure B-1.

ALABAMA 1965-1980

Total Employment and Manufacturing Employment

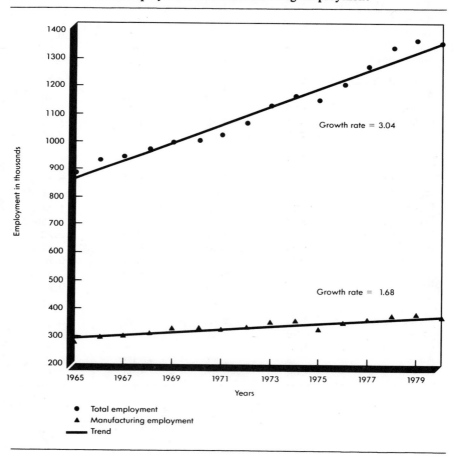

Figure B–2.

ALASKA 1965–1980

Total Employment and Manufacturing Employment

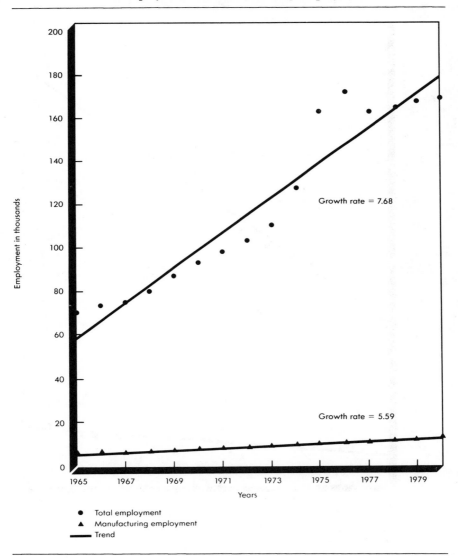

Figure B-3.

ARIZONA 1965-1980

Total Employment and Manufacturing Employment

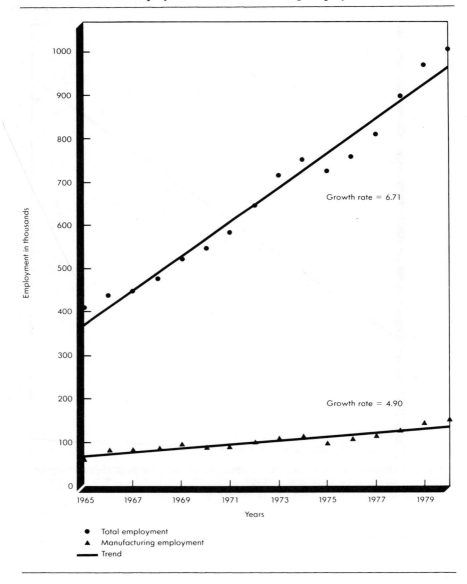

Figure B-4.

ARKANSAS 1965-1980

Total Employment and Manufacturing Employment

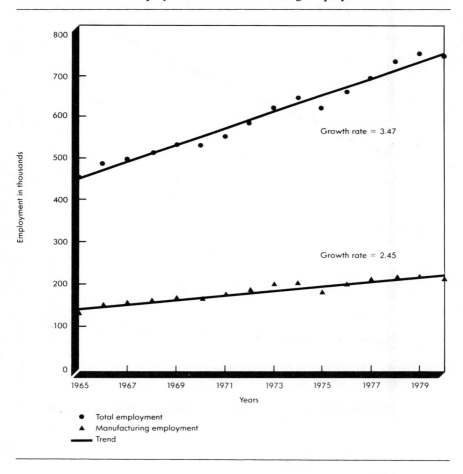

Figure B–5.

CALIFORNIA 1965–1980

Total Employment and Manufacturing Employment

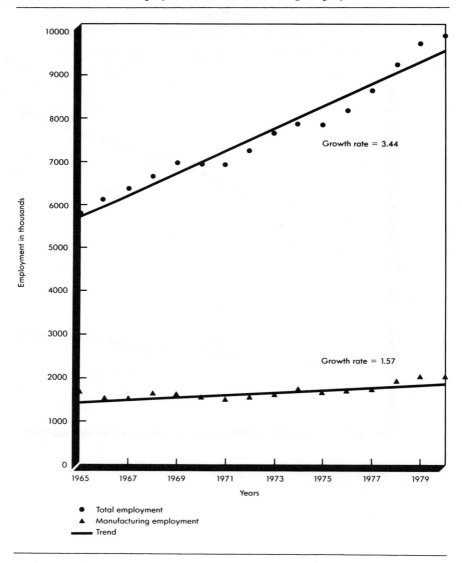

Figure B-6.

COLORADO 1965-1980

Total Employment and Manufacturing Employment

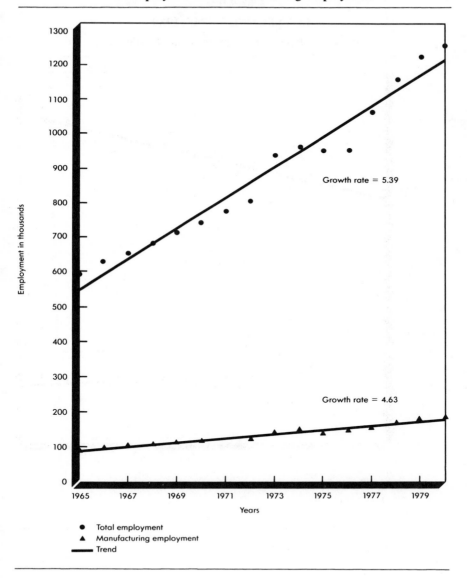

Figure B-7.

CONNECTICUT 1965-1980

Total Employment and Manufacturing Employment

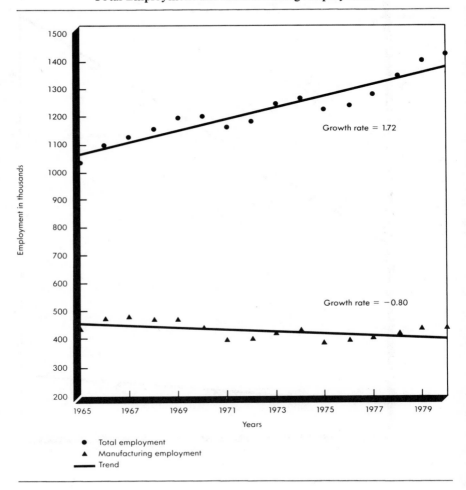

Figure B-8.

DELAWARE 1965-1980

Total Employment and Manufacturing Employment

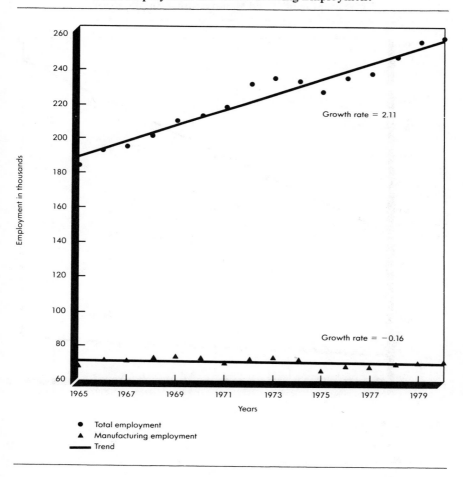

Figure B-9.

FLORIDA 1965-1980

Total Employment and Manufacturing Employment

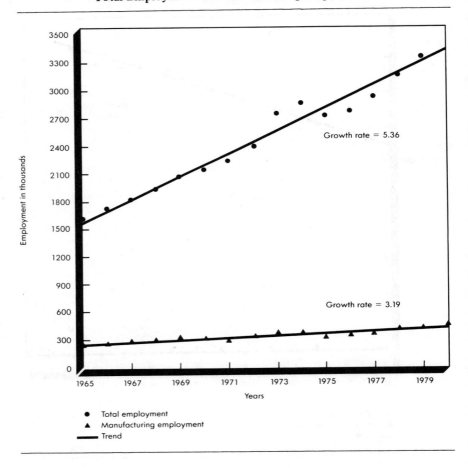

Figure B-10.
GEORGIA 1965-1980
Total Employment and Manufacturing Employment

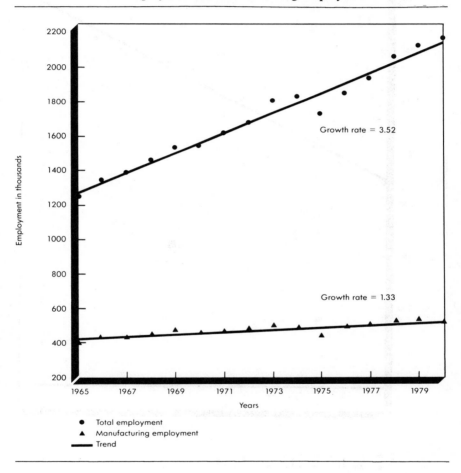

Growth rate = 3.52

Growth rate = 1.33

● Total employment
▲ Manufacturing employment
━━ Trend

Figure B-11.

HAWAII 1965-1980

Total Employment and Manufacturing Employment

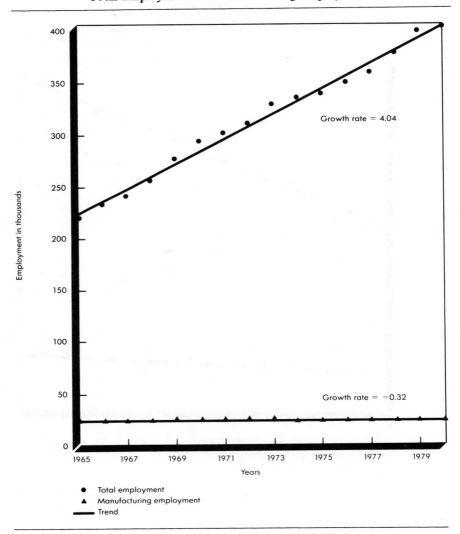

Growth rate = 4.04

Growth rate = −0.32

Employment in thousands

Years

● Total employment
▲ Manufacturing employment
▬ Trend

Figure B-12.
IDAHO 1965-1980
Total Employment and Manufacturing Employment

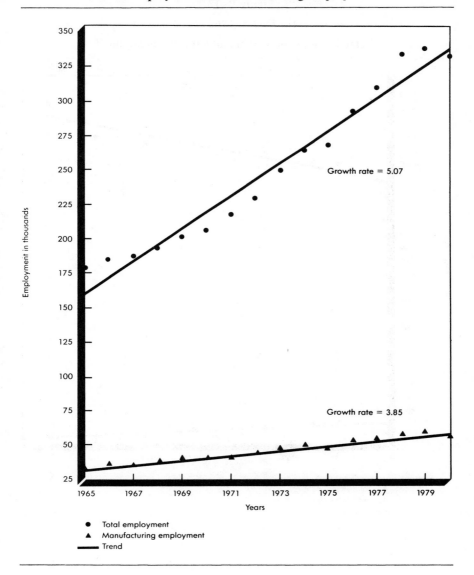

Growth rate = 5.07

Growth rate = 3.85

Employment in thousands

Years

● Total employment
▲ Manufacturing employment
━ Trend

Figure B-13.

ILLINOIS 1965-1980

Total Employment and Manufacturing Employment

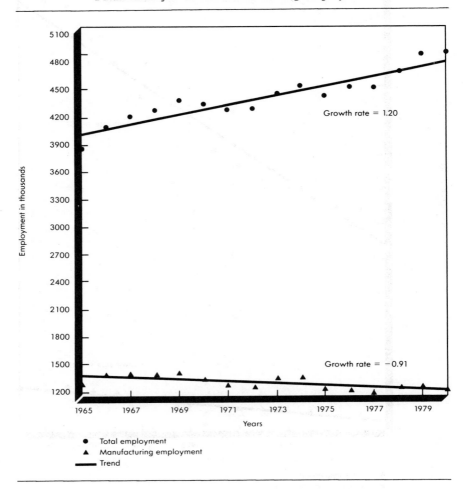

Figure B-14.
INDIANA 1965-1980
Total Employment and Manufacturing Employment

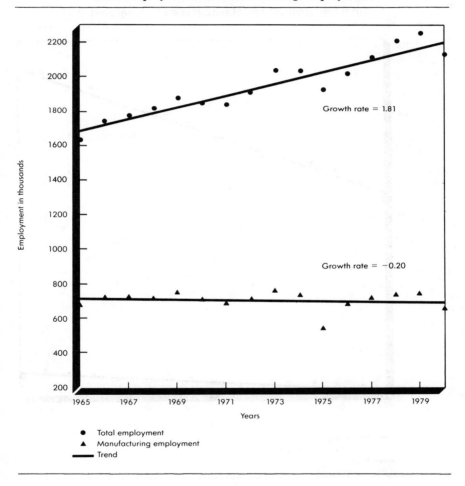

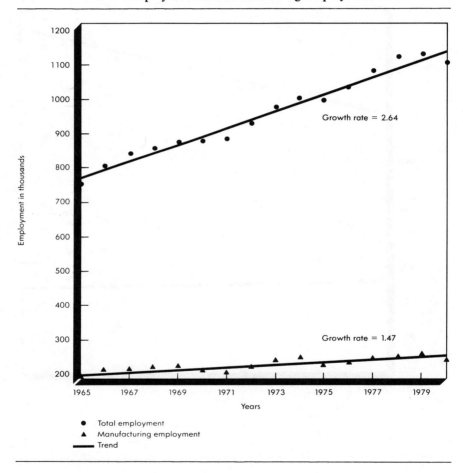

Figure B–15.
IOWA 1965–1980
Total Employment and Manufacturing Employment

Figure B–16.
KANSAS 1965–1980
Total Employment and Manufacturing Employment

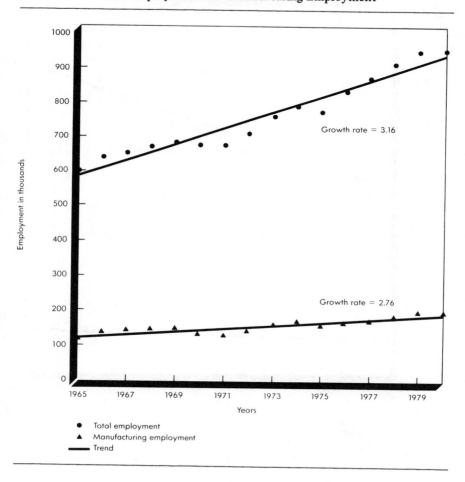

Figure B-17.

LOUISIANA 1965-1980

Total Employment and Manufacturing Employment

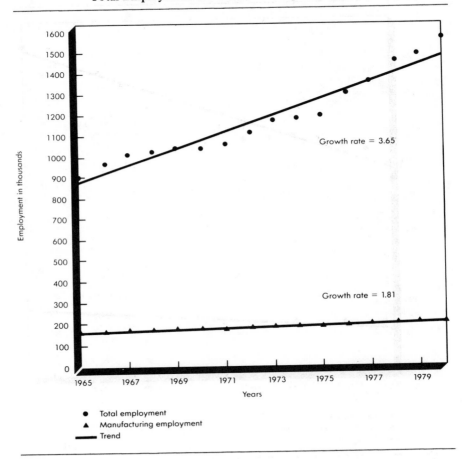

Figure B-18.

MAINE 1965-1980

Total Employment and Manufacturing Employment

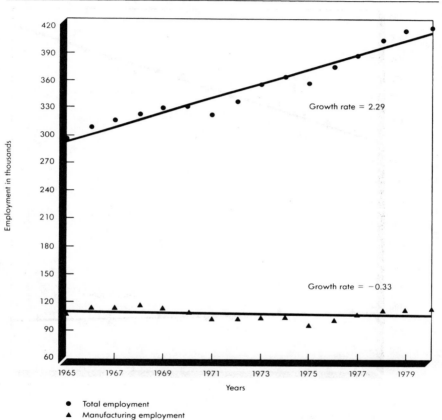

Figure B-19.
MARYLAND 1965-1980
Total Employment and Manufacturing Employment

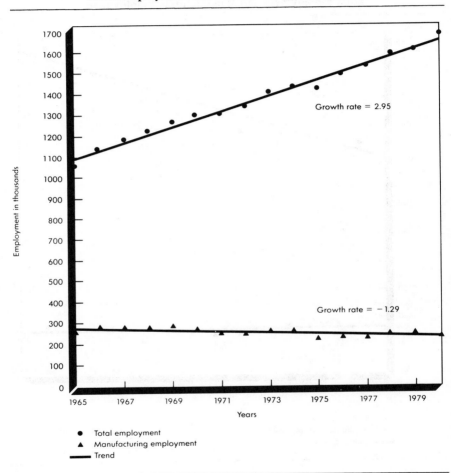

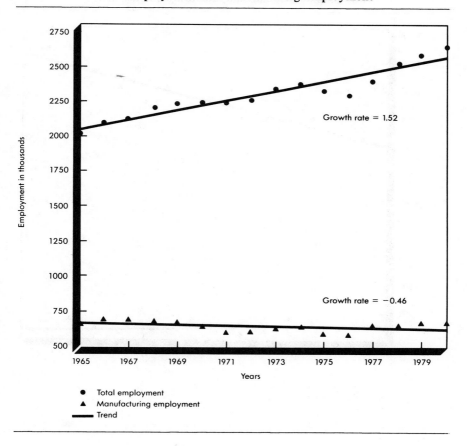

Figure B-20.

MASSACHUSETTS 1965-1980

Total Employment and Manufacturing Employment

Figure B-21.

MICHIGAN 1965-1980

Total Employment and Manufacturing Employment

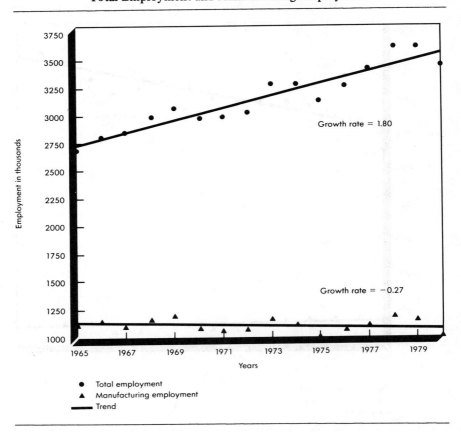

Figure B-22.
MINNESOTA 1965-1980
Total Employment and Manufacturing Employment

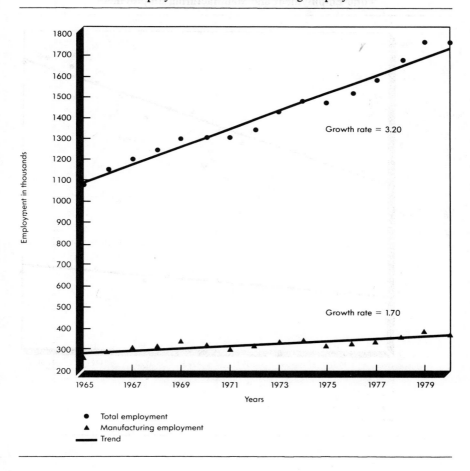

Figure B-23.

MISSISSIPPI 1965-1980

Total Employment and Manufacturing Employment

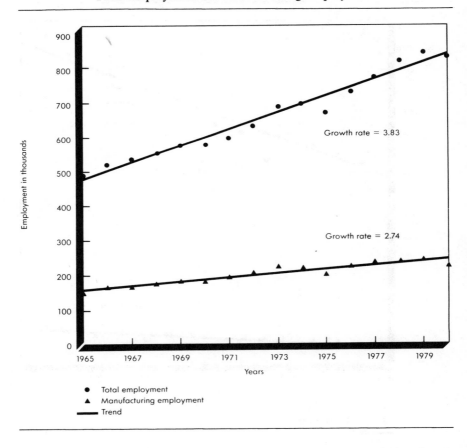

Figure B-24.
MISSOURI 1965-1980
Total Employment and Manufacturing Employment

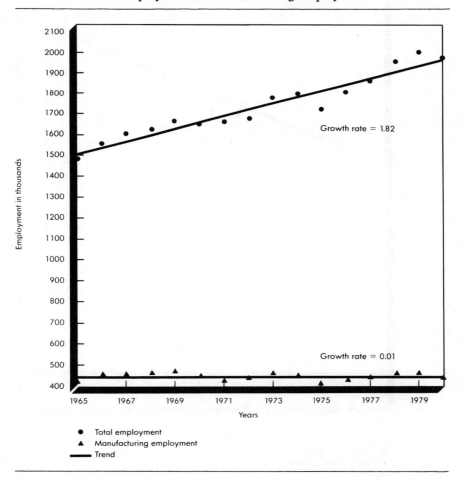

Figure B-25.

MONTANA 1965-1980

Total Employment and Manufacturing Employment

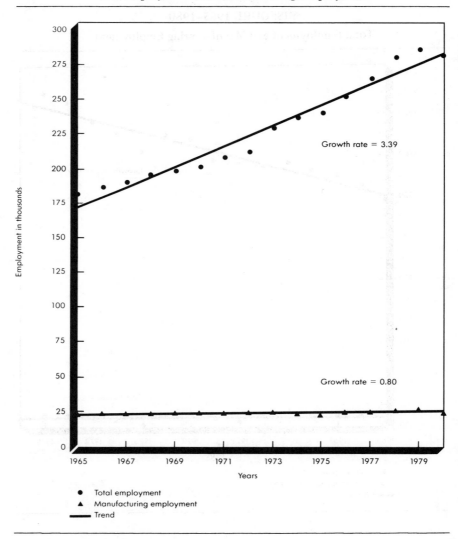

Figure B-26.
NEBRASKA 1965-1980
Total Employment and Manufacturing Employment

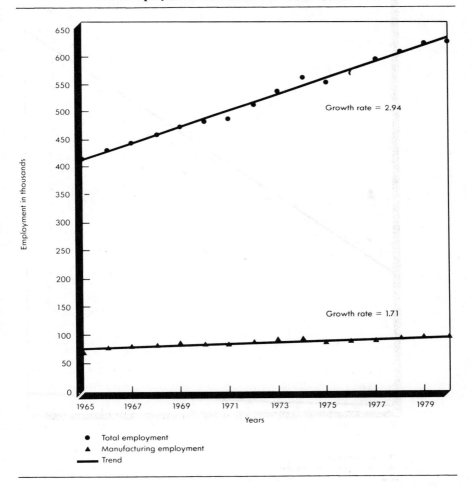

Growth rate = 2.94

Growth rate = 1.71

Employment in thousands

Years

● Total employment
▲ Manufacturing employment
▬ Trend

Figure B-27.

NEVADA 1965–1980

Total Employment and Manufacturing Employment

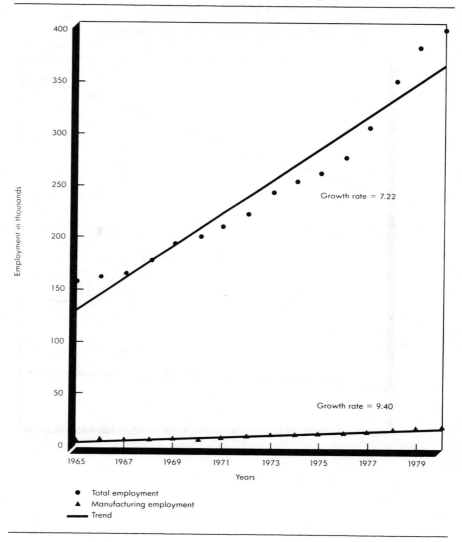

Figure B–28.
NEW HAMPSHIRE 1965–1980
Total Employment and Manufacturing Employment

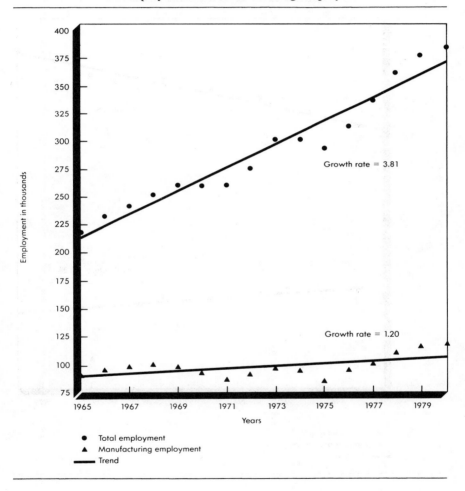

Figure B-29.

NEW JERSEY 1965-1980

Total Employment and Manufacturing Employment

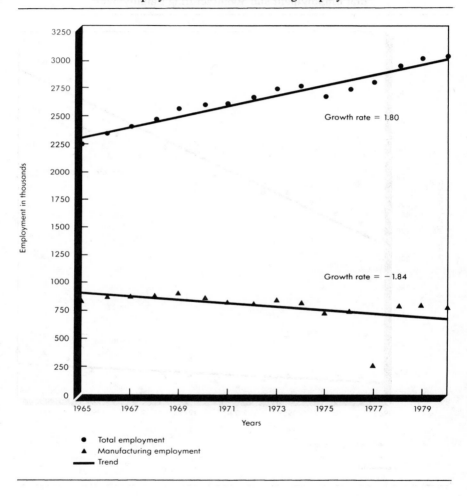

Figure B-30.
NEW MEXICO 1965-1980
Total Employment and Manufacturing Employment

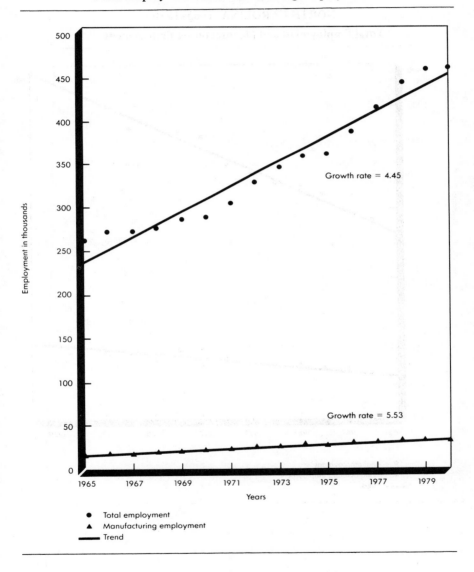

Growth rate = 4.45

Growth rate = 5.53

- ● Total employment
- ▲ Manufacturing employment
- ▬ Trend

Figure B–31.

NORTH CAROLINA 1965–1980

Total Employment and Manufacturing Employment

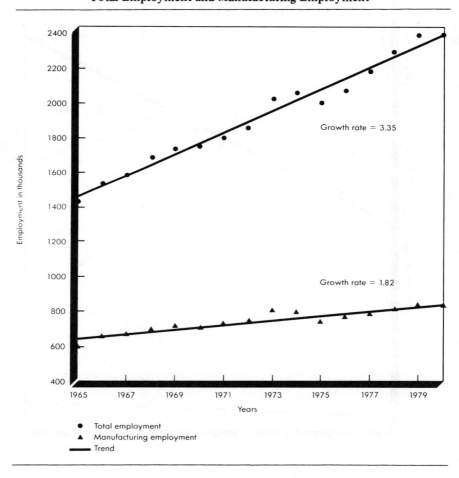

Figure B-32.
NORTH DAKOTA 1965-1980
Total Employment and Manufacturing Employment

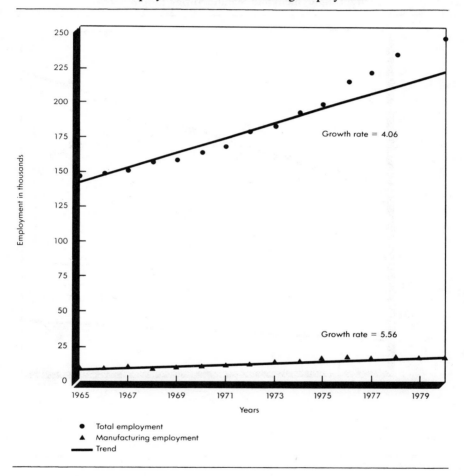

Growth rate = 4.06

Growth rate = 5.56

Employment in thousands

Years

● Total employment
▲ Manufacturing employment
▬ Trend

Figure B-33.

OKLAHOMA 1965-1980

Total Employment and Manufacturing Employment

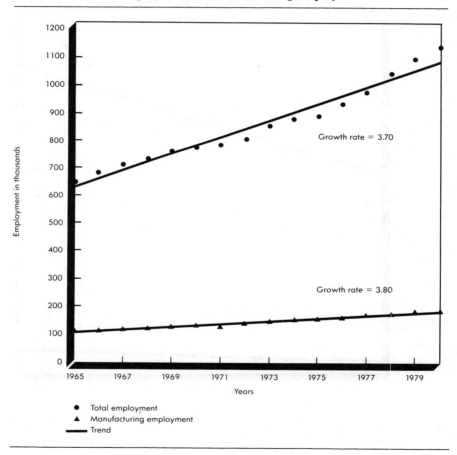

Figure B-34.
OREGON 1965-1980
Total Employment and Manufacturing Employment

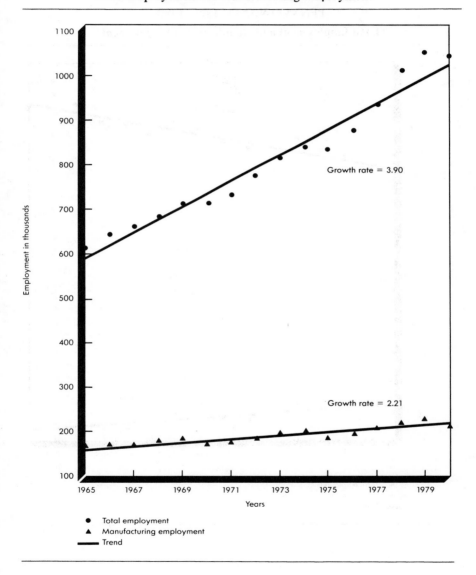

Growth rate = 3.90

Growth rate = 2.21

Employment in thousands

Years

● Total employment
▲ Manufacturing employment
━ Trend

Figure B-35.

PENNSYLVANIA 1965-1980

Total Employment and Manufacturing Employment

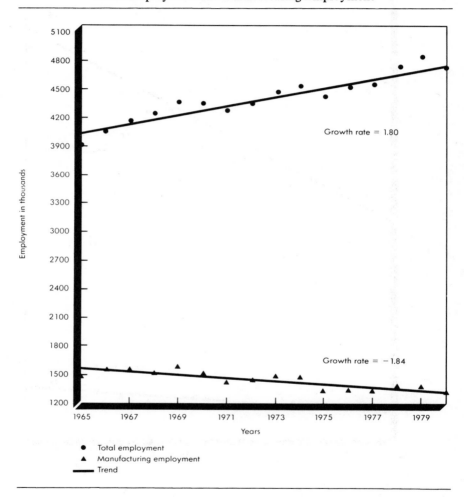

Figure B–36.
RHODE ISLAND 1965–1980
Total Employment and Manufacturing Employment

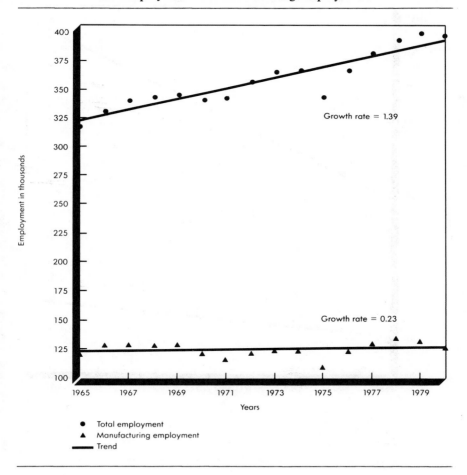

Figure B-37.
SOUTH CAROLINA 1965-1980
Total Employment and Manufacturing Employment

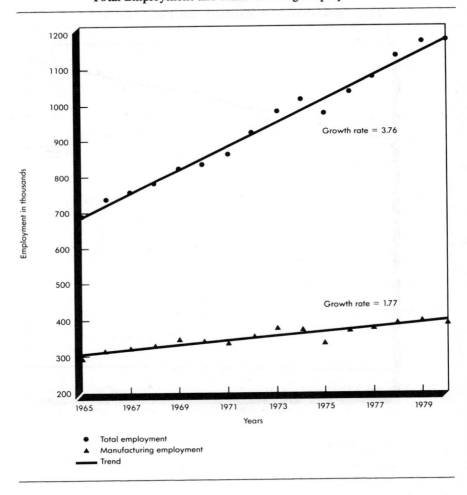

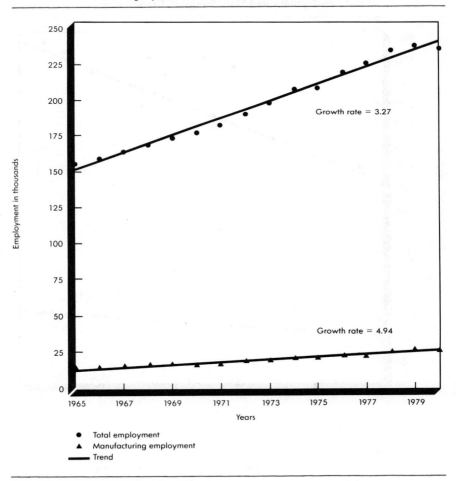

Figure B-38.

SOUTH DAKOTA 1965-1980

Total Employment and Manufacturing Employment

Figure B–39.
TENNESSEE 1965–1980
Total Employment and Manufacturing Employment

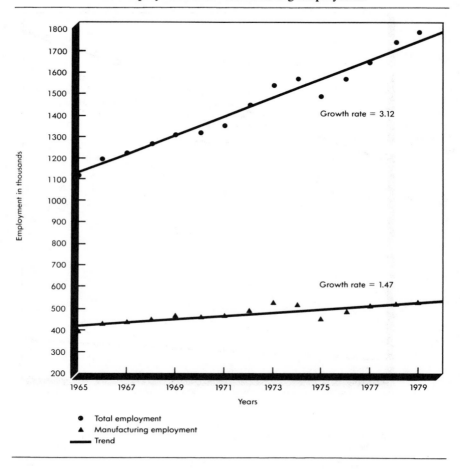

Figure B-40.
TEXAS 1965-1980
Total Employment and Manufacturing Employment

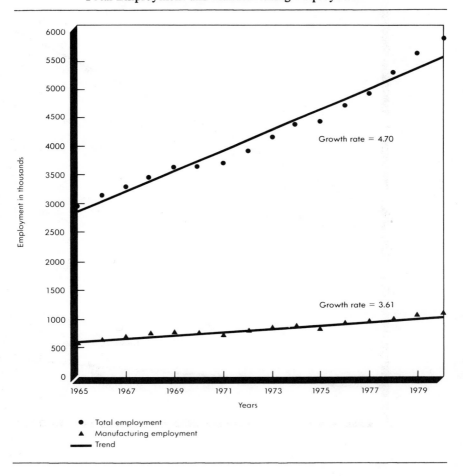

Growth rate = 4.70

Growth rate = 3.61

Employment in thousands

Years

● Total employment
▲ Manufacturing employment
━ Trend

Figure B-41.
UTAH 1965-1980
Total Employment and Manufacturing Employment

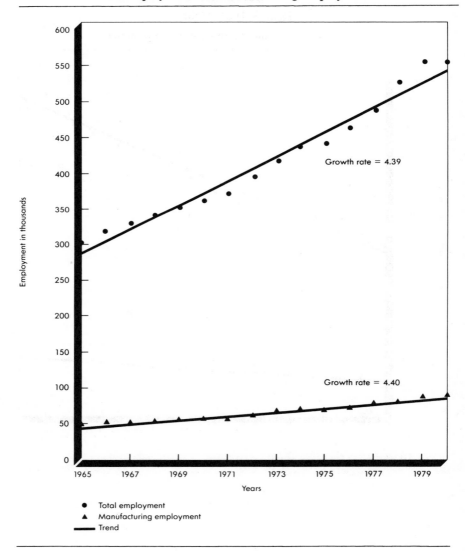

Figure B–42.
VERMONT 1965–1980
Total Employment and Manufacturing Employment

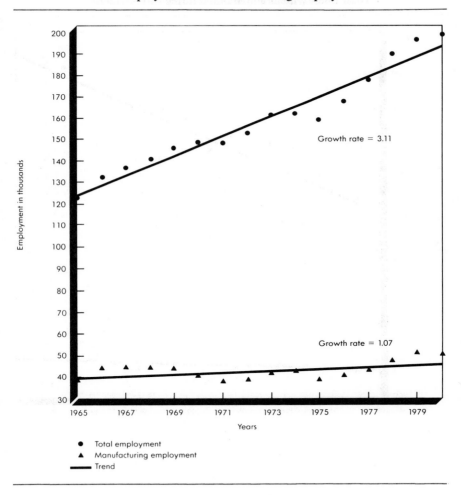

Growth rate = 3.11

Growth rate = 1.07

Employment in thousands

Years

● Total employment
▲ Manufacturing employment
— Trend

Figure B–43.

VIRGINIA 1965–1980

Total Employment and Manufacturing Employment

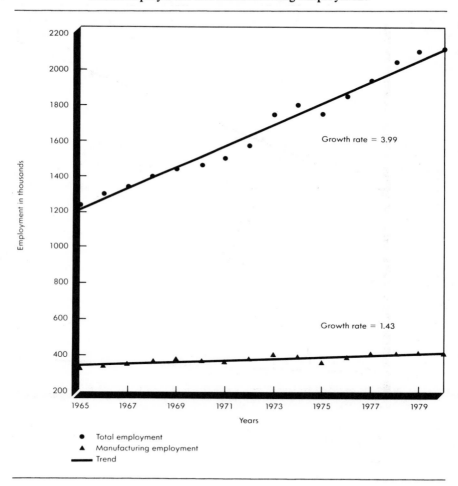

Figure B-44.
WASHINGTON 1965-1980
Total Employment and Manufacturing Employment

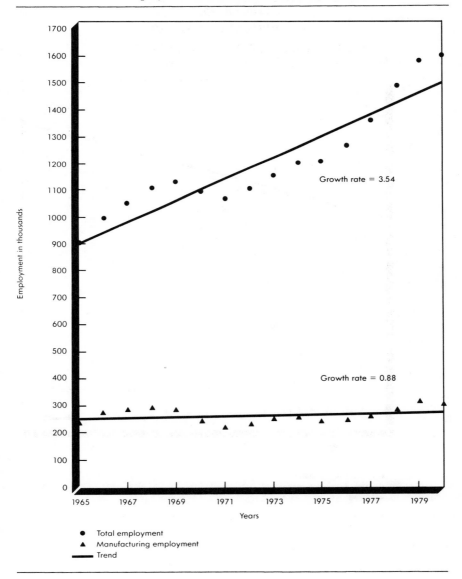

Growth rate = 3.54

Growth rate = 0.88

Employment in thousands

Years

● Total employment
▲ Manufacturing employment
▬ Trend

Figure B-45.
WEST VIRGINIA 1965-1980
Total Employment and Manufacturing Employment

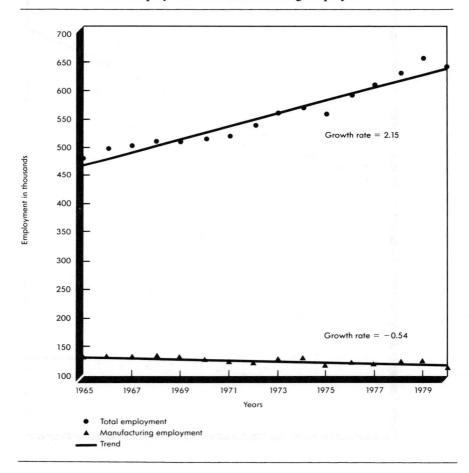

Growth rate = 2.15

Growth rate = -0.54

• Total employment
▲ Manufacturing employment
— Trend

Figure B-46.
WISCONSIN 1965-1980
Total Employment and Manufacturing Employment

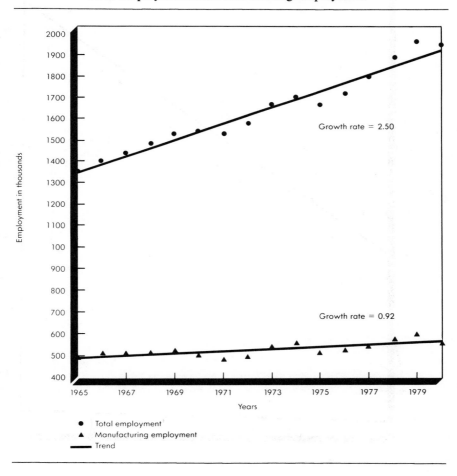

Figure B-47.
WYOMING 1965-1980
Total Employment and Manufacturing Employment

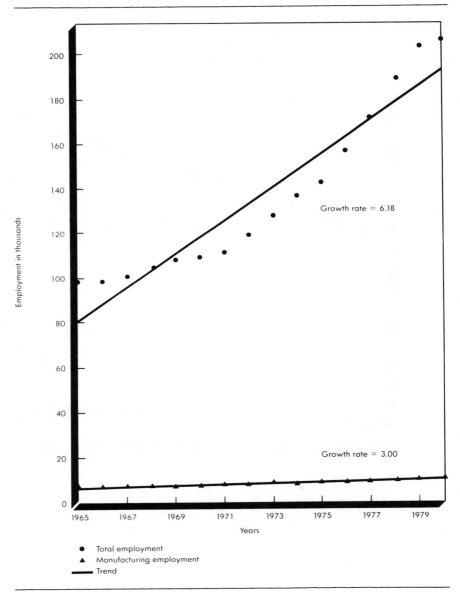

Growth rate = 6.18

Growth rate = 3.00

Employment in thousands

Years

● Total employment
▲ Manufacturing employment
━━ Trend

Appendix C

SUPPORT OF PLANT CLOSING LAWS

LABOR SUPPORT OF PLANT CLOSING LAWS[1]

In the text we noted that unions have backed plant closing laws. The support for such a contention can be deduced directly from union-backed publications on the subject, which have been scrutinized throughout the volume, and indirectly by way of empirical test. The purpose of this appendix is to provide empirical evidence on union backing of plant closing laws and to develop our explanation for the unions' position. The thesis is that plant closing laws are backed principally by two groups that can benefit most by them, unions and state and local governments. Tied directly to these groups is a third member of the supporting political coalition: elected representatives whose political fortunes rise and fall with those of their constituencies. These groups' support stems from two sources: First, they seek plant closing laws as a means of protecting their monopoly rents, not as a means of preventing firms from seeking labor markets where competitive, market-clearing wage and tax rates are naturally lower. In addition, following the recent work of Maloney, McCormick, and

---

1. This appendix is a slightly revised version of a paper published by the author and Bruce Yandle, "State Plant Closing Laws: Their Union Support," *Journal of Labor Research* (January 1982).

Tollison,[2] plant closing laws can be probabilistically predicted to emerge and be enacted where their costs can be externalized or imposed on residents of other states. Second, we have argued all along that new capital will avoid restrictions. If plant closing laws are enacted in one area of the country, then new capital will move to other areas, distorting the country's regional growth patterns. Although plant closing laws have only infrequently and in a modest way been enacted by states, plant closing restrictions have effectively been imposed by imaginative interpretation of union labor laws by the National Labor Relations Board and the courts. Unions have effectively attained plant closing restrictions; capital is being diverted away from heavily unionized areas of the country, the North, for example, and moving rapidly (or more rapidly than it otherwise would) to nonunionized areas like the South. In short, a contention of this appendix is that unions have effectively achieved plant closing laws, are suffering employment and membership losses as a consequence, and are attempting to regain a part of their bargaining position by imposing, by way of legislation, the same *dis*advantage on everyone else.

Union Support for Plant Closing Laws at the State Level

To explain the political attractiveness of plant closing legislation, the simplistic argument that the legislation is a "regional phenomenon," spawned by, for example, cultural or geographical forces, is explicitly rejected. In short, we (Bruce Yandle and the author) predict that although most of the laws have been entertained in legislatures above the Mason-Dixon line, their consideration does not, after statistical adjustments have been made, have a regional bias. Rather, we contend that the proposed legislation is founded on economic forces that have no inherent regional bases. Support for the legislation emanates from two principal sources, unions and state and local governments that have let their wages and taxes get out of line with other states and that seek to protect their monopoly positions. Supporters of restrictions on plant closings hypothesize that plant closings are a

2. Michael T. Maloney, Robert E. McCormick, and Robert D. Tollison, "Exporting Economic Regulation" (Blacksburg, Virginia: Center for the Study of Public Choice, Virginia Tech, 1981).

consequence of the attraction of low wages in other areas of the country. We contend, conversely, that industry is effectively pushed out of business or its original location by noncompetitive pricing behavior on the part of labor unions and state and local governments that attempt to exploit their monopoly positions.

As noted above, our focus provides an additional application of the regulatory theory of Maloney, McCormick, and Tollison.[3] From this particular theoretical perspective, plant closing laws are an attempt to "export" regulatory costs. That is to say, the legislative consideration of plant closing laws can be predicted to emerge in those states most capable of exporting the costs of restrictions, which, as must be evident from the provisions listed, can be substantial. Restated, our thesis implies that plant closing laws will tend to emerge, and be enacted, in states where noncompetitive labor and other costs are exported to other areas of the country and the world, places that could be good substitute production locations (since such locations would be close to the markets for the products).

Furthermore, the legislation is likely to be backed by those political groups within each state that have the most to gain by the legislation — that are in the best position to export the costs of the closing restrictions to other groups within the state and, better yet, for the political acceptability of the legislation, to other groups in other states. Successful unions are in such a favored position; the wage advantage of unions is, to the extent it exists, a function of the unions' capacity to externalize their wage demands. We suggest that unions tend to be successful in industries that have a location advantage, that is, where production cannot be readily moved to another part of the country. The proportion of a state's workforce that is unionized is a reasonably good indication of the unions' success in externalizing their wage demands. Where union membership is on the decline, even greater pressure to hold on to monopoly rents by restricting capital outflows can be anticipated. Similarly, state and local governments can support restrictive legislation as a means of "capturing" their tax base, which is another way of saying that the costs of government are exported.

Given unemployment insurance (UI) programs, plant closing is not likely to be backed solely by labor groups. High unemployment rates within a state can mean high unemployment insurance pre-

3. Ibid.

miums within that state both for firms that do and do not experience layoffs. Although the UI system is constructed so that firms experiencing high unemployment pay the highest premiums, firms with limited unemployment are still under the UI system, adversely affected by it. These firms can be expected to see plant closing laws as a means of shifting the government-created costs of unemployment back to the firms experiencing unemployment and, better yet, to people in other states through higher product prices.

Pressures on state UI funds were particularly severe during the recession of the mid-1970s, the period leading up to the time when discussions of plant closing legislation were initiated at both federal and state levels. Indeed, the unemployment funds of some states were drawn down completely. As shown in Table C-1, during the period between 1972 and 1978, 25 states obtained interest-free loans from the federal UI fund, and 20 of those states are still in debt to the federal fund in 1978.

Finally, state disparities in population growth rates can lead to a change in federal government representation. Politicians can be expected to protect their jobs by attempting to contain their constituencies. Assuming that the "people-follow-jobs" theory of migration explains, at least to some degree, recent disparities in regional population growth rates, one means of containing political representation is by restricting plant closures.

More formally, the probability of a plant closing law being introduced in a state legislature is related to the percent of the labor force belonging to a union (U_i), the change in the percent of the labor force unionized (CU_i), the per capita state and local taxes as a percent of income (T_i), the state's activity in borrowing unemployment insurance funds from the federal government (UIA_i), the per capita debt to the federal UI account (UID_i), and the change in the population (P_i), or

$$P_i = f(U_i, CU_i, T_i, UIA_i, UID_i, P_i) \; .$$

It is anticipated that U_i will be positive because (1) unions can be expected to protect their monopoly rents; (2) unions are a reasonably good proxy for the ability of labor to export the costs of restrictions on everyone else; and (3) organized labor provides political muscle for elected officials. CU_i is also predicted to be negative because declining union membership, independent of the *level* of membership, may be partially corrected by plant closing laws. T_i is

Table C-1. Advances to States and Status of Indebtedness[a] (advances received in millions of $).

State	1972	1973	1974	1975	1976	1977	1978	Repayment	Balance
Connecticut	31.8	21.7	8.5	203.0	137.0	75.0	37.0	66.2	447.8
Washington		40.7	3.4	50.0	55.3			12.4	137.0
Vermont			5.3	23.0	9.2	10.3		1.4	46.4
New Jersey				352.2	145.0	141.7			734.9
Rhode Island				45.8	20.0	9.0	96.0	3.7	102.1
Massachusetts				140.0	125.0		31.0		256.0
Michigan				326.0	245.0	53.0			624.0
Puerto Rico				35.0	22.0	18.2	13.5		88.7
Minnesota				47.0	76.0	49.0			172.0
Maine				2.4	12.5	8.0	13.5		36.4
Pennsylvania				173.8	379.1	373.3	261.0		1,187.2
Delaware				6.5	14.0	16.1	10.4		47.0
District of Columbia				7.0	26.6	25.4	8.4	2.9	64.5
Alabama				10.0	20.0	26.7		12.8	43.9
Illinois				68.8	446.5	243.3	187.9		946.5
Virgin Islands				2.5	5.6	2.8			10.9
Arkansas					20.0	10.0			30.0
Hawaii					22.5				22.5
Nevada					7.6			7.6	0
Oregon					18.5			18.5	0
Maryland					36.1	25.5		62.6	0
Florida					10.0	32.0		42.0	0
Montana					1.4	7.9	1.2		10.5
New York						155.8	180.0		335.8
Ohio						1.9		1.9	0
								Total	$5,344.0

a. From "Advances to States from the Federal Unemployment Account," U.S. Department of Labor, Employment and Training Administration, August 31, 1978.

expected to be positive because states with relatively high taxes must find ways to keep their industry. States with a high proportion of the labor force unionized are likely to be states with proportionately large manufacturing sectors (states and localities with proportionately large service sectors are not likely to have to restrict firms from moving since service firms tend to be tied to the local economy). We anticipate that UIA_i and UID_i will be positive because a higher level of borrowing of federal UI funds predicts higher unemployment insurance premiums, a cost *surviving* firms (those with lower unemployment experience ratings but with premiums adjusted upward for the closings of other firms) may seek to avoid by imposing the unemployment costs of plant shutdowns on the affected workers and firms through severance pay and community restitution requirements.

To test the stated predictions for each of the variables in our model, we assembled data for each of the fifty states and the District of Columbia and used a log regression procedure. The logit technique used as a dependent variable a zero-one dummy variable — legislative consideration, no/yes — and estimated the expected value of the probability that a given state will discuss formally plant closing legislation. The variables used in our tests are:

L_i 0, 1, depending on whether or not legislation was introduced between 1979 and 1981,

U_i Percentage of state and labor force organized, 1978,

CU_i Percentage change in proportion of state labor force organized, 1970–1978,

T_i All state and local per capita taxes as percent of per capita state income, 1978,

UIA_i 0, 1, depending on whether or not a state borrowed from the UI account,

UID_i Per capita debt to the federal UI fund, 1978,

P_i Percentage change in state population, 1970–1980,

R_i Regional dummy variable; nine standard areas: New England, Middle Atlantic, East North Central, Mountain, Pacific, West South Central, East South Central, and South Atlantic.

L_i is the dependent variable in each of the tests.

The model contained all of the variables hypothesized to affect the probability that a plant closing law will be introduced in a state legislature, and the results are reported in Table C–2. Note first that,

Table C-2. Logistic Regression Results (dependent variable: law).

Variable	Coefficient	Chi-Square	Significance
Constant	−13.188	4.67	.030
Union	.384	5.61	.017
Union Growth	−.330	2.04	.153
Tax Rate	43.106	.60	.438
UI Activity	4.209	3.35	.067
UI Debt	−50.867	3.16	.075
Population Growth	−.124	2.97	.084
Region	−.062	.03	.862

Model Chi-Square: 51.04; Predictive Accuracy: .769.

as predicted, the regional variable is not significant, nor are state and local taxes as a percent of per capita income, contrary to prediction. Considering the other variables, however, observe that UI debt has a negative sign and is significant. A positive sign was predicted, but we now interpret the negative sign as suggesting that states viewed their UI indebtedness as a grant. Clearly, given that the funds were interest free, when, by historical standards, interest rates were very high, a significant grant is implied. Simply put, the debt represented a cost of unemployment that already had been "exported" to national taxpayers.

Each of the other variables has the predicted sign; however, union growth is significant at only the 15 percent level.[4] On the other hand, the strength of union membership, UI borrowing, and population growth in the model strongly supports our coalition theory.

To interpret the partial effects of a unit change in an independent variable on the probability of the legislative consideration, coefficients must be transformed by $P = B_i P (1 - P) X_i$, where B_i is the beta coefficient and P is the mean probability of the dependent variable (.272). By making these calculations and interpreting each of the partial coefficients, we find that a one unit increase in the percentage of organized workers increased the likelihood that legislation will be introduced by 8.9 percentage points. (The expected value for all states is 37.2.) A change in the percentage of organized workers across 1970–78 of one unit—say, from 20 to 21 percent—de-

---

4. Two offsetting forces may be at work on the union growth variable. On the one hand, a decline in union membership may spur a union to intensify its lobbying efforts for rent-protecting legislation. On the other, the decline in union membership spells fewer votes at the command of union leaders, making any union lobbying efforts less effective.

creases the probability of legislative discussion by 7.6 percentage points. A one unit increase in the percentage of per capita income accounted for by state and local taxes increases the probability by 10 points.

If a state borrowed funds from the federal government unemployment insurance account during the 1972–78 period, there was a 98-point increase in the likelihood of legislative consideration. And if a state increased its UI debt by $10 per capita, there was an 11-point decrease in the likelihood that plant closing legislation would be introduced. Finally, a 1-point increase in the rate of population growth during the 1970s reduced the probability of legislative consideration by 2.9 points.

Using the results of the model, we estimated the likelihood that each of the 51 political units considered in the tests would entertain plant closing legislation. Those estimates along with the zero-one dummy variable indicating whether or not a bill had been considered are shown in Table C–3. With respect to these estimates, several states whose legislative activity is not predicted well by the model should be noted. Maine, for example, entertained legislation, and in fact later passed a limited closing law, but the model assigned a .335 probability to the event. New Jersey also entertained legislation, while our model assigns a likelihood of .702 that the legislation would be introduced. On the other hand, Maryland did not consider plant closing legislation, yet our model predicts that event would occur with a probability of .963. Alabama is the only other outlyer. That state considered a restrictive bill; however, our model assigns a probability of only .412 to that occurring.

By examining the entries in Table C–3, one can identify states that may stand at the threshold of debate concerning plant closing legislation. These are Maryland, Rhode Island, and Nevada, each of which has a predicted probability of debate in the greater than .40 range.

At the outset of this study, an alternative theory to explain the prevalence of state plant closing legislative initiatives were described. The analysis supports strongly our theoretical arguments and enables us to identify states that may emerge in the struggle to confine factories in a short-run effort to save jobs, tax revenues, constituencies, and monopoly rents.

Table C-3. Estimated Probabilities of Plant Closing Legislative Discussion.

State	Law	Estimate	State	Law	Estimate
Northeast			*East South Central*		
Maine	1	.335	Kentucky	0	.262
New Hampshire	0	.001	Tennessee	0	.013
Vermont	0	.011	Alabama	1	.412
Massachusetts	1	.972	Mississippi	0	.002
Rhode Island	0	.430			
Connecticut	0	.044	*West South Central*		
			Arkansas	0	.003
Middle Atlantic			Louisiana	0	.001
New York	1	.999	Oklahoma	0	.001
New Jersey	1	.702	Texas	0	.000
Pennsylvania	1	.984			
			Mountain		
East North Central			Montana	1	.983
Ohio	1	.999	Idaho	0	.001
Indiana	1	.938	Wyoming	0	.000
Illinois	1	.976	Colorado	0	.003
Michigan	1	.998	New Mexico	0	.001
Wisconsin	1	.953	Arizona	0	.004
			Utah	0	.000
West North Central			Nevada	0	.233
Minnesota	1	.969			
Iowa	0	.102	*Pacific*		
Missouri	1	.942	Washington	1	.995
North Dakota	0	.004	Oregon	1	.946
South Dakota	0	.031	California	1	.674
Nebraska	0	.037	Alaska	0	.000
Kansas	0	.015	Hawaii	1	.866
South Atlantic					
Delaware	0	.165			
Maryland	0	.963			
District of Columbia	0	.001			
Virginia	0	.004			
West Virginia	1	.993			
North Carolina	0	.000			
South Carolina	0	.000			
Georgia	0	.002			
Florida	0	.002			

BIBLIOGRAPHY

Allaman, Peter M., and David L. Birch. *Components of Employment Change for States by Industry Group, 1970-1972.* Cambridge: Joint Center for Urban Studies of MIT and Harvard University, 1975.

Bennett, James T., and Thomas J. Dilorenzo. "The Political Economy of Corporate Welfare: Industrial Revenue Bonds," *Cato Journal* (Fall 1982).

Birch, David L. *The Job Generation Process.* Cambridge, Mass.: MIT Program on Neighborhood and Regional Change, 1980.

_____ . "Who Creates Jobs?" *The Public Interest* (Fall 1981).

Bluestone, Barry, and Bennett Harrison. *Capital and Communities: The Causes of Private Disinvestment.* Washington, D.C.: The Progressive Alliance, 1980.

_____ and _____ . *The Deindustrialization of America: Plant Closings, Community Abandonment, and the Dismantling of Basic Industry.* New York: Basic Books, Inc., 1982.

_____ , _____ and Lawrence Baker. *Capital Flight.* Washington, D.C.: The Progressive Alliance, 1981.

_____ , _____ and _____ . *Corporate Flight: The Causes and Consequences of Economic Dislocation.* Washington, D.C.: The Progressive Alliance, 1981.

Brown, Lynn. "How Different are Regional Wages?" *New England Economic Review* (January/February 1978).

Ersenkal, Caryl Ruppert. *The Product Cycle in Regional Growth: An Application to South Carolina.* Clemson, S.C.: Clemson University, Department of Agricultural Economics, 1981.

Ford, William D. "The National Employment Priorities Act of 1979," *Congressional Record: House* (August 1979).

Gordus, Jeanne Prial, Paul Jarley, and Louis A. Ferman. *Plant Closings and Economic Dislocations.* Kalamazoo, Mich.: W.E. Upjohn Institute for Employment Research, 1981.

Green, Mark, et al. *The Case for the Corporate Democracy Act of 1980.* Washington, D.C.: Americans Concerned about Corporate Power, 1980.

Haggard, Thomas R. "Plant Closure and Relocation: The Legal Issues," Columbia: University of South Carolina Law School. Discussion paper presented at a Liberty Fund Symposium on plant closing legislation, May 1982.

Hekman, John S., and John S. Strong. "Is There a Case for Plant Closings?" *New England Economic Review* (July/August 1980).

Irving, John S. Jr. "Closing and Sale of Business: A Settled Area?" *Labor Law Journal* (April 1982).

Jusenius, C.L., and L.C. Ledebur. *A Myth in the Making: Southern Economic Challenge and Northern Economic Decline.* Washington, D.C.: Department of Commerce, 1976.

_____ and _____. "Where Have All the Firms Gone? An Analysis of the New England Economy." *Economic Development Research Report.* Washington, D.C.: Department of Commerce, 1977.

Kelly, Edward. *Plant Closings: Resources for Public Officials, Trade Unionists and Community Leaders.* Washington, D.C.: Conference on Alternative State and Local Policies, 1979.

_____. *Industrial Exodus.* Washington, D.C.: Conference on Alternative State and Local Policies, 1978.

Lynd, Staughton. "Reindustrialization: Brownfield or Greenfield." *Democracy* (1981).

Mathews, Nancy T., and Richard B. McKenzie. "New Plant and Employment Gains in North and South Carolina during the 1970s." *Review of Business and Economics* (October 1982).

Mazza, Jacqueline, and Bill Hogan. *The State of the Region, 1981: Economic Trends in the Northeast-Midwest.* Washington, D.C.: Northeast-Midwest Institute and the Northeast-Midwest Congressional Coalition, 1981.

McKenzie, Richard B., ed. *Plant Closings: Public or Private Choices?* Washington, D.C.: Cato Institute, 1982.

_____. *Restrictions on Business Mobility: A Study in Political Rhetoric and Economic Reality.* Washington, D.C.: American Enterprise Institute, 1979.

National Lawyers Guild. *Plant Closings and Runaway Industries: Strategies for Labor.* Washington, D.C.: National Labor Law Center, 1981.

O'Connell, Francis A. Jr., and Richard B. McKenzie. *The Politics and Economics of Barriers to Plant Closures: Unions, NLRB, and the Courts.* Clemson, S.C.: Clemson University, Department of Economics, 1983.

Premus, Robert, and Rudy Fichtenbaum. "Labor Turnover and the Sunbelt/Frostbelt Confrontation: An Empirical Text." Washington, D.C.: Department of Commerce, 1977.

Shostak, Arthur. "The Human Cost of Plant Closings." *The Federationists* (August 1980).

Sullivan, Michael, Peter Tropper, and David Puryear. *Tax Incentives and Business Investment Patterns: A Survey of Urban and Regional Implications.* Washington, D.C.: Northeast-Midwest Institute, 1981.

U.S. Congress, House. "Corporate Governance Act of 1980," H.R. 7010, 96th Cong., 2nd Sess.

_____. "National Employment Priorities Act of 1979," H.R. 5040, 96th Cong., 1st Sess.

U.S. Congress, Senate. "National Employment Priorities Act of 1979," S. 1608, 96th Cong., 1st Sess.

_____. "Employment Maintenance Act of 1980," S. 2400, 96th Cong., 2nd Sess.

_____. "Employee and Community Stabilization Act of 1979," S. 1609, 96th Cong., 1st Sess.

Verway, David I. "A Critical Examination of the Dun and Bradstreet Files." Paper presented at the Southern Regional Science Association Annual Meeting, Nashville, Tenn., 1979.

Yandle, T. Bruce. "The Emerging Market in Air Pollution Rights." *Regulation* (July/August 1978).

INDEX

ABOUT THE AUTHOR

Richard B. McKenzie, currently Professor of Economics at Clemson University and Senior Fellow at the Heritage Foundation, received his B.S. in business administration from Pfeiffer College, his M.A. in economics from the University of Maryland, and his Ph.D. in economics from Virginia Polytechnic Institute and State University. He has served as Visiting Research Associate at the Center for the Study of Public Choice at VPI and State University (1976–1977) and has taught economics at Appalachian State University (1972–1977) and Radford College (1966–1972).

Dr. McKenzie's primary research interests include public choice and public finance, applied microeconomics, and the economics of education. He is the author or editor of numerous books including *Bound to Be Free, Economic Issues in Public Policies, An Economic Theory of Learning* (with R.J. Staff), *The Limits of Economic Science, The New World of Economics* (with G. Tullock), *Plant Closings, Restrictions on Business Mobility*, and others. His articles and reviews have appeared in such scholarly journals as *Ethics, Journal of Economic Education, Journal of Economic Issues, Journal of Labor Research, Journal of Political Economy, Policy Review, Public Choice, Public Finance Quarterly, Regulation*, and *Southern Economic Journal*. His informed opinions have been published by leading newspapers such as the *Christian Science Monitor, New York Times*, and *Wall Street Journal*.